Stanley Spencer
The Man: Correspondence and Reminiscences

Stanley Spencer

The Man: Correspondence and Reminiscences

Edited by
John Rothenstein

Ohio University Press
Athens, Ohio

For Oscar Nemon
and John Tanner

Published in the United States
by Ohio University Press, 1979

First published in Great Britain in 1979
by Paul Elek Ltd, London

ISBN 0-8214-0431-8

Library of Congress Catalog Number 79-63683

Printed in Great Britain

Contents

List of Plates

The author and the publishers would like to thank all those who have been so helpful in supplying photographs and granting permission for reproduction, in particular Mr Nicholas Tooth, the staff of the Stanley Spencer Gallery in Cookham and Mr Richard Carline.

Introduction

Early in 1975 some of Stanley Spencer's Cookham friends and neighbours, later joined by others, acutely unhappy about some writings and broadcasts on him, encouraged me to compile a book which would give a less distorted picture.

When one visits Cookham today, although nearly twenty years have passed since his death, it is almost as though Spencer still lived there, walking over the Moor pushing his perambulator loaded with his painting equipment, at work before an easel on Odney Common, having tea at The Copper Kettle or sitting in some friend's house talking far into the night, so positively is his presence felt. He is all but alluded to as a cherished neighbour.

I was honoured by this encouragement, for I was devoted to him as a friend and an ardent admirer and supporter of his work, both as director of public art collections and as a writer, and was much attracted by such a project.

Yet what, I asked myself, were my qualifications? There are some who knew him far better, such as his former brother-in-law Richard Carline – but he was already engaged on a book on Stanley's early life and writings. Others had disadvantages of various kinds; they had known him only towards the evening of his life, or else were disinclined to write at length.

I was acquainted with him from 1923 until his death thirty-six years later, although there were longish periods – when I was in the United States or he was in Port Glasgow or Gloucestershire – during which we never met. But in the autumn of 1938 he spent six weeks at our house at Fellows Road, Primrose Hill, in London, and shortly afterwards several months at nearby Adelaide Road. He formed a deeply trusting friendship with my wife, and I, although I spent all my weekdays at the Tate, came to know him well. There were other times, especially in the 'fifties, when we met frequently.

For personal and professional reasons we were often in touch, but I was not among his intimates, who in any case were mostly women. In the company of a friend, however, he was apt to talk with extraordinary candour.

I have indicated the scope of our relationship. Those who disagree with, for example, my selection of letters may say: 'He may have known him for many years, met him often, but was never among those closest to him'. However, I believe I knew him well enough to make this attempt to show something of his strange combination of the simple and the complex. This belief was shared, at least by his brother Gilbert, who in his *Memoirs of a Painter* (1974, p. 185) wrote: 'Among the guests [at dinner with Lord Astor] at Cliveden was John Rothenstein, whom we had known almost since his childhood, and one could not but wonder how Collis's name had been introduced when there were people like John well placed to gather first-hand information from those of us, brothers and sisters, still alive and not uncritical, in the strongest position to give help.' Gilbert I did not in fact consult, since besides numerous references to Stanley in the book just cited, he had written a biography of his brother, *Stanley Spencer* (1964), and had been able to give full scope to his sympathetic understanding of Stanley's character and his memories of him, especially of his early formative years. For this particular undertaking I preferred more detached impressions from his friends and neighbours. The present volume, therefore, concludes with recollections from a number of them, to several of whom I am indebted for help in other respects.

On first acquaintance Stanley Spencer appeared to be a simple, even immature village boy – indeed he retained an element of boyishness until later middle age – who possessed extraordinary talent as draughtsman and painter. No impression of his character could have been more erroneous. In spite of his manner and appearance he was, as quickly became apparent, one of the most intellectually and emotionally many-sided of men, yet one who retained characteristics of the village boy. Although in no doubt about his stature as an artist he continued so to regard himself, describing people whom he considered his social superiors as 'toffs' or 'swells'.

His ideas and emotions he expressed in a torrential, virtually inexhaustable – though often to his listeners exhausting – flow of talk. For some years I was unaware that these were also expressed in a continuous flow of writings: diaries, miscellanea and letters, many of them of a hundred pages and more, but not until after his death that these amounted to some three million words or more, an output larger than that of many professional writers.

Much of his writing, like his talk, was compulsive, and from some time around 1930 he became obsessed by the ambition to assemble an immense autobiography which would include almost all his writings, from which, he used to say, 'nothing of me would be left out'. Nothing about himself, neither his most intimate thoughts and acts nor his fantasies, would be too insignificant to be preserved and recorded. (He once told me that he never threw away any piece of paper relating to himself, whether an invitation card or even a bill.)

This writing was even more wide-ranging and intimate than his endless talk. It consists of a vast mass of autobiographical fragments; a very lengthy one, for example, expresses his preoccupations with religion, with sex (the two often closely related), his affections, hostilities, suspicions (often unjustified), rages, eager sociability, delight in solitude, wild vanity, discerning assessment of his own artistic talent, as well as long lists of his works. It underlines his conviction that the significance of every feature of his paintings and drawings, down to the smallest detail, was fully explicable by its creator alone, and his fear that some aspect of it would elude the spectator, who, unlike his Victorian predecessor, responded to aesthetic qualities rather than to subject.

Yet such was the ambivalence of his character that even his passionate desire to write this vast autobiography from which 'nothing of me would be left out' did not escape it. In a letter to his second wife, written in 1938, he wrote:

... if it were truthful it might be interesting but quite and completely unprintable ... I would have to ... criticize myself, which would not be interesting as I am not good at it and I feel ... I am mistaken therefore in regarding myself as a suitable subject for ... autobiography.

And he once said to his brother Percy, pointing to the big wooden case in which his papers were stored: 'You can burn that!'

So extraordinarily varied, contradictory and frequently inaccurate is his writing that it is possible, even easy, by selection for a specific purpose, to represent him as almost anything from a mystic to a sadist. It should, however, be borne clearly in mind that he would write what others dream, and on waking forget, or mention only to intimates – or psychiatrists.

The long-cherished projected autobiography could never have been written. Stanley, master of many gifts, lacked the essentials to its realization: consistency, conciseness, sense of the rational. To it he applied his all but superhuman energy, numbering and renumbering thousands of pages – and he failed. His failure was fortunate, for there is a radical difference between the personality who emerges from the greater part of the writings and the Stanley Spencer known to his friends and acquaintances. Like others he expressed, verbally, from time to time, his irritability, vanity, anger, suspicion, conspicuous in his writings, but these writings only rarely disclose the high spirits and sense of fun, his affection for his friends and his generosity, shown, for example, by gifts of drawings to his friends and Cookham neighbours, mostly of their children. These gifts were numerous and made in spite of intense pressure of work, ill-health and the acute poverty he suffered until the last four years of his life.

One of my own most valued possessions is a pen-and-ink 'Self-Portrait' – one of his best – that on our first meeting at his studio in The Vale of Heath, Hampstead, he handed to me as though it were no more than a cup of tea and this at a time when there seemed not the remotest chance of my being of any service to him.

Nor do his writings, except on rare occasions, express the detachment about his own work of which in conversation he was capable, but rather his vanity, sometimes unqualified. The Introduction he wrote for the catalogue of his 1955 retrospective exhibition at the Tate was one such rare occasion: in it he expressed his sorrowful awareness of the decline of his visionary powers (see page 149). Yet he was usually ready to discuss his work with detachment and respond to criticism. Of his 'Glasgow Resurrection' – surely unsurpassed by any of his later imaginative works – he said sadly to my wife and me, one day in 1950: 'It lacks the real religious feeling of my early paintings', and such observations were not infrequent.

Spencer was indeed extremely self-absorbed and far from lacking grave faults – and follies for which he paid grievously – but he was a humane, generous and honourable man, an obsessed, although even by the most tolerant criteria an incorrigibly unorthodox, Christian, a man who showed resilient and cheerful courage in the face of crippling emotional and physical distress. His possession of these qualities few who knew him would be likely to deny, and few men of comparable eminence made fewer enemies.

It is earnestly hoped by the contributors to this book that there will emerge a less distorted impression of the man – the artist has from his early years received discerning appreciation – than he has been hitherto accorded.

At the risk of overemphasis of the character of so large a proportion of his writings I feel bound to insist on how relatively little they reflect the character of the man as he was known to his friends and acquaintances. To them this is a truism. But in the course of time they will no longer be alive to testify. Only the immense accumulation of Spencer's writing in the Tate Archives or elsewhere will survive, and it is to them that students of Spencer will have recourse. For instance, even Maurice Collis, who could have consulted many of those who knew him well, neglected to do so (he and his daughter, although neighbours, knew Spencer only slightly); he wrote, 'The chief authority for this biography is his own written word' (*Stanley Spencer*, 1962, p. 15).

Of course there is much to be learnt from these torrents of written words. This could hardly be otherwise, but they are distorting mirrors and they need much subtlety in the handling. Scholars should accordingly treat them with the utmost circumspection. They should be aware, to take a trival example, that although his usual memory was extraordinarily retentive, especially where it related to his early days in Cookham, it was far from infallible. Its fantasies have already been referred to.

Spencer's character was bafflingly many-sided: he exhibited many qualities, good and bad. Two were constant: devotion to his art and indifference to material possessions beyond the barest necessities, indeed to what all but the very poorest would regard as intolerably inadequate.

Otherwise this simple-seeming man could act with entire unpredictability. But only in the rarest circumstances did he act with cruelty. Certainly this term could be justly applied to his treatment of Hilda while he was courting Patricia; and his feelings towards the woman who, in his correspondence with Dudley Tooth, was termed 'the interference' were on occasion vengeful, but again only temporarily. Although, like many others, he was subject to fits of rage or irritability, he did his fellow men less harm than most, and many were his acts of kindness and generosity.

⸱ Like most others he could be untruthful, and forgetful (his versions of his treatment by the Jesuits at Campion Hall, Oxford, for example, are entirely false, but, far from having 'the buried self' attributed to him in the concluding paragraph of Louise Collis's *A Private View of Stanley Spencer* (1973), much of the grievous trouble he suffered was a consequence of the candour with which he was prone to discuss, not only with friends but with mere acquaintances and even strangers, his most intimate concerns. His uncompleted autobiography shows an eagerness to take the whole world into his confidence.

From the vast morass of words that Stanley Spencer left at his death I have selected in the first instance letters concerned with his first wife, Hilda. This I have done because she was the central person in his life, and so remained even after she was dead. But even of these I have selected only a minute portion. To publish them *in extenso* would not only be physically impossible; read in bulk, Stanley Spencer's compulsively written letters, the obsessive and monumental egotism his writings express, would batter a reader into insensibility. I have, perforce, therefore, selected only a few. My criterion of selection has been simply the degree to which they are, if not entirely representative of the man wielding the pencil or pen, at any rate less wildly distorting than what has been discarded.

The extracts from letters are usually printed here with the eccentricities of spelling, punctuation and so on to be found in the manuscripts. Such minute corrections as occur – and they are rare – were made only for the sake of readier intelligibility.

Acknowledgements

A number of Stanley Spencer's letters are published in this book, mostly in part, with the permission of his daughters, Shirin and Unity Spencer, and those of Hilda Spencer with the permission of Mr Richard Carline, her brother, a number of the many written by her to Stanley Spencer, all hitherto unpublished. At their insistence a small number of deletions have been made but in no case do these deletions alter or obfuscate the story. I am indebted, too, to Messrs Arthur Tooth for the loan of the long correspondence, also unpublished, between Spencer and the late Dudley Tooth and members of his firm, and for permission to publish them, in whole or in part; to the Stanley Spencer Gallery, Cookham, for the loan of photocopies of Spencer's letters to Desmond Chute; to the Tate Gallery's Archives Department for allowing me access to the vast accumulation of his writings in its possession and facilities for their study. (A few of the letters to Hilda come from these archives. Spencer's interest in himself and his writings developed in him a habit of making carbon copies.) I should make clear that the extracts from the writings here published – almost all of them from the Carline collection – are a minute fraction of the total. I am indebted, especially, to Mrs Joan George for suggesting the names of friends, particularly of neighbours, of Spencer's, who should be invited to contribute their impressions and recollections to this book, and for introducing me to several of them. I am also deeply indebted to Mrs Caroline Leder for her invaluable research assistance and for her selection of relevant portions of the Carline correspondence, generously made available to me by Mr Richard Carline.

The first draft of the book proved far too long for publication. To my wife and to Vincent Turner, S.J., I am indebted for its abbreviation and reshaping and for many suggestions.

To all those who in their various ways have contributed their help I wish to express my deepest gratitude.

For permission to publish the photographs of paintings and drawings that illustrate this book I wish to thank in particular Mr Richard Carline who went to considerable trouble to locate photographs for me and to Anthony D'Offay who supplied a number of the photographs here reproduced. In all cases the owners of the originals are acknowledged in the captions.

Chapter 1

Cookham and Early Friendships

Stanley and Gilbert Spencer from their earliest years have often been regarded as phenomena who emerged, if not exactly from nowhere, at least from an environment unlikely to produce or to foster men of such outstanding talent. They belonged, in fact, to an artistic family distinguished by talent, although not visual talent, and in the case of certain members of it by unusual eccentricity. Their father William Spencer noted on the fly-leaf of the family Bible that he was born on 16 September 1845 (and his wife Annie Caroline, born Slack, of Irish descent, on 15 September 1851) the elder of the three children of Julius Spencer and his second wife named Gosling from Seaton, Devon, a Cookham governess. Julius Spencer came to Cookham from Wooburn in Buckinghamshire, settled, about 1830, in Vine Cottage, established himself as a builder and became village constable.

It was he who built the two identical semi-detached adjoining villas, Fernlea (later Fernley) and Belmont for his sons William and Percy Julius respectively, on their marriages, where both of them remained for the rest of their lives. He also built Cliveden View, to which he moved from Vine Cottage.

To the William Spencers were born twelve children, William, George, Horace, Annie, Harold, Florence, Percy Julius, Sidney, Stanley (born 30 June 1891) and Gilbert (born 4 August 1892), besides Gertrude and Ernest, who died in infancy. All those who survived were marked by a high degree of individuality and several of them by gifts of a rare order.

Their father was a talented and enterprising eccentric who used to ride a lady's bicycle around the village reciting Ruskin. He was determined that his family should achieve success. Like his father, who had set up the village choir, he was a versatile amateur musician; he was organist at Cookham church; he gave piano lessons. Without any formal musical education, he set up his brass plate on his gate-post: 'W. Spencer: Professor of Music'.

This, however, was a trivial error by a man who showed so rare a capacity for infusing his family with a passion for music. Will and Harold became pianists and violinists, the former served as Piano Master at the Cologne Conservatoire; Percy played the 'cello and Sidney the piano and organ. This passion was also shared by Stanley and to a lesser degree by Gilbert, who wrote: 'We grew up with it naturally and could listen and talk at the same time' (*Memoirs of a Painter*, 1974, p. 12). Second to music came literature. William Spencer ran a lending library in the house, Stanley and Gilbert serving as assistants. Between the library and the volumes the family owned, Fernlea was filled with books, including classics such as *The Pilgrim's Progress* and works by Ruskin. William also regularly read the Bible to the children, though, Gilbert tells us, 'the emphasis was on the beauty of the language and imagery. Most of his quotations pointed strongly towards mercy and forgiveness' (*Memoirs of a Painter*, 1974, p. 78). This observation is pertinent, for Stanley's religious paintings reflect the beauty of the Bible's imagery rather than its moral teaching. The works of Ruskin also had a significant influence on his attitude towards his art.

William Spencer was a highly unorthodox Anglican, who caused scandal by violent attacks in verse on the Athanasian Creed in *The Maidenhead Advertiser*. The family was, however, closely attached to the Wesleyan Methodist Church, to which their mother belonged. The chapel they frequently attended was opened, in 1962, as the Stanley Spencer Gallery.

In comparison with music and literature the family's interest in the visual arts was tenuous, although at one time Will, addicted to drawing, was tempted to become an artist. Stanley's formation as an artist, however, owed much – he used sometimes to say 'everything' – to his early environment. He meant the rudimentary character of his education under his sister in a nearby garden shed, which gave him the leisure to concentrate on drawing, which began to express itself by at least the age of thirteen. The absence of conversation about the visual arts enabled him to develop his own highly individual ideas uninfluenced by elders whom he held in high regard. Their father's preoccupation with music and authoritarian disposition 'drove Will to such long hours of practice . . . that ultimately [his] health was seriously undermined and . . . he had to be kept in a highly expensive nursing home' (*Stanley Spencer by his Brother Gilbert*, 1931, p. 34).

Stanley, though free from the pressures that undermined Will's health, was also deeply absorbed by music and literature. Such was the identity of interests of this close-knit family that his primary passion for drawing only gradually emerged. Richard Carline, his first wife's brother, believes that in his earliest years drawing ranked only third among his interests. But emerge it did, and besides drawing himself he studied the Victorian reproductions that hung on the walls of the house, and the illustrations to its children's books (he told his brother Gilbert that he would like to draw like Arthur Rackham) and the Bible.

They also took weekly lessons in drawing from Dorothy, daughter of William Bailey, by whom three watercolours, *Cookham Bridge*, *Willow Trees* and *Cookham Church & River*, also hung in the Spencer's house. Bailey was a builder and plumber as well as an amateur artist who devoted himself to depicting local landscape. According to Gilbert it was Bailey's pictures of Cookham and their own reproduction of Fred Walker's

Geese in Cookham Village that 'inspired in us a preference for local scenes which never left us' (*Memoirs of a Painter by Gilbert Spencer*, 1974, pp. 15, 16).

The cumulative effect of Spencer's study of this miscellaneous assembly of reproductions of Victorian drawings and paintings, trivial as they mostly were, and a few minor originals, was to evoke his powerful innate sense of the importance of the subject matter of a work of art. For him a subject in which the imagination played a dominant part was crucial: he stated it constantly in his talk and writings, and landscape painting he came to regard as a distasteful means of making a living.

In 1907 he attended Maidenhead Technical Institute, where he drew from plaster casts; but 'It was more,' he said, 'from looking at the walls and the shelves and books that I learned than from the masters.'

The following year he attended the Slade, remaining there until 1912. While there he had the opportunity of studying original paintings by the early Italian painters who moved him most – they were also the subjects of special exhibitions in these years. But of unique importance for his study of Italian painting was the series of booklets published from 1905 from Gowans and Gray. These consisted of fifty-four numbers, each containing fifty to sixty black-and-white plates without an introduction, and costing sixpence. 'My brother Stanley,' Gilbert Spencer told Gowans in 1948, 'owed his education to you.' Stanley possessed a number himself and several were among his belongings when he died. A note in a scrap-book written in 1946 shows his enduring admiration for these books, as well as his confidence in his own stature as an artist. 'I still wish a Gowans & Gray little book could have been done', it reads; 'I once had some tiny photos of the *Zacharias and Elizabeth* (1912–13) and *John Donne [arriving in Heaven]* (1911) and other pictures and tried them on a page in an early Italian Gowans & Gray. I think it was a Fra Angelico. I wanted to see if it would satisfy me at all in the same way and in many ways it was up to standard.'

In Roger Fry's celebrated Exhibition of 1910, 'Manet and the Post-Impressionists', some forty works of Gauguin were on show. How closely Spencer looked at these is evident from his own early work – massively rounded forms, for instance, near the picture surface and a consequential indifference to perspective.

During his four years at the Slade, and shortly afterwards, this young man – he was seventeen when he entered it – painted a succession of masterpieces: *Two Girls and a Beehive* (1910), *John Donne arriving in Heaven* (1911), *The Nativity*, (University College) and *Joachim among the Shepherds*, (the last two of 1912). *Apple Gatherers* was probably his next work, the preparatory study having also been made at the Slade in 1912 where it was a Sketch Club subject.

All these works were not only made in Cookham but represented local figures, literally or allusively, and all in Cookham settings.

The Nativity was awarded the Melvill Nettleship and Composition

Prizes by the Slade in 1912, and in the same year *John Donne* and two of his drawings were included in the Second Post-Impressionist Exhibition.

Nobody at the Slade appears to have been aware of his painting, and when he brought these two examples up from Cookham they created a sensation and evoked the highest praise from Tonks, who in a letter to Spencer's family wrote of Stanley that 'he has shown signs of having the most original mind of anyone we have had here at the Slade'.

Spencer used to say that he went to the Slade only to learn to draw, which, unlike painting, had to be taught. Whatever the validity of this claim, which, like almost everything he said about the art of his time, applied only to his own, the effect of his years at the Slade during one of its most brilliant periods seems to have brought to a climax the inspiration he experienced in Cookham – the Cookham he described years later as 'possessed by a sacred presence'.

The fact that he was known as 'Cookham' at the Slade suggests recognition of his uniquely intimate association with the place of his birth and upbringing. Indeed until the war he scarcely ever left it except for the Slade, from which he returned the moment the last class had ended.

After leaving the Slade he continued to work in Cookham, painting about two-thirds of *Swan Upping at Cookham* (the Tate Gallery) in 1914, which he was unable to complete until after the war, in 1919.

During the Cookham interlude between the Slade and the War he was able to complete further major paintings: *The Visitation, Self-Portrait* (the Tate Gallery), *The Resurrection of the Good and Bad* (all in 1913) and *Mending Cowls, Cookham* (1914) and *The Centurion's Servant* (1914–15) both at the Tate Gallery. From 1915 until 1917 he served in the Royal Army Medical Corps, first in Bristol, then, until the end of the war, in Macedonia, for the last year in the 7th Royal Berkshire Regiment.

These early years might well be described as Stanley Spencer's visionary years. His biblical imagination, or more precisely his simultaneous dual vision of Cookham people and happenings and of Bible stories – a vision of its nature precarious from lack of intellectual under-pinning – was at its most intense, undistracted by the confusion of competing preoccupations, simple, single-minded and innocent.

In 1916 he met a Downside boy, Desmond Chute, who subsequently became a Catholic priest. It was a friendship that he always treasured. He began a correspondence with Chute that runs from 1916 till 1922 and was briefly resumed, after a break of a few years, in 1926. Most of Spencer's letters were written during his service in the army, from Bristol and several camps in England, but mainly from Macedonia. In the early 'thirties, probably, he wrote an account of his first meeting with Chute, when he himself was serving as an RAMC orderly in a Bristol hospital: 'He was a young man about 16, a Roman Catholic. Brilliantly clever, and with all that spiritual outlook and vision and mystery looked and longed for. His mother was a friend of the Colonel of that Hospital . . .

and he used to sneak away into the wards . . . to find me whenever he came with her. He found me as usual swathed in sacking and scrubbing floors and when he first approached me and I looked up from the floor and saw him approaching me much as he would approach an altar, I felt his love and regard for me. I felt here, though I shall continue thus – some sort of deliverance. From that time until the end of the war he never ceased in his kindnesses to me. He completely [filled] what of spiritual life I could have. Took me to hear good music. Read – translating fluently as he did so Oddysey, etc. Wrote marvellous letters full of wonderful atmospheres.' He also sent Spencer Bach and Beethoven scores.

It was to Desmond Chute that in March 1917 Spencer wrote from Salonica a letter that was published two years later in a short-lived and occasional Catholic magazine, *The Game*, edited by Hilary Pepler in close association with Eric Gill and Edward Johnson. Since this periodical is now inaccessible, and since Spencer's letter is one of the most revealing that he ever wrote, it deserves to be printed again.

(Salonica)   (March 1917)
I am walking across Cookham Moor in an easterly direction towards Cookham villiage, it is about half past 3 on a Tuesday afternoon and I have just seen mama to the station. Walking upon to the causeway between the white posts placed at the eastern end, is Dorothy Bailey; how much Dorothy you belong to the Marsh meadows, and the old village. I love your curiosity & simplicity, domestic Dorothy. I can now hear the anvil going in Mr. Lanes blacksmith shop, situated on the right of the street, & at the top end of it, as I walk towards it. The shop is over shadowed by a clump of pollarded elms which stands just outside the old red bricked wall which is built round Mr. Wallers house. Appearing above the elms & part way between them & a Ceda tree which rises from the garden enclosure formed by the wall, are Mr. Wallers malt houses with their slate roofs & heavenly white wooden cowls: the work of the cooper; I love to think of that; Every thing is so dull, the sun shines, the sky is blue, out there is an occasional young girl with some wreath which she is taking to her mothers grave. She has a pair of new shoes on, all shiny black. So unhappening, uncircumstantial & ordinary. The girl is going to the new Cookham Cemetery built halfway along the lonely road leading from Cookham to Maidenhead. Mama is safely packed off to Maidenhead & now I can let the bathchair swerve all over the causeway and go where it likes while I enjoy the eternal happiness of this life irrisponsible. And now as I enter the villiage I hear the homely sound of the Dox-ology, which the children of the 'back lane' school are singing. The 'back-lane' cuts at right angles across the top end of the villiage, and being semicircular in shape it appears again at the bottom of the villiage. The sound of the childrens voices as they come teeming along the lane; prisoners set free; comes across the top end of the street & hits the Thames side of the street causing echo upon echo which getting in between the maltings becomes very hollow. I am now walking down the street. Mr. Tucks milk cart is standing outside his shop having just returned from one of its rounds. The ice is being taken under the arch by the side of Mr. Caughts butchers shop, it

is being dragged along the ground by a big kind of pair of calipers. He has an awful yet fascinating way of clutching this ice. I enter our house, close the front door and look down the passage. At the further end the door leading into the kitchen stands wide open and the kitchen is flooded with sunlight. The plates and dishes on the tall dresser, in serried ranks along the shelves arranged, one plate overlapping the other glisten sparkeling bright in the sunlight. The shadow of the maid shifts about over different parts of the crockery as she buises about getting tea. I go into the dining room, the cloth is laid & I sit down to the piano & look at my Bach Book. Tea at length comes in and I sit down and take 3 pieces of bread and butter and a big cup of tea. Then I have some more. Then I get up and look through the dining room window down our garden to the bottom of it where rises a big Walnut tree which spreads out over our garden and over the gardens on either side of us and over a big orchard at the bottom of the garden but I am more particularly looking at the yew tree which is framed by the Walnut tree forming the background. This fir tree has many apatures, openings etc which greatly excites my imagination. They all seem holy and secret. I remember how happy I felt when one afternoon I went up to Mrs. Shergolds and drew her little girl. After I had finished I went into the kitchen which was just such another as our own (only their kitchen table and chairs are thicker and whiter) with Mrs. Shergold and Cecily. I nearly ran home after that visit, I felt I could paint a picture and that feeling quickened my steps. This visit made me happy because it induced me to produce something which would make me walk with God. 'And Enoch walked with God and was not.' To return to the dining room I remain looking out of the big window at the Yew tree and the Walnut tree which nearly fill the space of the window, and then turning to Sydney ask him to play or rather try to play some of the Preludes. He does so, and though haltingly, yet with true understanding. And now for 2 or 3 hours of meditation. I go upstairs to my room and sit down to the table by the window and think about the resurrection then I get my big bible out, and read the Book of Tobit; while the gentle evening breeze coming through the open window slightly lifts the heavy pages.

I will go for a walk through Cookham Church yard I will walk along the path which runs under the hedge I do so and pause to look at a tombstone which rises out of the midst of a small privet hedge which grows over the grave and is railed round with iron railings. A little to the right is a simple mound, guarded at either end by two small firs both are upright and eliptical in shape. I return to our house and put it down on paper. I think still more hopefully about the resurrection. I go to supper not over satisfied with the evenings thought, but know that tomorrow will see the light, tomorrow 'in my flesh shall I see God'. And so I go to sup: Mama is home from Maidenhead where her business has been chiefly in making bargins at 6½d. Bazarrs and in nearly getting run over. There are cherries for supper cherries and custard. It is dusk and the cherries are black and I have a good gossip with Mama or any one good enough to give me some gossip. Then I go out and walk up to Annie Slacks shop and sit in the shop and watch the customers. After the great doings of the night are over and the shops closed I must have one deliberate walk round by the Crown Hotel down the Berries road along the footpath to the river-side then along by the river through Bellrope meadow to the Lethbridges garden end of the meadow and then I stand still and the river moves on in a solid mass, not a ripple.

I return the Berries Road way to the village and when I come to that part of the road where you can look across to the backs of the houses running down the north side of the street I stop again. Then I return home and go straight up to bed having Crime and punishment under my arm and a candle which would last a life time. I get into bed and after reading for about 2 or 3 hours I blow out the candle, and whisper a word to myself 'Tomorrow' I say and fall asleep.

I do not ever remember the exact moment of waking up any more than I know the moment when sleep comes.

But although the moment of waking is not known; yet the moment when you become aware that it is morning; when you say 'its morning' is the most wide awake moment of the day; I lay on the bed and look out of the open window accross the road to Oveys Farm, then I turn my eyes to the room and let them rest on the wall paper which is covered with small roses. The reflection in the western sky of the sun rising in the east, casts a delicate rosy bloom on to this part of the wall. Now everything seems fresh and to belong definitely to the morning. The chest of drawers now is not anything like the chest of drawers of last night.

The front of our house is still in shadow and casting shadows accross the road but the Farm house opposite with its long red tiled roof is recieving the full blessing of the Dawn. The white doves are circleing round and round the farm yard; now over the barn, now casting shadows slanting up the side of the roof of the old farm house now rising up, and nearer and nearer, now they are over our house I can hear their wings going. A slight breeze comes in through the window. Annon they appear a little off to the left and slanting downwards. Then they rise a little to the farm roof and then 'banking' a little they alight on it and bask in the sun.

The sun has now just reached the street and the shadow of passing vehicles sweeps slowly across the ceiling. I hear a rumbling cart coming. It is coming round by Mr. Llewellens house. I hear the stones scrunching under the wheels, its the mail cart. I know when it reaches the Bell Hotel because the scrunching of the stones suddenly ceases and you now only hear the plop plop of the horses hoofs, and a muffeled rumble of the wheels. I hear Mr. Johnsons little boy call 'Harry, Harry!' down below in the street, and annon I hear his scuttering feet across the gravel as he runs past our house. Our back iron gate swings open and hits the iveyed wall out of which it is built, with a bang; then quick steps up the passage, then the sound of the milk can opening and of the jug drawn off the window cill. After fully enjoying the thought of all the varied and wonderful thoughts I am going to have during the day I get up & go & look out of the window Mr. Francis the baker is returning from doughing. He is white all over with flour. He has long hair white with flour, and a white meek face. I go and call Gil in the little bed room. Out of the window which looks towards the west is Elizer Sandalls garden. Then Elizer walks down the ash path, she lowers the prop holding up the cloths line and begins hanging cloths on stretching her skinny arms to do so, the rooks are flying overhead; they are going over to Mr. Lamberts Rookeries. I go down stairs, and takeing a towel I strole into the street. I walk down to the bottom of the street and call a friend, we all go down the Odney Weir for a bathe and swim. My friend has an Airdale terrier, a fine dog with magnificent head neck and shoulders. He jumps leaps and bounds about in the dewy grass. I feel fresh awake and alive; that is the time for visitations. We swim and look at the bank over the rushes I swim right in the pathway of sunlight I go home to breakfast thinking as I go of the beautiful wholeness of the day. During the morning I am visited and walk about being in that visitation. Now at this time everything seems more definite and to put on a new meaning and freshness you never before noticed. In the afternoon I set my work out and begin the picture, I leave off at dusk feeling delighted with the spiritual labour I have done.

Another letter from Salonika to Chute (March 1917) runs as follows:

. . . So now I have no Bible only a Testament. 'The Garden of the Soul' which you gave me I gave to a very earnest Catholic in exchange for a soldiers edition of the Ordinary of the Mass. . . . He lent me a book called 'Catholic Belief' and though it was just an uninspired explanation of the Catholic Belief, it led me to understand a great deal. What you say about the Protestants is true. But I do not look upon the Protestant Belief as an existing thing at all, & therefore out of argument, I think that what my friend Jacques said about the Protestants is true. That they are 'mean, unforgiving, hate the poor to get drunk and think soap is a virtue.' I quote this because it is deeply true. That is what the protestant has become, because he has, as you say lost the personal idea of God, and *only because of that*. But the protestant will be forgiven because he is ignorant. For instance if he once realised the awful necessity of understanding that Christ said *I am* & not *in me* is the way, he would not remain in his ignorant former belief. . . . In my bedroom at home when I woke up I used to look out of the open window across to the Farm house opposite. I simply had to sit up and look in front of me and the long red roof of the farm (Ovey's Farm) with the lovely white pidgeons basking in the early morning sun would be right in front of me . . . I go for a bathe . . . I saunter back home to breakfast across Odney Common (once thought to be called the Isle of Odin) and as I walk I think of what joy is before me in a whole day. I was longing for the day the night before because I am going to do 'that', I would say, and when I do it, it seem varitably to make the day a 'whole' day. A day full of prayer. . . .

In January of 1919 Eric Gill persuaded a reluctant Stanley Spencer to spend a week-end at Hawksyard, the Dominican Priory in Staffordshire. Gill described him there (on a postcard to Chute) as 'having a fearful wrestle – chiefly with himself' and as being 'in a curious mixed state of mind of pride, prejudice & humility & reverence'. But the visit was not a success nor could there ever have been any intellectual sympathy between Spencer and Gill. Moreover, despite fairly frequent references, in his correspondence with Chute, to the Catholic Church, requests for Missals, his interest in Augustine and John of the Cross and his delight in Crashaw, his refusal to attend Church of England parades and his attendance at Catholic parades instead – none the less Stanley Spencer's becoming and remaining a Catholic is entirely inconceivable. It was the Church of

Giotto, but no man could have been less fitted, by temperament or intellect, to belong to any institutional religion, the Catholic least of all.

Far as he was from being a conforming Methodist, Methodism was the only faith of which I recall his speaking with a degree of sympathy and this was owing to his childhood and boyhood associations with the Methodist Chapel, now the Spencer Gallery in Cookham. But there was no place that he loved more than Cookham Parish Church; he delighted in the exhibition of his work held there and in the Vicarage in 1958 and responded with the utmost affection to the benevolent friendship of Michael Westropp, its Vicar at the time of his death. None of this, how-ever, made him anything approaching an orthodox Christian, though he believed in God and Christ more passionately than many Christians, and spoke not infrequently of his terror of Hell.

In the early 'twenties there was a break in Spencer's correspondence with Chute. But in August 1926 Spencer wrote to him again and with no less affection than before. In a letter from Wangford, Suffolk, of 17 November 1926 he refers to Chute's 'request to me to continue Joachiming' [i.e. to make more religious paintings such as *Joachim among the Shepherds*]. Stanley's letter also contains an extraordinarily candid, though over-modest, analysis of his own character:

. . . I think one catches sight of ones own vulgarity when one for a moment gets hold of something vital. I feel really that everything in one that is *not vision* is mainly vulgarity . . . It has always puzzled me the way people have always preferred my landscapes. I can sell them but not the Joachims. This fact of recent years has a *wearing* effect on me. I began to wonder if my Joachims were ambiguous but later in this letter I will explain certain strayings and wander-ings that I have done since the war. It was inspiring to be asked to do a Raising of Lazarus. I think the only way to paint a 'picture of this incident' would be to do as Christ did, *first* to rejoice & thank God, & then do the picture. That is the real artistic vision when you are certain & sure about things & ideas before they have been given to you & before you have the least idea what they are like. That's the stuff to gie 'em. In this private chapel war picture scheme I am doing [the murals in the Oratory, Burghclere], I asked my patron [Mr. J. L. Behrend] if I could do a Bible for the building & he seems keen on the idea. I would like just to do a Gospel. What a funny thing it is, as soon as I contemplate the doings in the Gospel, I am fired at once, & yet I am not entirely in love with Christianity. I think it's this, that one can love Christ without fearing that one's going to be brought up with a sudden jerk, whereas with any other passion one fears a coul-de-sack. But several things during the war years since the war have done a considerable amount of havock to my 'faith' as an artist. You see, where you get real vision & artistic feeling you will notice that the vision appears not simply in one kind of product but in *every* kind. If brother Gil does a landscape its got the same quality as his Crucifixion & the same quality as a drawing of his of a head. This kind of spiritual uniformity seems to ratify the truth of Gil's vision to me. But with me, if I do a drawing of a head it's utterly worthless, it's nothing but a Slade drawing of a head. . . . If I do a . . . resurrection or a visitation it's got something marvelous about it. This *unevenness* is very disturbing & in fact makes me dubious of myself altogether. . . . If what an artist does comes from the stem of Jesse it should be clearly apparent in *everything* that artist does. Being quite sure that this is so I naturally distrust as a result, what *seems* to be good in the kind of work of mine that you specially like. I feel that such things may have a species of imagination in them but *not* artistic imagination. Its awful after 4 years at the Slade to find oneself not in possession of an imaginative capacity to draw but instead to find that one has contracted a *disease*.

My capacity to draw & paint has got *nothing* to do with my vision, its just a meaningless stupid habit. This all sounds horribly anyliticle but still it is what has put me off badly during the years since the war.

The John Donne picture is £5 to you, sir . . . [a study for the finished painting sold in 1911]. I quite agree (damn it) that my landscapes: especially . . . one I have done (a big one) of a heap of stinging nettles . . . have both given me more insight in landscape painting & I really enjoyed doing them. . . . I had real feelings about it & something is growing inside me as a result of having painted it, this last fact is what had made me feel that my desire to be able to paint landscape is not without some reason. . . . This half a hemisphere of nettles attracts me & I feel as if I had discovered another planet. It is strange that I feel so 'lonely' when I draw from nature, but it is because no sort of spiritual activity comes into the business at all. Its this identity business. There are certain things where I can see & recognize clearly this spiritual identity in something, but if I am drawing & dont see this clearly, its all up. In fact the only impulse I have to draw or paint is that I know that somewhere in all these things there is that miraculous spiritual meaning that just in a flash of a second could change boredom of drawing into a tremendous experience. . . .

This is the last letter Spencer wrote to Chute, at least the last that is known to survive. There does, however, survive a letter from Chute (Rapallo, 2 February 1927) which further contradicts Spencer's conviction that Chute lost interest in his work, for it concludes, 'you may go on doing landscapes as long as you don't give up the other, better stuff!'

Thus, apparently, ends a correspondence that shows Spencer at his happiest, the most responsive and serene of any in which he was ever to engage. Desmond Chute was ordained priest at Downside in 1927, but ill health and developing tuberculosis hindered his work as priest and artist. He bought a house at Rapallo and spent the rest of his life there.

Chapter 2

Hilda: Courtship and Marriage

A friendship at the Slade between Spencer and Sydney Carline resulted in the most deeply felt and in every sense the most significant relationship of Spencer's life, namely with Carline's sister, Hilda.

Sydney was a member of an exceptionally and variously talented family of painters. The first was George F. Carline (1855–1920), a stylish academic and illustrator; Anne, his wife (1862–1945), did not begin to paint until she was sixty-five. Certain of her paintings are reminiscent of Lowry's (which she is unlikely to have seen); others show the influence of cubism, originally interpreted, and a one-man exhibition of her work was held in Paris in 1939. Sydney (1888–1929), their third child, served (1916–1919) with the Royal Flying Corps and in 1918 and 1919 as one of its Official Artists, as was his brother, Richard. Sydney was Ruskin Master of Drawing at Oxford (1922–29). It was he who in 1915 introduced to Spencer his brother Richard, the painter (born 1896) and Hilda (1889–1950), who like her brothers studied at the Slade.

The Carlines, however independent as painters, as a family were closely knit. Mrs Carline, Hilda and Richard lived at 47 Downshire Hill, Hampstead, where they created an environment in which many fellow artists felt at home and were stimulated by the creativity in the air. Among those who used to visit them, after his return from Macedonia, was Spencer. Yet so closely knit were the Carlines that even when he became a member of the family by marriage he was never unreservedly accepted as one of them and in consequence resented their clannishness. Moreover, he was passionately attached to Cookham, sometimes, even, to the point of jealousy.

Hilda was a highly original woman, deeply preoccupied with social justice, though not politically minded, with what became known as Women's Liberation, and especially with Christian Science as well as painting. Owing to the early recognition of Stanley as a major painter, her work was inevitably overshadowed by his, though her work, and that of her brothers and father, is represented at the Tate. Declining health, accelerated by the ordeals she was to suffer, resulted in a corresponding decline in its quality and volume.

At its best, it was moving, in such a painting, for instance, as *Melancholy in a Country Garden* (1921), depicting her mother in mourning after her father's death; the sorrow of the solitary figure made the more poignant by the luxuriance of the plants she stands among.

23

It was towards the end of 1919 that Spencer first visited the Carlines. In a memorandum written in 1942 in Cookham he gives an account of their momentous encounter:

Hilda I had met at the Carlines as she came round to me and Jas [the painter James Wood] and the rest of us with the soup I thought how extraordinary she looked. I felt sure she had the same mental attitude towards things as I had. I could feel my true self in that extraordinary person. I saw life with her and in that visit where her manner was of one familiar to everyone *except* me, I could see me in her manner to everyone. I felt a longing for her as at once I saw a life with her. But I heard that Gil had been meeting her at the Slade . . . and was himself taken with her. So I lay low and waited.

However deeply he felt for her, his approach for a time remained tentative in view of her close though not enduring friendship with Gilbert. In the summer of 1922 he joined the Carlines on a three-month painting expedition to Bosnia where he had the advantage of Hilda's regular companionship, as well as the evoking of wartime memories of Macedonia.

Stanley was moved by Hilda not only as a woman but as a painter. On one of his early visits, although almost penniless, he bought one of her paintings of sheep because, he wrote, 'There is something heavenly in it.' This response to her painting was not only a result of the emotion she originally generated in him; he continued throughout every vicissitude of their relationship to admire it and to encourage her, whenever her impulse dwindled, to pursue it.

Their relationship evolved slowly but her independence, especially her attachment to Christian Science and the candour with which she criticized his work, was apt to obstruct their tacit engagement, but their relationship remained close. It became closer still when, in the spring of 1923, he briefly attended a drawing class at the Slade and stayed with the Carlines. In the summer he visited Henry Lamb at Poole, Dorset, where, as related elsewhere, he discussed with Louis and Mary Behrend his plan to make paintings of his war experience, a scheme for which they ultimately built the chapel at Burghclere specially to house them. At the end of the year, while this was in course of consideration, he returned to London, again staying with the Carlines before settling early in 1924 in the not far distant Vale Hotel, first in Lamb's studio, then in one of his own. Hilda and he visited one another at the Carline's house and the Vale; she appears five times in the major work on which he was engaged, *The Resurrection, Cookham*. In the meanwhile their relations became closer: they endlessly recalled their past lives and endlessly argued, even quarrelled, about religion, on account of her fervent attachment to Christian Science. Finally in February 1925 they married at Wangford, Suffolk, continuing to live at Vale Studios until *The Resurrection, Cookham* (1923–27, The Tate Gallery), was completed.

24

From 1928 until the summer of 1932 Stanley Spencer was engaged on the decoration of murals for the Oratory of All Souls, Burghclere. The first two panels were painted at Vale Studios, Hampstead, and the last at Cookham, the rest at Burghclere. The undertaking was arguably his greatest achievement. It was the kind of project – vast in scale, consisting of a superb altar-piece, measuring 21ft × 17½ft, eight arched lunettes 7ft × 6ft, eight Beaufort Hospital scenes 6ft × 3ft and two other panels 28ft × 10ft – which he aspired to repeat for the remainder of his life. Although his paintings belong to a different world of achievement from his writing they have one element in common: both are autobiographical: in spirit, and, though sometimes obliquely, in subject, expressions of his passionate desire to leave to posterity memorials of his life, human relations and environment on a vast scale but also in minute detail, so as to avoid 'something of me being left out'.

The vast and infinitely various correspondence between Stanley and Hilda began about 1922 and he continued to write to her for years after her death. Some of his letters relate to the children or some other domestic subject. Others are different in purpose and though addressed to Hilda are fragments of the projected autobiography or 'book' that continuously preoccupied him from about 1930; still others are spontaneous expressions of ideas, observations and notes on his own works. Many were unsent or else personally delivered, and many are of immense length. Some were argued over and annotated by Hilda. There follow extracts from this vast correspondence between them. They represent a minute fraction of the whole, but they have been selected from material in the custody of Mr Richard Carline to illuminate the characters of Stanley and Hilda and their changing relations. Unless otherwise indicated, they may be presumed to be written by Stanley. The first set of extracts runs from 1922 until marriage in 1925. Their frequent letters often crossed, so that although these extracts are in chronological order replies are not always in sequence.

19 High Street, Petersfield, Hants (15 & 22 June 1922)
[Written from lodgings, near the Muirhead Bones.]
    Its lovely to say things to you & I long to see you again, its lovelier to hear you say things. When I met you for the first time (when my coller stud broke) I remember the moment the thing that must have been filling me with delight was thinking '& all that probably says quite a lot of things, I wonder what the things she says are like', I have an 'over the wallish' feeling about what you say. I would love to hear from you; if you would kindly lift me up & let me look over, it would be almost as marvellous to me to hear you speaking now at this moment, as it would be if St. Peter suddenly began to speak in Masaccio's picture of St. Peter casting his shadow. Would the 'magic' disappear if you were here, speaking? In the case of looking at a place somewhere distant from where you are standing one feels how wonderful it would be to be just there when one is there however lo, the feelings gone, it was a mirage. . . .

Petersfield (19 October 1922)

I will let you know what I decide to do with respect to where I live and such like. I am certainly not going to stay here; I hate it more and more.

. . . I was thinking when I said that of what Henry had said about the way I hurl myself at people and then break away from them.

. . . It may seem very strange that it should be so but between you & me there is a relationship that to me is perfect. . . . I hate to feel that I have caused you suffering. I find it very difficult to write to you Hilda, you will know why it is. The last part of your letter was beautiful; you have had a wonderful effect on me too Hilda: you have put a new song into my mouth, oh, I must not go on. Would you like me to lend you my Oddysy? You *might* have time to read it.

10 Hill Street, Poole, Dorset (1923?)
[Written while staying with Henry Lamb.]

Why I like writing to you is because I feel I can say what I like & because I always feel so alive & natural with you. I don't think ah, I must not say that or this or she wont understand, even though you dont often understand. . . . You know I love your work it is one of the few things I can say honestly about you but I do long to see you do a picture like your little one of Cora and you and the sheep, and I long to look through your work again. Could you not do a little picture of a real spiritual experience? You came very near to what I mean in the pic: you did of Mrs. Carline in the Garden at Byways. All this depends on your will to be happy. That is the great secret. . . . I feel that you also fail to express yourself in landscape as compared with your ideas, like for instance the one Henry has here of yours of Cora & Collin going down a dark lane. . . [C. F. Collin and Cora Stoop were fellow-students of Hilda's at Tudor-Hart's art school in Hampstead, 1914–15, and subsequently married.] But I want to paint a landscape with the same desire and feeling in me that I have when I do a big picture, & I never got it. You see a place effects me much as sometimes a person effects you . . .

Poole (June 1923)

. . . it is obvious that you think I do big pictures to enhance that feeling of importance that you once alleged I liked to have; when you said I thought there would be a big black blot left where I had been. Both you and Mrs Lewis obviously thought that my tendency to be always talking about myself and my big pictures, showed that I was suffering from swelled head self importance pride & all the other virtues: instead of realizing it was just the natural exuberance & desire to tell everybody everything. If I had a job you would not hear so much but when all these things are buzzing in my head & I am unable to put them on walls, I relieve myself by talking about them.

Until you can get the idea out of your head that you know better than I do what is good for me, I cannot attach any importance or get at all interested in any thing you think. I would like to read your play through though I dont think I shall like it, I suspect it has some of this propergander in it. . . .

. . . from things you have said in your letters, that you thought I showed lack of feeling, simply because I was unsympathetic & hard hearted & perverse – o ye of little perception – where as the real reason was that I knew that my feelings were not for you. I rather deplore the hope of ever knowing who they are for.

Poole (4 July 1923)

I have written to you a huge letter but as I hate it I dont want to send it. . . . From what you say in your letters, it is painfully obvious that you have never understood in the least the feelings I wish to convey in those big pictures of mine. You never would have thought that painting big pictures was just a matter of inclination, a different inclination, from doing small ones, if you had had the least notion of the feelings in my pictures.

Such a sentence as this in your letter completely blights my desire to talk to you about pictures at all. And this is a pity as you have a kind of knowledge about pictures which although it is under the influence of the French school, interests me.

Poole (18 July 1923)

I should like nothing better than to be with you all again, but the roving spirit is not in me, though the Pyranees I should think would be very wonderful. [The Carline family, including Hilda, were going away for some months.]

. . . You must know that no matter how kind Henry or Mrs [Augustus] John might be to me, that somehow I dont feel happy in this atmosphere, and that no one, no matter how much better they may understand me, can provide me with the atmosphere you provide, or give me the power to live that you seem able to do. I hope you will forgive me for saying this much of my feeling – I find it a great strain to have to smother my feelings about you.

Poole (19 July 1923)

[Referring to Stanley's still life of a Hyacinth, which Hilda admired.]

. . . I just did that when I was bored and had nothing else to do, & that has been the sort of circumstance under which I have painted *all* my landscapes. Your feeling like this would lead me (if I agreed with you) to the painful conclusion that all my imaginary pictures were the tortured product of a madman. . . .

Poole (July 1923)

. . . I dont mean that I think you and I ought to be the same kind of artists; could not if we would but it does mean that at least ¾ths of my life can't be communicated to you & that is rather a blow. . . .

Poole (July? 1923)

I still *hate* being in Poole & I still intend to stay here hating Poole, myself, your ideas, and. . . . It is rather comical that I hate myself & love my ideas; whereas with you I hate your ideas and love you. I in no way esteem the still life of the Hyacinths. If you were as honest as I am which you are not, you would acknowledge that you hated my ideas as much as I hate yours, however the proof that you are out of sympathy with my ideas is indiscreetly exhibited in the fact that you like the still life which is absolutely devoid of any idea of mine hense your liking for it. Dick had the intelligence to dislike it.

Poole (August 1923)

[Referring to his letters to Hilda] . . . my whole point in writing them is to be a comfort to you if possible (it is true Hilda I can hardly bare to think of you being miserable; altho perhaps I cause you the most misery) & also to keep me so to speak in communion with you. I have no communion with anyone else. . . .

. . . but you know that altho I am often harsh & seemingly unkind & scoff a good deal, that really I am very able to understand you or am I not?

. . . And now I must stop as I must write a letter to Miss Hilda Carline. P.S. Could you call me *Stanley* & *not* Stan

[Stanley & Gilbert had just been staying with Darsie Japp (painter, b. 1883).]

. . . I remember you said in your letter when I left 47 [Downshire Hill], that I had set up a 'fuggy muddled atmosphere' & that you felt more like yourself & natural when you are away from me.

I can quite understand that I would give you this feeling. I remember your saying I was not real; & it was true.

Undated

Books read aloud to each other

Don Juan, Byron.	Vale of Health
The Light of Asia. Sir Edwin Arnold.	V. of H.
The Oddyssey	Wangford 1924
Alice in Wonderland	Wangford 1924
The Horse Stealers (Tchekov)	Wangford 1925
Richard II	
Europides: *Media. Ajax. Hercules* & others	at V. of H. Studio
Sophocles: *OEdipus Tyrannus. OEdipus at Collonus. Antigone* & others	at V of H Studios
Queen Victoria (Strachey)	At Hollands, Ashfield
China (Havelague)	Chiefly at Poole
Gullivers Travels	Wangford 1926
Two collections of Grimms fairy tales	Wangford 1926
Lady Inger of Ostraat)	
League of Youth) Ibsen	at Vale of H. Studio
Romersholme)	
Candida. Shaw.	Petersfield 1922
The Cherry Orchard)	
Uncle Vanya)	
The Sea Gull) Tchekov	Wangford 1926
The Bear)	
The Proposal)	
Reminiscences of a Retired Diplomat	Sir F. St. John – Wangford 1926
This old man. by Mrs. Muirhead Bone	Vale Studios

Still reading:

Oxford Book of Ballads

Chinese Empire (Hue)

The Idiot Myschkin (Dostoevsky)

The Manor House, Garsington, Oxford (summer 1923)

. . . I was rather relieved to get your letter; you seemed to me more cool &

clearer in your mind; and that clearness was due to your being away from me. I quite agree that I did excite a fuggy hectic atmosphere there and that it was having a nasty effect on you. . . .

I feel convinced you will agree with me that to carry on as we were doing at 47 would have been fatal to us both. I know I am almost entirely to blame over this business although I feel that these sort of things are almost bound to occur in a life.

Poole (Autumn 1923?)

. . . Of course I am really rather worried about our relationship. You see I just wonder wether you ought to try to be like me. I dont want you to be, and it seemed to me that when you said you were beginning to see things with my eyes & that you did not feel sure you were the right thing, it struck me that somehow you were never intended to be like me or have my outlook and that in trying to get into my way of looking at things was making you feel less how you wanted to feel; less like yourself, and less natural. . . . You know in a way I still believe Dick [Richard Carline] is the man best fitted to healp you; only he wont of course now. I feel about myself & about most of my friends like Lamb & the [Augustus] Johns etc, there is something *artificial* & I believe when you are with me sometimes you feel this & feel you cant breath freely. You mentioned this to me once in a letter that you sent me just after I left 47 Downshire Hill. You said you liked to be with nice simple natural people, after being in the muddled feverish unnatural atmosphere that I created. I thought when I read this, yes, at last Hilda is speaking the truth.

Poole (1923?)

. . . It is futile for me to pretend I have not the feelings about you I have. You are the most secret & greatest joy of my life, you are like redemption to me. I think of you all the time; because it brings everything to life when I do. I miss being looked at by you. I see nothing & nothing happens down here. . . . I now know if I have you I shall find my life is full. If I belonged to you I feel you would do wonderful things both with your self & me. Could I make your life more real & more happy if I made you a birthday present of myself? You know I used to think that the sort of person I ought to marry would have to be a very clever witty and altogether thoroughly developed character so that I could boast and swagger with her to all eternity but I suddenly said to myself yes, but what is all this wit learning and sense got to do with me specially to where is the great joy of making each other, when the person you have married is already made.

4 Vale Hotel Studios (2 December 1924)

I have often thought that I would become much happier if insted of enlarging on faults in you, I enlarged on just what to me was true in you & in every thing, that gradually and naturally fault after fault would disappear. Is there no basis upon which we could rely which would guarantee me from wanting to bang you on the head? As far as I can see I am wasting my own strength when I am pulling you to pieces and doing neither you nor myself a particle of good, but if on the other hand I agree *not* to have a quarrell I am or seem put into a false position & as soon as I feel this falsness I want to throw it off & I am only seem able to do so by banging you, & that doesn't really do it.

3 Vale Hotel Studios (5 December 1924)
[Regarding a certain 'loss of vision']:

As I pointed out to you in my letter; I know it was not Cookham that gave me ideas but just the degree of consciousness that God (I only say God because that is the nearest to what I should imagine) has brought me to. I must hope for this consciousness to return & not in the meantime fill up the emptyness with Cookham 'padding' because there will then be no room for the consciousness.

(1924?)

How I became aware of the great help you were to me was like this. It was very simple; I noticed that when I was with you I was no longer fearful of *myself*. I could penetrate into all the ramifications of my spirit without fear.

(1924?)

I often wish that though we see each other every day we could nevertheless continue to write to each other. . . . I wish we could both celebrate and chronicle every second of each others life. I dont feel this is a letter, it is not it is a wonderful spiritual journey that we are both taking together. I have often wanted to do pictures of the progress of the soul. I could give a wonderful description of mine from early times. The first instinct I had was the feeling that I should have to cast off my shoes 'for this is holy ground'. It was when I did the calf picture that Jas [Wood] has, that I became aware of the miraculousness of things.

(1924?)

I hope this will be the last time you go chasing about over Europe with Dick; though I know it won't be. I know you like going all over the place really. I don't, I hate it, & I am thanking myself for having the good sense not to come with you this summer. Of course when there are wars then I like to go all over the place as everything is too disturbed for me to feel I can settle down and work, but apart from this I could walk up & down the garden parth at 47 Downshire Hill for ever and ever. . . .

The correspondence is resumed some four years after they were married in 1925. It may be helpful to give a brief account of the context of their married life.

The Burghclere paintings were completed in 1932, but Spencer had visited Cookham often in the course of the two preceding years, when he renewed his acquaintance with Patricia Preece, whom he had first met in 1929. He bought Lindworth, a spacious semi-detached house on the High Street, where he settled in Cookham with his family in the spring of 1932.

The Burghclere paintings were immediately and widely recognized as a major achievement: a great autobiographical series of a character that it was his lifelong ambition, never fully realized, to carry out again. As is related elsewhere in this book, his affairs were placed in the capable hands of Arthur Tooth, he was elected an Associate of the Royal Academy and he was re-established in his beloved Cookham.

This year, 1932, seemed to him and to those who knew him and his work to be the beginning of a spectacular professional career and the consolidation of a relatively serene family life, in a place which, he used to say, was 'inspiration' and where, when circumstances compelled him to live elsewhere, he was always, with a few occasional and fortuitous exceptions, eager to return.

It was, on the contrary, a time when his life was about to be disastrously transformed and when he was convinced that a deterioration in his work was becoming apparent.

During the Burghclere years Hilda frequently visited her family. She was with them for the birth of Unity; she also went when she was needed to nurse them through severe illness (her brother Sydney died in 1929, George in 1932). Of her marriage there were two daughters, Shirin, born in 1925, and Unity, born in 1930.

Hilda's absences from their home, Chapel View, coincided with a time during which her husband's reputation as a painter was steadily increasing; he was sought out by hostesses, and flattered by many young and attractive girls. He admitted to Hilda that these presented temptations. On the other hand he was physically overstrained by the enormous task he was carrying through, and his health was further undermined by the consequences of kidney failure – stone in the kidney for a period of years, with the necessary surgery in 1934. All this exacerbated a native quarrelsomeness, so that for the first time his letters to Hilda show ill temper and ill nature and are at times cruelly critical. He contrasts her listlessness, for example, with the high spirits of the girls who were flattering or courting him. Mostly, however, his letters remain deeply loving.

The following extracts date from a period four years after marriage when they were very much apart.

They begin with a long letter of January 1929. He had just returned from Hampstead, where he had spent Christmas with the Carlines. In it he airs many resentments and some extreme fantasies – that, for instance, had he married a really creative intellectual companion he would be a more disciplined man. 'One of my first and best instincts about falling in love was the feeling of wanting some one to whom I could feel grateful, to whom I could always be giving and expressing gratitude, that exercise of gratitude has the effect of revealing more and more of our spiritual nature. Its the feeling I have always had about Christ and that is why I am rather keen on the Christ aspect of God.' But in this respect Hilda has been a disappointment and he confesses that he has made a start on 'the comparison business'.

... When one feels that ones presence & behaviour & conversation is giving intense pleasure to & enlivening ones friends one also notices that expressed pleasure in the friends is enlivening & inspiring to oneself, but the only proof that each is giving pleasure to the other is by the *expressed* enlivened inspired behaviour of each. You may declare that I give you pleasure & that my presence & talk is inspiring to you, but what is the use of that to me? I want the signs the indisputable proof that my company is an inspiration to you. So far I have had definite proofs to the contrary. You ceased to want to paint or draw as soon as you met me you became just the reverse to what you should have become. I was bright & loved bright & happy dispositions. So of course you (except when I was out of the way) became more & more wretched & hang dog & lacka-daisicle every day. How nice for me? Every one watching & noticing.

... Love in me is definitely & distinctly a religious intuition. The only way I can give it any direction or idea how to proceed or grow is primarily through religion. I mean by religion the inspirational & emotional experiences of Love that arises in & through the contemplation of Christ, or listening to a Bach organ piece. And with me my admiration for the different women you rather despise me for admiring, my admiration for Mrs Hutchinson's capacity for sympathy & her apetite for life her greed to extract pleasure from the people around her, all this is admirable & it is the same thing that I admire in Elsie [the maid at Burghclere] & in the [Patricia] Preece Girl & in a girl that came to the Chapel yesterday. She came to the Chapel with her father whom she dragged all over the Chapel first to one picture then to another. It is when I feel that this joyfulness & readiness to have a good time is clearly the result of a forthright instinct & desire for real life, that I then know they are on the threshold of experience that hunger & thirst that is going to be filled. The Preece girl hungered & thirsted but the [Dorothy] Hepworth girl did not. The Preece girl expected much & was always getting far more attention & interest than the Hepworth girl who could only find human beings awfully good models to draw. One felt with the Hepworth girl that all the nice parcels & surprise packets & hapenny dips that one usually finds oneself in possession of when faced by some hungry one such as a Preece or an Elsie, were some how not wanted & everything got slowly stored away in to some foggy recess. I was going to say that my admiration for these sort of Janet Hutchinson, Margaret Slesser (safety in numbers you know) women arises from this aforesaid religious intuition. I mean that my finding such people attractive is partially due to a natural liking I feel for hopeful dispositions, responsive natures, & people having a great zest & apetite for life. All of which qualities may seem little in themselves but all of which are very important stepping stones to heaven. ...

Hilda to Stanley
Downshire Hill (2 February 1929)
... The same things puzzle me as you, & I just wonder how it is going to come about, but the fact of our both puzzling over the same questions & looking to the same solutions & in the same direction, shews that we are doing something together. What I have been doing mostly has been trying to get rid of all those faults of mine that you refer to, in fact trying to find a way of really

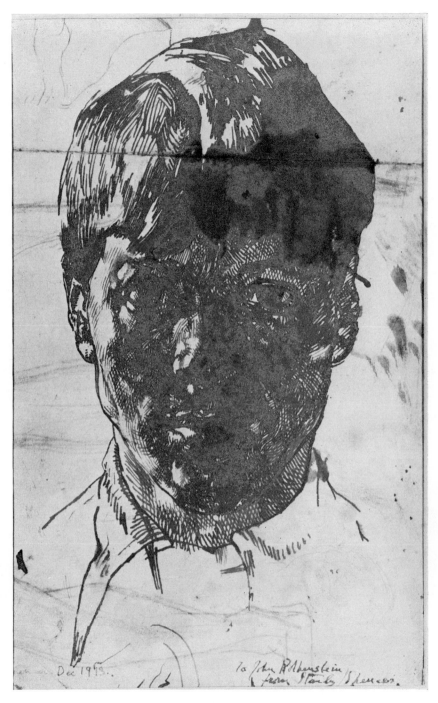

1   Study for self-portrait, by Stanley Spencer, pen and ink,
December 1913. *Private Collection*

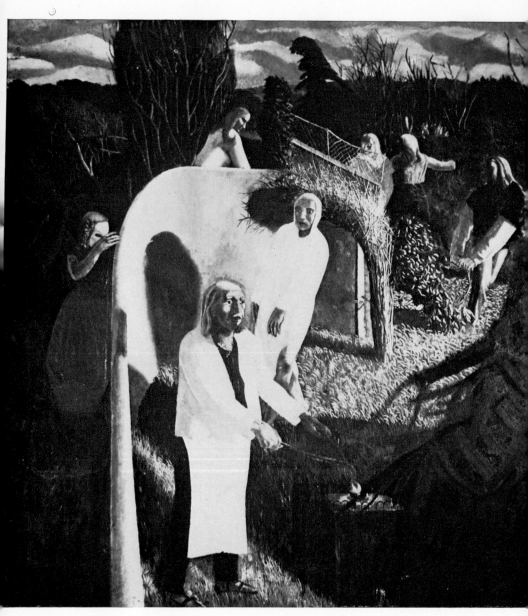

2   *Zacharias and Elizabeth*, by Stanley Spencer, oil, 1912.
Photo: David Rowan. *Private Collection*

being what I am, then I should be more convincing ; visible & of course happier & more knowing what to do.

I always feel that I get on terribly slowly, so you wouldn't perhaps feel that there was very much to shew for it all, but I am feeling happier & less crushed & more hopeful & more powerful, & I was feeling *very* far from being happy or hopeful when I came here, so I don't want to be despondant about my slowness, as I always tend to get in despair about myself because I am so slow, & I felt more hopeless this time than ever before, *much much more*. At any rate I am getting on & I am better in health. . . .

It is nice getting a real letter from you. It is the first one since we have been married. I think it is easier thinking things out away from each other for a while, for the reason that you say, that one doesn't get bothered by the untrue aspects of each other, and one gets more to the real point. . . .

Syd [Carline) is very anxious for you to come up to his private view on Thursday, but I don't suppose you will want to come up for that. *It would be very nice* to see you though if you did feel like coming up for the day or a day & a night. . . .

Hilda to Stanley
Downshire Hill (February 1929)
[Evidently in reply to a critical letter from Stanley written while the family were upset about Sydney Carline's death.]

Why don't you look into other people's minds and even size up what *they* may be feeling or what *their* impulse is, or *their need* is. Why do you work everything round about yourself as though you were the magnet round which everything worked & you were the motive for every action.

Surely some kind & sympathetic thoughts could be given me free of charge.

Dear, I ought not to write like this when I know you were not feeling well & were so uninspired.

But it came as rather a shock & blow to read your letter on my return [from Sydney's funeral].

Chapel View (February 1929)
[After visiting Hilda.]

I don't know when I have had such a happy time with you as I have on this visit. . . .

Chapel View (20 February 1929)

Sometimes I feel impossible difficulties about you but other times quite welling over with happiness & joy at the thought of all the possibility of life & joy that you suggest. At these precious moments when I can visualize you & can feel the feeling of how completely possible our life may become together. I feel I want to rejoice with you for ever & ever, to take your hand & sing 'Hallelujah'. . . .

Chapel View (22 February 1929)

As soon as I feel confidence in myself I find everything I experience on the same *scale* as my Cookham feelings. A lot of my feelings for you being antagonistic to my Cookham feelings has been largely due to the fact that you for ages & at different times have been associated in my mind with my visionless & unconfident side.

Chapel View (1929?)

I would like to talk of that picture you thought you might some day paint of you & I before we met & after. I want to do a picture on the same theme as it might show just the differences & similarities of each others atmospheres. As I have that scheme of domestic bliss compositions I thought these ought to be a centre part of a scheme of pictures, on the left would be just me in Cookham & on the right you in Hampstead & Wangford. . . .

But I have a nasty feeling that you dont like painting because you dont like the feeling that I am *liking* you to paint that you think there is something wrong in my relying so much in my feelings for you on your painting. . . .

In your painting I can see, understand & love you & I can see how & where you & I are joined together. In a great deal of what you say & think I get the feeling of being one with you. But I can only get this feeling when I feel sure of the vitality & soundness of what you say or do. The more near I come to loving you the more dangerous your erraticness becomes to me so that I naturally feel a greater momentary hatred for you. But it would make me much happier if I could feel God approved of our union. It seems so disturbing to think how badly we began. . . .

[Critical of Hilda's idea of ceasing to paint and taking up architecture.]

You must forgive & if possible take notice of some of these raving fits I feel obliged to have occaisonally. . . .

It is very important to write to each other & when you are back I may continue to do so for a purely superficial but important reason. We get muddled & across each other when we talk & then forget what we were going to say. . . . It will probably have the same steadying influence as reading the Bible.

I am feeling more possibility in our situation & this makes one feel more powerful & able to bare your temporary feebleness. Its when I myself feel feeble or on the wrong track that I find it so difficult to support my feelings for you & I have had a long period of almost not wanting things to come right, & of longing for some healthy (spiritually & bodily) girl that would be a comfort to me & give me all the things that in your present state you have not apparently been able to give.

Chapel View (1930?)

The way you have painted Elsie's skirt is a revelation to me of qualities I always hoped you had.

Chapel View (2 March 1930)

Oh duckie what ever the rights & wrongs of our situation is I do get such cosy happy feelings when I am writing. I just love sitting down at odd spare moments just to have a little communion. I am just now returned from the Chapel for tea & am waiting for the kettle to boil. I have done a tremendous lot to day & after tea I shall go & do some more until about 7, & then I shall come back & continue this letter on & on & on. Its such fun. . . . I think I will write to you a letter everyday when you are here & Elsie can bring it up to you in the morning. . . . This evening it was so nice & quiet I would have

written a whole writing pad but I have done such a lot in the Chapel to day &
yet this morning I badly wanted to spend the whole day just writing to you.

I think the reason why it does not occur to you that it is cruely blunt of you
not to see that you should make your soul a fit & habitable place for me to live
in, is because you feel no desire to inhabit my little mental abode as you are
already a resident in the handsome magnificently appointed desirable residence
called Christian Science, so that you have no way of feeling what sort of feeling
my longing is. But you do seem a marvelous present to me & I never cease to
really take a real imaginative & vital interest in you.

Hilda to Stanley
47 Downshire Hill (March 1930)
  . . . And why should I have to mould myself by you, & *only* want what you
want. You want me to be individual & at the same time you simply can't bear
me to be. You simply can't bear me to want anything you haven't previously
wanted me to want. You want me to be the most faithful copy of you that
anyone could be. . . .

Hilda to Stanley
47 Downshire Hill (28 March 1930)
  . . . As I know definitely that I can't at present have you in any real way, I
want instead all sorts of unreasonable things. I like to have you do things for
me rather than anyone else, because I like to have you about. . . . I want to be
with you, if only merely in the same room & not talking a word, . . . I want
every kind of scrap of you I can get, in every way or form. . . . But I think the
chief point of difference actually is that I *believe* in my need for you, & you
don't believe in your need for me. . . . Your need for me is only a practicle one
actually, the truer need that you feel is not definitely centred on me, it could
be supplied equally well and better by some one else if you were not married
to me. So that what you need of me only exists because of the practicle fact that
you are married to me & so can't be married to someone else at the same
time. . . . If such a remote possibility might occur that I should feel so desperate
about the line you took that eventually I left you, that wouldn't worry you
either, it might even please you. Although one doesn't actually think of these
things, you know that in the back of your mind this is the consciousness that is
there. . . .
  . . . With regard to you & me; I have often thought that nothing can ever
come right until you actually beleive in our marriage as definitely right.

Chapel View (1930)
  Sometimes when I come in quite bright & brisk & I catch sight of you
looking miserable or indifferent or uninspired I feel as though you had caught
me by the sleeve and swung me round away from life & joy. . . .
  The thing that I hope is that these terrible obstacles can be overcome
without our having to leave each other or any other rotten procedure. . . .
  If I could feel that God is as desirous for your well being as he is for mine &
that he has *certainly joined us together* it would give me such confidence & happiness I should be much less sensual than I am. I don't believe in divorce but I
think separation is possible & it is this thought that worries me & depresses me.

Chapel View (6 May 1930)

... Louis [Behrend] said he thought you & Mrs Carline & Dick were a *naturally* refined family & if anything over intelectualized & that this he thought accounted for the difficulty you have in feeling comfortable with just anybody.

Hilda to Stanley
47 Downshire Hill (7 May 1930)

It is so nice to hear what the Behrends say for instances, & it gives me such a freer feeling, & makes one realize that they are not just intellectuals, but real people, otherwise the *perfectly ordinary* remarks I have made about pictures at times, would have gone quite unheeded. One of the chief things I have been bothered about at Burghclere has been the feeling that one had got to be interesting & if they don't mind the fact that one isn't interesting & only says ordinary things it takes quite a weight off one.

Chapel View (May? 1930)

I have just had tea now & have just painted the cauldron in the chapel. I am still in the chapel but it is too dark to paint any more. Yesterday & today I have done a lot. As far as looks are concerned, what I have just done seems more stimulating than anything else in the chapel. The little person is meant to be me that is holding up between two flat pieces of wood a big bunch of bacon. And it was very amusing trying to get the difference between the unfried rashers in the box & the fried rashers in the dixie. But the incident was not big enough to display my talent to its fullest. The tea in the cauldron due to the movement of the men carrying it is lurching up the side. ...

... I have just switched over from the other letter back to this one so that I really for the moment continue from the other letter. That letter is one of the currant account letters & this is a deposit account one.

Dear darling Hilda, you are a precious hope to me. ... I long to love you dear Hilda why cannot I do so completely. In spite of your sometimes sad outward appearance (only véry superficial that is) you still are to me the most revealing person of true essential joy I know. ... Oh darling why is it that over some things about me & about anything you are the surest & most unerring judge I know & yet on some things like other peoples needs you are so blind & consequently rather unjust unresponsive & unsympathetic. ...

[Regarding *The Centurion's Servant*] I had a great deal of feeling for the shape of bed. Added to the interests was the to me moving fact that our servant used to carry on conversations with the servant next door through the wall.

So that all the associations connected with this picture were very happy, as had been the case with every picture I have painted. The picture had no sort of connection with the War. ...

Chapel View (24 May 1930)
[He had just heard of Unity's birth; pleased the baby is a girl.]

... It seems nice to think that all yesterday evening up until very late I was in the other very big letter I am writing to you, describing an idea I have of mothers and children all together in a place with Virgin & Child as the central idea. I don't want to send that big letter yet so will just send this off.

Chapel View (4 June 1930)

One cant I know exactly make endearing remarks to a canvas before you begin to paint on it but I felt I could kiss the canvas all over just as I began to paint my apple picture on it.

... There is a lot of what you would call Christian Science in me & that if my creative ability feeling happened to be in that direction it would be surprising to find how great the influence was. I must do a Science picture of just people conscious of & rejoicing in perfection, it will be like a lot of people sun bathing, basking in Gods love. ... It is amazing that Christian Science had a big share in inspiring most of my after the war pictures. It didn't have much to do with the Christ carrying the Cross or The Betrayal, but it had a little suggestion of it in the Unveiling War Memorial. But the Tate Resurrection has a lot of Science inspiration in it. Of course I have *always* loved peace & happiness & absence of alarm or fear but In my resurrection Christian Science has helped me to establish & assert that feeling. In the end wall of the Burghclere Chapel Resurrection the influence has been greater still. The joy I felt on first understanding Christian Science was a new & tremendous & never before felt joy, the joy of understanding. ... This is a description of my experiences of the first dawning of Christian Science on my mind & of no other religious experience, I had ever had, & this is the substance & main spring of inspiration in the drawing of the different groups of men in that picture: There are the aware men, the conscious men the ones studying & and the ones rejoicing & expressing gratitude some to Christ & some by making demonstrative gestures to the crosses they are holding. ...

The other day I was reading your description of your conception of the raising of Tabitha. ... It showed that Christian Science in you could contribute in a unique way to your compositional sense. ... I believe even out of Christian Science thoughts you could evolve an original way of doing things. What you felt the last supper signified (as you described in a letter) when one began to think of it in that way all sorts of new & revealing possibilities from a pictorial point of view are surely possible?

Chapel View (20-c. 23 June 1930)

I really do wish I had a way of visuallizing the truth Christian Science reasoning side of my imagination conjointly & together with the sort of atmosphere side. ...

But its so lovely just sending my thoughts to you: sending them 'home'. And when they arrive they always find pals & pair off. ... This difficulty I seem to have of being able to retain as clear a vision of you when you are here or with me, that I can when you are away is rather, in fact exactly like the difficulty I have about painting from objects; with the object in front of me I mean.

With the object in front of me & with you with me I have to see a lot of things that I have not imaginatively comprehended & dont like & the remedy required in each case is identicle; confidence, that one can see only perfection wherever one looks ... or wether I look at you gardening or what ever you do that I dont like; if I see only the perfect you which ever way I look. ...

Chapel View (June? 1930)

What I do sometimes when I read your letters is to imagine that I myself am thinking the thoughts & writing the letter. As I say, the fear of your unlikeness to me has in the past made me a bit blind to your outlook & to the things you have said. I could write much better answers to your letters now than I did in the past.

I have been reading bits of old letters of yours just now. . . .

I dare say I could do a lot more that you want me to do now than I could have done last year even. I might even be able to be a Christian Scientist if you make it clear what you want me to think. All I have against it is what you have against it and this is that it does not seem to comprehend & include all the fine religious artistic & imaginative qualities that one has always known of but which some how have not yet become identified with Christian Science. . . . I dont mean that I think that there would be any dramatic or drastic becoming a Christian Scientist but that feeling love for what you are wanting me to be will be like a gradual discoverer of what I really am. . . . [Stanley's pencilled note: 'read it March 2, 1944'.]

Chapel View (May – end of June 1930)
[Begun before Unity's birth; continued afterwards.]

You can't expect to have any harmony which is what you & I both want between us when to my symphonic efforts you keep up a dreary beating of old tin cans which is all your sewing & gardening means to me. Of course if you did a reasonable amount of creative work in proportion to the amount of sewing and gardening; then the gardening & sewing would please me. . . . I do hate the feeling of not painting pictures during the baby having periods & waiting until the children have grown up like Gwen Raverat. It makes painting all wrong & the having of babies wrong too. I have not forgotten that you have done 2 paintings last year & its a great thought to me that you did. . . .

It was by seeing things through that 'in Church' atmosphere that I painted most of my pre-war pictures. I remember the Swan Upping picture coming through this feeling. I would be in Church & while in Church all outside the church was heaven so that I thought of people going on the river, . . . My religious consciousness began my feeling for *places* & that was later related to a child memory of a cosiness. But this cosiness feeling has rather bothered me lately. . . .

Somehow I itch to do a picture of the same style & size as my usual big pictures but somehow all my present ideas seem sort of long continuous endless things. I would not mind this if I could feel they were as intense. But they dont seem to be. I believe one of the causes of this is that having grown up & having more developed sex feelings than I had before the war or having concentrated on those feelings for a longer period than I had before the war they made the earliest feelings of religion & Cookham so almost die out as to be memories of consciousness rather than consciousness itself. But I dont think they are memories. I think they are true eternal feelings to which I have become partially blinded due to the preponderance of inferior desires.

. . . It was quite marvelous to see how far more positive you had become as a result of nurses simple & persistent kindness to you. It gave me the feeling that you will only thrive where there is not a vestige of criticism. This is rather awkward as I am continually as you know having outbursts & I can notice the difference in your face at once when this happens.

... I wonder if you could ever fit into my Cookham feeling it isnt a matter of being Cookhamish its merely a matter of being on an equality with it; just a matter of fulfilling yourself. ... Of course to you Cookham itself may seem very worldy & I myself need protecting when there but that is because I need some one who pulls their weight as much as Cookham pulls its weight. Cookham is such a positive place that it makes the production of imaginative efforts an absolute need. ... Most of my pictures depend on atmosphere, the place feeling & one of the most important equipments for understanding & sensing of these atmospheres & place feelings is the intelect. ...

... That is what is so funny about you; I when I am alone with you never want any one else yet directly there is a chance for you to be alone with me you at once fish round to see who you can have to come & stay. I was absolutely astonished when 8 days after we married you asked Gil to come & stay. ...

... My wanting to marry you was originally the keeness I felt watching your growth as an artist & being able to share in the joy I felt it would give you. ...

But in order for me to be with you I have to devitalize myself & become interested in gardening or sewing. If I should not do that then I am to be cut off from you because your life outlook that can stand month after month of doing nothing is not my mind or life outlook which could not possibly stand it. With everything you do & think I have got to feel in myself a possibility of *doing the same thing myself*. ... But when I want to be with you I can only see (with a few exceptions in some of your letters) you out in the garden (I would not mind if it was only for odd parts of the day) or sewing or doing nothing or being angery or irritated about something.

... I dont think I should get a bit keen on you physically if it was not for my spiritual feeling about you. ...

Its very humiliating to me when I see that all my golden words & helpful remarks etc make you go thinner and thinner while the nurses kind remarks etc. make you fatter & fatter. I should have thought that nearly every word of this letter would have added an inch of fat to your cheeks & a tube of rose madder to the colour on 'em.

I shall quite miss this letter, as I already miss the other 2 I wrote.

[This letter is a hundred pages long. Inscribed 'I read it Nov. 16 1950. Stanley'.]

Chapel View (1930)

[No letter from Hilda that morning.]

... I must just invent one to make me feel I have one. [Writes out an imitation Hilda letter.] ... Somehow M.S. nor Miss Roberts could never quite give me the significance of Cookham that the Bailey girls did or any other Cookhamite, such as Mr Worcester, Pa, Mr Croper, or Mr Francis, or Mr Pym, or Mr Jim Pym, or Mrs Bailey, or Mr Hatch. Its just heaven reciting those names. ... But I remember one of the things that worried me rather & that was that my in love feelings such as I had with Dot Worcester [Wooster] never quite came up to the sort of high religious Cookham atmosphere – & you remember how I used to try to drag them up to that pitch by bringing them Dot & Emmy into my pictures; a good way but it never quite did the trick. I began to have the longing for Dot to show some artistic or literary or creative feeling, but she had not & all this really robbed Dot of the Cookham significance I had previously felt about her.

[1930]

. . . I have been in a room & I have been conscious that I was emanating delicious lovely 'Stanley' qualities: all the time bits of me thrown freely about the floor like bits of bait. I have seen some hungery ones rush to pick them up & seeing that has made me love to supply more. One throws the food to those that have their hands ready to catch. I go to throw a morsel to you & your hands are at your side & your face turned away; probably asleep. You seem to have no use for what I have to give. SOUR GRAPES. If you just had an idea of what that stuff was that I give to all the attractive girls (I dont give it to them any more than to any one that will take it) & did not adopt the attitude to all that 'bright' side of me, of superiority or indifference you would see Mrs. Hutchinson or Elsie walking off with the very *best* bits of Stanley produced that afternoon. I know those qualities are not the only best qualities but if you don't love them you are not loving a great mass of highly lovable me. Its not in the least my fault that this happens I often bring you out in a very wonderful way & would do so more only you seem to prefer to relapse into somniference, & every time I try to bring you in or say something that would tempt an angel right down from Heaven you show a dogged reluctance. But its more this business of bringing me out you dont seem in the least degree CURIOUS or interested or *wanting* to know what I think. You like it when I tell you what I think but what about that real vital apetite that I have got, to know what you think & that Julia Strachey & Peggy Andrews & Elsie & Mrs H. & Kate & Margaret & Mrs Behrend & God knows who, have got to know what I think. I can only think of 2 girls who do not want to know what I think B. . . . D. . . . M. . . . . I have said all this duckie because it does show that my falling in love tendancy brought about this way & also shows that it could be rectified. I feel some times that when you have seen me getting very stimulated in the society of some girls that you have said to yourself 'Well I am certainly not going to compete with those idiots for the kind of stuff they are looking for in Stanley' & you have visualized a sort of undignified scramble. . . . I only write this because I really do believe it would be helpful & help to clear things up.

Chapel View (25 July 1930)
[Hilda intends shortly to return to Chapel View. Stanley suggests they 'ban' extra people in the house, leaving just themselves, the children and a woman to help during the day.]

. . . If you & I got to bed earlier & *went to sleep* (I am preaching this sermon against myself) I would wake up early enough to do all the main work of the day before breakfast. . . . I know I have always been for having a maid but only because you never did anything & every thing went to bits & to do my work & the main work of the house was too much. But I dont like all this 'posh' basis we are doing things on I hate the 'wealthy' atmosphere.

. . . If I was just doing gardening or butchers errand work driving would be the only thing I liked but driving will never go with Zacharias & the atmosphere of the bible, or any real atmosphere at all.

. . . I am not a bit surprised that I bought the car when I did: there was no prospect of home life at all or happiness with you all the time hating the place & wanting all the time to be hopping off I felt utterly degraded & thought as the vulgarians say well I guess I must get a kick out of life somehow. At that time I felt desparate & would have joined the air Force for two pins. . . . I know that I had at the time I bought the car a longing to be able to drive, and during the war I had a longing to be able to shoot & used to enjoy the Rifle Range practice. . . .

. . . Aren't *you* ever attracted away from me. . . . I think when one feels that strain one should just let oneself drift apart. . . . I feel you are as passionate as I am, only I wish you understood it a bit more.

Chapel View (1930?)

Looked at from a practicle & material point of view there has continually been evidence or what could be taken as evidence, that I had a deterrent effect upon you. First. When away from me you brighten up, improve in morale & recover mental poise & balance. Second. You are much more stimulated to inspirational efforts by anyone rather than me. . . . The atmosphere of Gil makes you want to paint Miss Silcox; the same makes you want to do Mrs Carline. The atmosphere of Jas inspires you to paint on Odney Common. The atmosphere of Dick was irrasistable & before I came on the scene & stifeled & chequed your desires to paint to be present in the room with Dick painting & you *not* was impossible. Then there was Christian Science & the inspiration you got from Practitioners. Last year when I sent you those two enormous letters all I got was that you had been made so happy lately by *just one thing* some practitioner had told you. . . . I feel that somehow perhaps my writing to you so much is really having the deterrent effect of taking away your desire to write rather than inspiring or stimulating you to do so. . . . I cant see but that my letters to you of these last two years must have a very inspiring effect upon you & in recent short letters you have shown that they have had some happy effect on you. . . .

Chapel View (7 July 1930)

I thought about a week agow that is about 460 quarters of an hour ago, that I would love to stick all mine & your letters . . . neatly all over the asbestos wall of the studio . . . what a marvelous feeling of communion of all our thoughts. We would be writing letters for the screen & making wallpaper.

. . . Down here the difficulties are more or less as follows.

1. Not enough time for us to enjoy & feel in each others presence. Too much interruption like being in the war.

2. No chance of being alone together, which in our present condition is necessary though it might not always be so.

3. We get annoyed with each other when one is feeling a possibility of happiness & the other does not see or sieze on the chance. This has happened both ways.

4. This difficulty is due to the fact that we cant feel together & happy & supported in each others beings all the time.

5. The getting depressed by your slack unvital appearance & consequently feeling attracted by the opposite in Elsie. During last winter when she was here you were in London I did not feel upset at all & had no difficulty in feeling you

in my thoughts all the time, so I really think that this difficulty which I believe is the greatest, is a thing that might be overcome by the very thing that makes me still able to love you & feel a vital interest in all your desires: namely that of being able to see myself & my desires & Gods thoughts THROUGH YOU. There is an important *fulfillment* lying at the goal of our concerted efforts & its this absolutely certain conviction I feel that makes our affair so different from these attractions that I feel. I have the utmost respect for these attractions & for the Elsies that unwittingly cause them, & I know that once I got right (getting the right degree of confidence in you & in God) all these attractions would not only not bother me but would actually enhance our feelings for each other. . . .
[Continued on return from spending day with Hilda at 47 Downshire Hill.]
. . . I know this morning we were saying all is over & all that sort of thing . . . but this afternoon it was apparant thats all; that a great feeling of peace has come to us. . . .

What I used to feel was that for you to be integral with me there would have to be in me a whole lot of stuff foreign to & at war with my best feelings.

But all this was due to a fear I had that what was best in me could be injured, could go bad, like fruit. I am now blissfully happy & feel the freedom in knowing how utterly impossible this is. . . .

Chapel View (15 July 1930)
There are a lot of art development in me that should be put to your credit, for instance I become *most* fertile in ideas when I am thinking about you. My really happiest feelings are when I feel I am with you. . . .

Chapel View (17 July 1930)
I wish you could see me as well as I see you duckie because I am sure I am very nice to look at. I feel my shape physically being such a complementary shape to yours somehow reveals to me something about our spiritual complementariness.
[Inscribed 'I read this lot Nov 16th 1950'.]

Chapel View (1930?)
Another depressing thing is my feeling of utter hopelessness so that I feel some times that it is almost wrong of me to give you so much, that I am making a mistake & you said it seemed such a waste that no one but you could share the wonderful thoughts & ideas I gave to you, & although I am unable to assert that I love you completely as you are somehow able to do to me, yet my love for you has made me able to find out what your needs were & able to supply them with what they want. You have never *deliberately* done anything for me. . . .

You once said 'I have no respect for you, I only love you . . .'.

[1930]
I want this letter to be given to you & for us to read together when you are home.
. . . I know I am not right yet, but you nevertheless are the dearest of all to me, most valuable, most meaningful. What I feel is that I can see my *way*

through with you & as soon as one knows the way the obstacles become less of a nuisance.

. . . It is quite obvious to me that when I first had feelings of falling in love I was visualizing some kind of person very much not your type at all. . . .

I ask myself the question is Hilda deserving of your complete love & affection? Well my reply is this. 'If what I had to give; the best that I had to give, *suited* & fitted Hilda like a glove. If I saw it was the very thing Hilda that these things gaze steadfastly at. If I only knew I was right in thinking I should love you above all. If, If, If, its so wearying. I know that nothing in this world would make me happier than to know that my love for you was a perfect thing & that I was right in persuing it. . . .

[Perhaps from an unaddressed statement.]

As far as I can see the only really significant love affairs I have ever had have been with *places* rather than with human beings.

This 'falling in love' with a place would *not* be to the exclusion of any thing else or any *one* else.

Chapel View (2 April 1931)

I went & saw the Preeces [Patricia Preece & Dorothy Hepworth] who received me with hospitality & kindness, but in assembling to talk in the drawing room their lovely forms so exemplified the art of the baroque as twer so to speak, a *leetle* disconcerting. But this time it was an entertainment; a glimpse of Preeces Shoulder: she was sitting on the arm of the chair I was sitting in, & a Mantegna's dead Christ on the sofa. If I twisted round to Preece my attitude became as twer, a burlesque of my inward attitude, so that I had to address all my remarks to 'Christ'. . . .

Hilda to Stanley
47 Downshire Hill (13 April 1931)

Everything felt very flat when you had gone, & continued to do so until gradually I forget that you *had* been here, & then I felt better. But there is not the same brightness in the house when you are not here.

Hilda to Stanley
Hartsholme, Thurlestone, Nr. Kingsbridge, S. Devon (June 1931)
[The countryside seemed unchanging until they reached Devon.]

I began to think that is why English artists go in for detail so much. The only way to get any meaning into the countryside is to concentrate more & more onto intimate things. [She therefore decided to paint Stanley.] I have arranged to paint you, surrounded by bursting flowers, crouching down in somewhat the position you were in in that absurd photograph of you in the hedge. . . .

There was one place that would make a marvellous setting for the sermon on the sea shore, ... For instance if Jesus was here now & was living in Thurlestone, he would not be doing the identical things that happened in the Bible. Another series of things would become just as hallowed – And in the same way things could be happening now just as meaningful, if one could realize the activity of Christ now. . . .

[Hilda described a farm she had seen & wished to paint.]

The whole universe of sheep under the trees, very tall trees. It is the sheeps heaven, & they have their places by right of virtue, & wander in & out in a wonderful sort of quadrill dance that they all know, & do without a hitch. There is a minor heaven, possibly a sort of nursery heaven, a little nearer the road way from the trees, where the geese all collect together, and sit in the long grass with a young one. They are just a little bit more frivolous on account of its being only a nursery heaven, but they are complete & are there by right, probably by right of happiness.

The cows keep to the trees, & keep watch. I imagine they are a kind of angel, & have a certain amount of jobs to do, as well as just being happy.

... I would like you & me to stay there & paint. It would occupy one probably for months painting & painting, & never moving more than a few inches.

Chapel View (24 July 1931)

... Your letter was very well written but the appreciation of what you do well is obviously someone's else's job not mine. ... Anyway you always manage to write when I am not particularly wanting to hear from you. I am too fed up to make any interesting comment on anything. ...

Hilda to Stanley
Devon (July 1931)

I am sorry you had to write when you obviously were not feeling like it. Every word in your letter was bristling with a sense of outragedness & futileness (as regards me). ...

Chapel View (28 June 1930 – December 1931(?))

Christian Science need only be like Tonks at the Slade; namely, simply seeing how & where one wants to go & consequently being able to keep you on the rails & able to tell you if you are going the wrong way. Of course I have for years had a complete & full knowledge of what my true direction is: I know to a fraction of an inch when I am deflected from that direction. All Christian Science might do is to make me a little more sure footed in that direction by making me not so fearful of being dragged away from it. ...

I would so love to do a drawing of you with your hair down; not because I think it suits you, although it gives you one special look I love, but because it would be such fun to do, & because the drawing I did of Evylyn Ballard gave me a feeling of how marvellous long hair was. I wish Shireen could grow hers long again now ... It gives one a wonderful feeling of infiniteness & endless-ness. ...

I noticed during the war that the continual being thwarted & prevented from working out any idea gradually made me give up trying & after I had given up trying for some time I discovered one day that when I went to try some notion I had no inclination & no desire ... I was still able to say some good things but there was no feeling that I badly wanted and longed to say it. I could even see quite marvelous things & not want to paint them. But the thing was how the duce am I going to get to want to paint when here I am not wanting to. Well being placed back in Cookham & the consciousness of its

44

infinite capacity and all the mysterious things that would be revealed to me by being able to join in the general happiness it conveyed made me feel I must do something to get there, ... & so I came back to art but for a long time I had to push away & disbelieve in my indifference. I did several rotten paintings before I did the Mules Travoy picture [1919, The Imperial War Museum] and I always felt that picture of mine was a triumph over some of the most horrible doubting periods I ever had. ... I have become a man of 40 since you have been away and I feel if there is any change in me it is nicer. ... Is there any way I could make myself more attractive to you. What about these kind of whiskers. It would be very difficult to look the pa and ma look like our pa's and ma's looked. ... I remember I rather loved it when you were 40. ...

... If we reached a certain degree of feeling for each other that we could feel the feelings we had when we were first at Mrs Lambert's [their landlady] & that marvelous night at 47 when I came into your room after we had gone to bed. ...

There are heaps of things that puzzel & worry me darling. One is this. That I feel this spiritual marriage, this oneness & consequent feeling of rejoicing with several women. I did not mind or bother a bit when yesterday when P.A. said any really happy or vital thought I felt I would like to hug her; the joy was so just the same as our joy & its slight difference seemed to make it harmonize better with our happiness. In a sense I take it for granted that I am really at times, when I feel that vital unity, married to all the women with whom I get that oneness feeling. I believe that *fear* of lust & the thought of such a thing existing does a terrible lot of harm.

... It may be a nuisance that with me a strong sex impulse plays a big part at these times but I think the more confident I get & the more I know the truth & source of these happy feelings the freer I shall become from any inconvenient or disintegrating or inferior desires. But one of the chief diffi- culties – & this is perhaps the cause of these right-yet-wrong things that happen to me, is that as you have seemed to me not to be able at present to recieve all I have to give, or at least not so ready & able as others to receive certain kinds of gifts; & I being bursting to give them I have found them wanting to slip into all the many Peggys I meet, so in they go duckie, but perhaps it isn't a home from home. I am glad to discuss this duckie because I have been so worried & puzzeled as to why it is I can never at any time (it has quite wounded me in these letters) been able to give you *all* my love which is what I long to do. ... If we can get a *chance* of having a more harmonious time together the difficulty I speak of will disappear, just disappear. ... But duckie I am only painting the blackest side of my difficulties and making them a deal blacker than they really are. ... Of course you have to bare in mind that I have gone & developed much further with you than I have with anyone like M.S. or P.A. & that in all probability I should have found barriers more impassable than yours. ... You know how each of those coming together of our feelings has all the excitement and thrill in it as our first night at Wangford. ...

You are another Cookham to me & I shall one day be getting the same degree (though a different kind) of feelings about you. My Cookham feelings were really this, that I felt this Ascot fashion Boulters Lock Sunday Bank Holiday terrific physical life could be so tremendous seen spiritually, & this desire on my part was intensified by the fact that Cookham had as far as nature aspects were concerned & as far as different jobs that were done there (boats and boat building etc.) an afinity with the Bible and the bible atmosphere. So that in a way all the things that happened at Cookham happened in the Bible. . . . Of course in this idealizing of Cookham people it was more just my own idealizing of them, my own feeling of perfection projected onto them but there was no demand for the Cookham people to feel what I felt or be in any way what I made them in my pictures. But in my feeling about you it is a demand that you should be & be conscious of the perfect Cookham conscious-ness I have of you. . . .

I wish I could do some really good pen and ink drawings, I did not think the Chatto ones [*Chatto & Windus Almanack*, with designs by Stanley Spencer, London 1927] were at all good though now and then I got rather a jolly effect, something that was really good. I think a sort of carnival (only not superficial) procession of you & me & all the pictures & things we have done; just showing ourselves off as hard as we can. . . .

Hilda to Stanley
c/o Miss Gilks, 18 South Terrace, Littlehampton, Sussex (June/July 1932)
[About their marriage, and Christian Science.]
I hope you will be able to contemplate a bit the thought of going to see Mr C. [a Christian Science practitioner; Stanley worried that he would thereby lose his own identity]. You said the other day that it would mean your entire capitulation . . . it must be that you are a tiny bit unconvinced & unsure of some of the you qualities. . . .

Lindworth (July 1932)
[Against coming to see Mr C.]
You are always putting me in the infernal position where I have got to *make up my mind* about some matter that has nothing to do with me. . . . The trouble is that you don't respect these dislikes that I have.
[Stanley might come, but only to pacify Hilda.]

Hilda to Stanley
Littlehampton (July 1932)
[Thanks Stanley for his letter; but she cried for an hour.]
But that is because I want you so terribly much, & I can think of nothing but how to get near you & I am all the time building up & longing and conse-quently am full of hope. . . . All this great perturbation is as much as anything due to your saying you cannot possible come to London even for a day; because it seems so crushing. It seems as if it is 'no' all the time, nothing but not; not a specially thought out 'no' either, but just merely 'no', 'no', 'no', 'no'. Just a chopper coming down on everything, dear heart.

Hilda to Stanley
47 Downshire Hill (7 November 1932)
[Longing to hear from Stanley, so long since she has heard, and to see Unity.]
I don't feel I can really describe all my activities & mental developments, as I am afraid you would either misunderstand what I meant, or dislike it, or feel upset or annoyed for some such reason; & yet I am really longing to tell

you lots of things; but I daren't run the risk; you would be sure to think I was getting at you, & construe some motive or meaning that was not there. . . . With ever so much love to you, dear love.

Hilda to Stanley
c/o. Mrs. Harter, Epsom (29 December 1932)
[After the death of George Carline, December 1932.]

I wonder why *you* can so readily do this: Giving with one hand & taking away with the other. Comforting at one minute, only to bang & hurt with the next. I am hardly able to think of your letter about George, or be comforted by your thoughts, because I cannot quite think of it separate from the latter half of your letter. [Of the letter here referred to, from Stanley, I have no knowledge.]

Your mentality puzzles me very much.

Is it that you *really* believe that I am indifferent to you, or to what happens? Or is it that you *want* to think that, & so, easily slip into doing so? . . .

I do all I can, & try all I can, to free our minds. . . .

But apart from this, I will take *not one step* towards any separation. I would not make one least effort towards it. If anything ever happened in that way, it would be entirely your act and your responsibility.

You would not expect me to assist in an act that to me is wholly evil, with not one exonerating quality in it.

You *are* my husband, my only husband, & nothing can make it not so. I am *your wife* for always.

No one else could ever be your real wife. . . .

In addition to this, you have no right to say or think, that I do not love you or want you.

You could not deceive yourself more, than in saying or thinking that. It is utterly untrue. To say that I am not allowed to love you would be true, & that it is made too dangerous for me, if possible to let myself want you.

Also it is not right to let anyone think that I am deserting you, when it is you who are deserting me. . . .

Chapter 3

Marital Breakdowns

In 1929 Stanley Spencer had met Patricia Preece. (She was twenty-nine years old, and had settled in Cookham two years earlier. She died there in 1971.) She also was a painter. With her painter friend, Dorothy Hepworth, she had come to live in Cookham in a cottage called Moor Thatch, belonging to Miss Hepworth. Over the following years she was accepted as a friend by Hilda and Stanley, both of whom felt great compassion for the poverty in which she lived. Hilda herself related very clearly the story as it developed in a long letter written (some years after the correspondence that follows) in reply to Dudley Tooth, as the person who was handling Stanley's finances, in August 1939.

When we first knew Patricia, she was very badly off, living with her girl friend in a house that they had rent free and having some groceries sent up every week from her parents, and 10/– a week to buy fresh vegetables. It seemed to us terrible and we used to feel very sorry for their difficulties. She had very little prospect of ever being better off as her parents were not likely to be able to leave her anything, her only hope being a rich aunt but I expect she was problematical. However badly she has behaved, I can't say I would like to see her return to anything like her former poverty. Anyway, I conclude she considered her only hope was to marry someone with money. I do not maintain this is an unforgivable sin in itself but one imagines a person marrying for money would at least expect to do something in return, especially if they have done all the engineering of it. Only a very unprincipled person would scheme to get the money and nothing else.

But I am now sure that Patricia had one thought only in her mind and that was to get the money and, finding Stanley a possible person, she set about to procure him, trying to keep the road clear to get rid of him when she wanted to. As it happened, Stanley turned out to be very difficult to get and it took her no end of effort and a great deal of time to get him. She vamped him to a degree unbelievable, except in cinemas. I often wondered how Stanley could stand up against it. If he went to her house, she always received him half or a quarter dressed, with perhaps a dressing gown on. She was always daring him to kiss her and, when he did not do so, said he was only a C.3 man. This taunt used to touch Stanley very much and he thought he really must be a C.3 man. One day she said 'Stanley, I am yours', meaning he might do as he liked with her but apparently he didn't like and he came home feeling furious with himself, believing what she said was true – that he was no use and worn out; this hurt his pride terribly. After walking up and down the dining room and talking about it all in an agonised way, he suddenly said 'I'm going back:

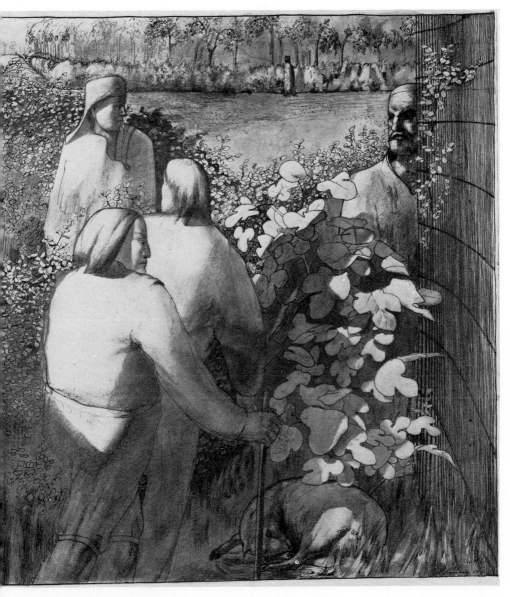

3 Study for *Joachim among the Shepherds*, by Stanley Spencer,
pen, pencil and wash drawing, 1912. *Tate Gallery, London*

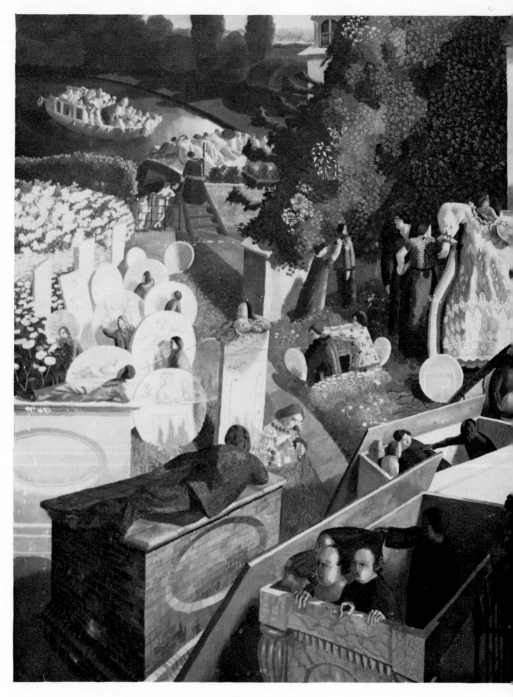

4   Detail from *The Resurrection*, Cookham, by Stanley Spencer, oil, 1923-27. *Tate Gallery, London*

I'm going to spend the night there'. I knew it would be useless for me to protest so I just held tight and, to my immense relief, in less than half an hour he was back. He said he wasn't able to go in, had walked round and round the house and had finally given up.

Of course, neither of us realised at the time that the reason was not Stanley's inability but *her* inability. At a later period her somewhat aloofness was never realised as a natural fear of something she did not want and could not participate in, but either as consideration for me or as greatness of character or some such reason. I can never understand how she could have appeared so eager during all those years when it must have been entirely put on.

Stanley always used to talk to me about this Patricia affair, often until two in the morning going over the question of whether he loved her, why he was so C.3. what he had said and she had said, what he felt and so on. [The place and time is Lindworth, 1932.] I mostly listened, sometimes explaining his thoughts or feelings a bit more clearly and occasionally veering him this way or that as the opportunity offered when there was a slight bent or wavering in his mind that could be increased. If I had known then what I now know about her physical inability, I know I could have changed the whole current of affairs, as there was so much that was confusing then and later that I could have explained.

Her whole line seemed to be an effort to arouse him physically. Later on, her conversation with him got more and more suggestive and, for an outsider like me a day of that conversation made me feel positively sick.

Actually I often felt terribly sorry for Patricia. For one thing, I concluded she was in great physical need and I knew what that could mean and felt terrible that she should have to suffer. Also she seemed to want Stanley and I used to think of her as, in the future, a lonely old maid thwarted of her one great love in life. It was only too easy to sympathise with her as I knew what I would have felt if I had not married Stanley, and *had* felt when the marriage was uncertain or unlikely. Yet I could never quite believe she loved him and that was my predominating thought in trying to get her away from him.

However, during these years, she still had made no real headway with Stanley despite his obvious interest in her, and then she used a slightly different method.

Stanley and she had been more or less inveigled into going to Switzerland [in 1933] by a man [Edward Beddington-Behrens] who seemed to feel that if any marriage had lasted more than a few years, it ought to be broken up. Both Stanley and Patricia thought that this man and his wife were going to be there too but the wife never went and the man, after being there a night, said he had to return to London on business. So there they were alone in this remote little village that was only approachable by mules. This was of course not Patricia's fault; she may have felt it might provide a hopeful situation even with the man and his wife, but she certainly did not know that they were going to be left alone there. She may however have indirectly influenced the situation by making it clear to this man that she wanted Stanley, as she was very friendly with this man. However, any supposition of that sort is pure fancy and at most was indirect without any direct intent as I have no knowledge at all on such a matter. Anyway fortune placed them in a position difficult to emerge from the same as when entering on it. I don't mean that they shared bedrooms, they certainly didn't. But the fact of sharing each other's daily life alone marks a new step which is difficult to retreat from. It marked the first big break from me, as when he returned he did not want me and I went away for a month feeling terrified of him. When I plucked up courage to return, to my relief he was apparently alright with me again.

Well, while in Switzerland, Patricia apparently made up to the hotel proprietor much to Stanley's annoyance; he complained to me afterwards that he thought it very rude of her to be constantly looking past him at dinner and smiling at the proprietor in much the same way as she had done to himself and had gone long walks with him, alternating with long walks with Stanley. In this way she made Stanley thoroughly jealous (she always got hold of his weak points).

This continued when they were back in England – working one off against the other. She used to come round with stories of the hotel proprietor's love letters to her and make his mouth water with all the lovemaking that was reputed to be in these letters. Nobody ever saw them but it never occurred to us to disbelieve her, and it certainly worked Stanley up a lot. She kept saying that this man was coming to Cookham in the spring when the birds are nesting and the conclusion one seemed to draw from it all was that she was desperate for some man and if it couldn't be Stanley it would have to be somebody else. The hotel proprietor was a married man but Patricia said he had not lived with his wife for the past year. All this had the desired effect on Stanley and made him feel very chivalrous so that if she was determined to have someone, he would rather it was him than the proprietor.

She always said that the letters contained money which she returned. Once she said he had sent £30. You can imagine how badly we felt at the thought of her actually receiving £30, needing it so badly and having to return it. Stanley was very affected on this occasion and gave her £10. I was a bit surprised at her feeling it alright to take £10 from Stanley but all wrong to take £30 from the other man, but anyway it seemed to put Stanley on another level and give him a sense of protection over her. Actually of course the whole story of the money may have been made up; no one ever saw the letters or what they contained, but they worked Stanley up more and more the nearer it got to spring. Towards Easter, things became more and more tense. Patricia kept saying the proprietor was coming in a few days and talking of what was going to happen; from what she said, one could only fear the worst and she led us to believe that he and she were going to be lovers. Finally he was supposed to have arrived in Holland intending to come straight to England, but his wife had tracked him down and asked him what kind of business took place in England on an Easter week-end. Then he said he would arrive in Cookham on Easter Monday and this brought about my departure from Cookham. Stanley said that if I was about he would not be able to keep a proper watch on Patricia, that his attention would be divided, that he did not mean to let Patricia out of his sight, that he intended sleeping in her kitchen and being with her whenever the man was with her and if they went for a walk he would go too, he was in such a terrible state of anxiety and worry that it was too painful to see him even and as I couldn't help him, except by being off his mind by going away, I did so. Actually I could not bear to witness his agony and anxiety.

Of course I was taken in too by all that Patricia said and appeared to feel;

it was only later that I knew it was all done purposely and that she could not have had all the desires and needs she pretended to have. But at that time we believed she was in a desperate way and Stanley seemed to feel that (though he didn't appear to want to) if anybody was to be sacrificed to satisfy her supposed needs, he would rather it were himself.

I know quite a bit about being in love with someone who is impotent as I was in love with such a person myself before I married, and I know what one feels and how easily one is deceived.

Well, to finish the story, I heard afterwards from Stanley that the visit was a washout, that the man eventually turned up just for a day and that there was nothing whatever to get worked up about. And, looking back, I think it was all a purposeful misrepresentation, that she could see the effect it was having on Stanley and worked on him over it. How she finally managed to bring him to the point after I left, I don't know, but I guess she misrepresented me, judging by his unaccountable fear of me, just before the divorce and she also prevented him from reading letters of mine and writing to me. However, I am afraid I don't really know what happened and it doesn't matter now.

It is what happened after that is the most significant. On looking back I am struck with the way she always seemed to protect herself in advance though I didn't see through it at the time. Why would she want to protect herself beforehand in this way if it was genuine love on her part; there would then be nothing for her to fear.

She must have known that there would be plenty of possibility, if she did get Stanley to marry her, of his being able to annul the marriage, and she wanted to be protected from that possibility. She knew she was a person incapable of marrying, that she was physically imperfect, and therefore she had plenty of planning to do to secure her position.

Eventually Hilda felt, reluctantly, that it was in Stanley's own interest to divorce him, though he did not ask her to do so. The decree nisi was pronounced in November 1936, made absolute on 25 May 1937 and on the 29th Stanley and Patricia were married at Maidenhead Town Hall.

Earlier letters continue to show a persisting emotional turmoil.

Hilda to Stanley
c/o. Mrs. Harter (1932)

I don't want to not do anything you suggest or ask, but you are asking a rather difficult thing.

I definitely don't want to go [to a party] with you & Patricia. In view of many things you have said it makes it more difficult to do so than it would have been formerly. . . .

I don't feel happy at the thought of coming home at all, there are so many things you have said from time to time, that it would be difficult to wipe out even ever. . . .

I am not against your trying to find out what you really feel about Patricia, I think it is necessary to do so, & in that case the sooner the better, & the more conclusively you find out the better. But I would definitely prefer not to be there while it goes on. Perhaps you do already know what you feel.

I have been talking to Dick about it, & he has told me one or two things about Patricia that surprised me – I don't know what you would feel about it, you might not mind, but in the back of your mind I think you would. My feeling is that you need to be careful & make very sure, & don't live in a fool's paradise, but try to find out definitely what she is like & what she feels. I don't suppose my opinion is of much value to you, but definitely, I don't think she would MARRY you. She might not mind something else to a limited extent, but I doubt if she would with you. On the other hand do you want to be mentally married to a person only, & could you even be *that* with her.

Hilda to Stanley at Lindworth
From Downshire Hill (7 January 1933)
I feel grieved to remember your face (& yet thankful that you can look like it).
But why do you give me things, I am not equal to. . . .
I should so much have preferred meeting Patricia in my own way: . . . I know you had not the least intention of hurting me, it was mere thoughtlessness; but it is a terrible quality to have, it can do so much harm.

Lindworth (11 January 1933)
In the early part of yesterday morning I *dreamt* that Patricia passed by the dining room window & up to the front door. I woke up to the awful fact that it was a dream, rather like waking up to find the war was on.

Hilda to Stanley at Burghclere
From Lindworth (1 February 1933)
I hope you have finished the Chapel by now, as it certainly would be nice to feel that was quite finished & off your mind. . . .
Apart from loneliness I am getting on very well. But I am so desperately lonely, that I just wonder how you were able to bear it when I was away, except that you weren't really alone, but quite considerately not alone. . . . Unity is as sweet and loving as ever, but as far as I can see a hundred children don't actually take the place of one Stanley.

Hotel Monte Moro, Saas-Grund, Valais, Switzerland (28 August 1933)
When I had been at Saas Fee about two days or more Mr. [E. Beddington-] Behrens said he thought he would telegraph to Patricia & tell her to come here. I was greatly surprised & needless to say more than delighted but I did not think she would come. I had made no sort or kind of suggestion about her coming: when I got on to the train at Gare de l'est, he said, 'And how is your friend Miss Preece?' I said, 'she has been ill & had just recovered but the Dr. had ordered her change & the usual things'. He made no reply & showed no interest & I felt awful. Although that was all I said I felt I had been saying it like a beggar. He handed me Patricias reply in silence & I read 'Delighted, coming etc'. She was under the impression that Mrs [Beddington-] Behrens was here also as *my* wire when he asked me said '*we* will meet you' . . . Patricia arrived, I then announced to her that Behrens was departing the next day & I think she was a little worried. She explained to me then that at the same moment as Behrens wire, came also a *charming* letter from you. She was in a

muddle as to what to do but had to decide at once as she would have to get Passports etc. Everybody of course said 'go'. . . . I am very very happy as well I might be. I must just look at these hundreds of goats. There is something almost ironicle about this situation: here I am, I should think not far from Neuchatel the place where you were. . . . Another touch of irony if you can bare it yesterday; to the sound of all this '(goat bells, roar of mountain torrent)', Behrens sang 'O Claire de la Lune'. . . . We both felt we would like him to have stayed *two* more days, but not more.

The air being so marvellous I had inwardly prayed that the thought might strike him to ask her to come out here I'm good at this hard praying, no one can stand against it. . . . Behrens wants to buy everything I do out here, but I really most want to do drawings of the peasants. . . .

Hilda to Stanley
The Hill, Wangford, Beccles, Suffolk (31 August 1933)
[She refers to Switzerland.] And it must be doing Patricia lots of good & you too probably. . . . With much love to you. Also love to Patricia & thank her very much for her card which I was delighted to get.

Lindworth (October 1933)
Your *cast* of thought is utterly unsuited to mine & mine to yours. And to see you trying to *put up* some appearance of understanding & enjoying what I am describing is so odious, so detestable, & so unconsciously insulting, that, some-times when I am talking about some quite simple but to me amusing matter, I feel your put on manner so intensely, that I just have to stop & a terrible choking sensation of rage has to be over come & I turn my head away so that I cannot see you & thus continue. *All* your affability to me is not a genuine product; you are not moved by me you have given a thing called God that job. . . . You cannot serve Stanley Spencer & Christian Science. . . .

I hate the way you live, the way you like to leave everything up to the last moment, the way you have so little appetite for real joy as to allow what little there is to be ruined by making everything as uncomfortable for yourself . . . as you can. . . . Its just the joyless feeling that gets me down. . . .

Hilda to Stanley (1933)
. . . I don't know what to say about the question of you and Patricia. I am tremendously anxious for the right thing to happen, and for you to have what you need and want. I am so much more anxious for that, than that I should have any of my personal wants. Although I have a lot of personal wants they have not been actuating me in this affair because I much more want everyone's happiness than just my own. . . .

Hilda to Stanley
47 D[ownshire]H[ill] (1933)
I hope you & Patricia had a nice birthday. When Patricia talks of not wasting the flying years, but collecting happy memories, I have certainly done so this week. [Hilda had visited Stanley.]

Lindworth (May 1934)
I thought my pictures [at the Royal Academy] looked quite academic &

commonplace & did not stand out at all. I saw Eddie Marsh there & he obviously did not care for my things. He introduced me to Winstone Churchill and Mrs. I saw no one else I knew, which sounds very grand. . . .

I got hundreds of notices. Patricia complemented me on the manner in which I stuck them in my press cutting book. She was prepared to say that much. She is like that to me as well as you; ie prepared to say nice things about me which are non-commital or of no great signification.

Lindworth (July 1934)

My affair with Patricia is my one & only social achievement; the true & correct reward for all the *best* work I have done. . . .

When I was wanting to see Will, she suggested I should go by myself & that she would wait about for me, but I was afraid I might loose her if I did that.

Lindworth (1 February 1935)

Could you do on 30/– less per week than you at present have from me.

The fact is I am much poorer through this illness [kidney trouble] is some reason, & I lost a lot of commissions; but that is not entirely the reason. The chief reason is that I so long to have more to spend here myself.

I like to spend money on what I *love* to spend it on & what I feel deserves to have it [i.e. Patricia]. But to have to pay only because of a moral obligation to do so is not very nice & like Income Tax I like to pay only what they have a right to demand. I think my present circumstances are very different from when I arranged to pay you four pounds a week. And then it puts such a check in my activities here.

If my circumstances improve I would try again to increase to £4 a week. [The weekly allowance was for Hilda and also for the two children.]

Hilda to Stanley
47 Downshire Hill (23 February 1935)

[Utterly shocked by the preceding letter and Stanley's attitude in general.]

It has brought on a complete breakup of health, & worse still of mind. I am better now in those respects than I was before Christmas. . . .

I am *terrified* of life, it is all too much for me. In the summer my eyesight nearly went, I could not look at things as I walked along a road, . . . because the moving things hurt them & eventually made me unable to distinguish things, unless I kept them shut all the time it was not absolutely necessary to have them open. . . . But all the time I had to keep forcing [myself], if I absolutely had to get anything done.

Switzerland was the best time I have had, in fact the only hopeful or happy time. . . . [Hilda had paid a recent visit there with Unity.]

Sometimes however I almost hoped to go out of my mind, as that I thought would break up my train of thought, & stop all recollections & puzzles or hopeless hopes & so on. I felt that that would be perhaps a sufficiently complete break up & when everything was forgotten in this way, I might someday begin gradually to build up once more. . . .

The kind of weak health or lack of health I have had this past year, handicaps one enormously. It makes everything five times the burden it should be, & makes nothing really well done, or satisfactory. But withall one is more or less master of oneself. But lack of mind; even the first dawnings of it! Takes away almost everything. . . . I feel it is the biggest physical loss one could sustain; except that if it were completely gone there might be just a blank.

I have also given up Christian Science; not because I believe in it any the less, but because I just can't do it. Although my mind will ramble on in its own way forever; I can't do any concentrated thinking. . . . Even in the summer, before going to Switzerland, I had practically given it up. . . . I am not happy about this, I miss it very much; & it makes me feel in a very precarious world.

I often think what a lot I have to be grateful for, that my physical needs are supplied, & that I do not have to do more than I can; that here all hard work is done by others, & I really have as easy a time as I need. And also you send me money, so, we don't have to lack anything we really need. I have often thought of this with gratitude; for conjointly with that, I have realised how impossible it would be to face any other situation. . . . Such a situation seems to belong to a moon world or a star world something quite outside my comprehension or possibility to deal with. Please Stanley, don't let such a thing happen . . . lack of livelihood would take away all chance of living. – I am *afraid*! . . . I am always very careful with your money. I buy nothing for myself. This winter I have spent £1 on clothes, very essential ones. Fortunately I have not had to buy any clothes for Unity, as what she has, still do. But I have had to spend somewhat on Dinnefords Magnesia, & Cod liver oil, as she was getting very poorly. . . . You probably don't believe I am careful. But when I was with you, I never was given any responsibility with regard to money. I never had a weekly allowance to do housekeeping with, or for my private expenses. I had to ask you for any particular item. And I had no clear idea as to what you had got & what it was justifyable to spend . . . .

[Have] . . . a longing for some place of my own, which could be like a home, something that was mine. Room to have some of my things round me, & for Unity to have some of her toys about. Here all my possessions, except those at Cookham, are packed into that tiny bedroom that has to accommodate Unity & me. I cannot even have my paintbox about it has to be packed away. . . . Not that I want to paint now at all. But my writing things that I really prefer now, have also to be packed away. . . .

My actions aren't free. I can't decide to have a fire in my bedroom & do some work. I can't organise anything in my life; & this is demoralizing; . . . . If one could say there is *one* compensation for a broken marriage, one would probably say that compensation was freedom; but I haven't even got that, not one scrap more than when I was with you, & as a matter of fact a great deal less.

Whilst I have been here I have had such an intense longing to get away from this house; when Mum talks about all the old associations connected with it, I feel I could scream, though the room is full of people. The associations are just what I want to get away from; I would blot out every recollection & association of the past, even happy ones, they are all unbearable now. . . .

When Dick and Mum are so complacent & unflurried about the *house*, & say, 'one wouldn't like to leave the old place!' I feel as if I am going crazy; I wonder whether they are mad or I. . . .

But there is another thing I have been longing for, perhaps more intensely than the house, & that is the prospect of renewed health. . . .

[She wants Stanley to come up & discuss the allowance question.] If we were legally separated, instead of your giving me your proposed £125 a year, or as up till now £200 a year, you would probably be expected to give me £400 a year. . . .

This is now 10 years since we were married. Patricia is now the age I was when we were married, or rather she is 2 months younger.

Hilda to Stanley
47 Downshire Hill (17 March 1935)
[Stanley's brother Percy will not act as go-between. Therefore Hilda is sending this letter 'in case you are interested to read it'.]

Firstly I would naturally have preferred, as I imagine would you also, to have had an amicable arrangement . . . I gather, however, that just those qualities of consideration, trust & confidence, are exactly what you neither wish for, nor would give. . . . I am cursing myself, (now that I realize it,) that I have been carrying on all this correspondence with Patricia, (thinking I was writing to you, & receiving replies from you!).

Hilda to Stanley
47 Downshire Hill (1 May 1935)
. . . If one were to weigh your conversations to other people about me, against my conversations to other people about you (which is the reflection of my thoughts about you), I can't help feeling that the balance would go very badly against you. . . .

My desire for you is for your happiness in the way you want it. As you know, as soon as I saw that it was impossible for you to pursue any course other than the one you were pursuing, I left you completely, never to return. And I did so without any fuss or recriminations, or making either of you feel uncomfortable or to blame. I made everything just as easy as I possibly could. (I wanted to.) Don't I deserve some gratitude for this, some confidence? . . .

Physically and mentally I am going under.

(Though this is only comparative as anything extreme is so improbable as to be impossible, and there are however so many degrees of dying, it is a long and increasingly painful way before one gets just there; what you are doing is nevertheless a degree of murder.

Hatred always is a mild form of murder, and in some cases it has a more murderous effect than others.)

. . . I cannot turn against what I have once loved and revered. . . .

Stanley to Hilda
Lindworth
[In folder with 1935 letters: postcard in an envelope: no postmark visible.]

. . . I will not send any reply to any letters & I will not send them. If you need anything from me please ask Mrs Harter (Sydney Carline's mother-in-law) to write as I dont want any correspondence with you.

Hilda (presumably to her solicitor, 14 June 1935)
. . . Also if I had not married him I would have been equally unhappy. . .
I was a great friend of Stanley's for a long time without having ever thought of marriage, the idea had never entered my head; though Stanley had apparently

always thought of marrying me. He said he decided to marry me the first day he saw me.

When, however he talked of marriage to me, I had to think of it, & when I had definitely come to the conclusion that I did want to marry him, there was no going back as far as I was concerned. . . .

However we were engaged & broke it off continually six or seven times or more, over a period of 3 or four years. . . .

And he unfortunately was not sure of his mind; & that uncertainty is another of his everlasting qualities, when I last saw him he was in the same state about Patricia, unable to know whether he really loved her or no, although he is so desperate about her, he has nevertheless been in a completely dithering state as to what his feelings really were. . . .

Actually I think the reason I have not actually lost over this marriage, is because I have put so much into it; because it was & is a life's job.

. . . And I think that is why this obligation remains: [for Stanley to keep Hilda]. He has broken a contract in such a way as to put me into a position I had never bargained for & would never have agreed to.

. . . With regard to earning my living, you know, I never have done so at any time in my life; it seems a bit terrible to start to try & do so now, unless it is unavoidable. At one time I did ask Tonks . . . whether he could find me some art work, but he was completely against my doing anything but painting. He had, as a matter of fact, a high opinion of me as an artist, & contrary to his usual practice with students, was discouraging of my earning a living any way but through painting. I then dropped any idea of other art work (such as teaching & so on, though I certainly never wanted to do anything like that).

Stanley was also at one time very ambitious for me, & was very anxious that I should be always painting. He said in fact that he first fell in love with my painting. . . .

Hilda to Stanley
47 Downshire Hall (23 July 1935)
[Hilda wishes to see Stanley rather than have a legal battle. She is on his side; will accept less money if he really cannot pay.]

You do realize, I suppose, that £2.10 a week, is quite inadequate to live on even in the way we are living, at the present time. . . . I have bought nothing for myself or Unity since you knocked my money down, except 3/s on some frilling. This however cannot go on for ever, & it has been difficult enough up till now. Clothes *won't* last forever however much one tries; my winter shoes have been almost impossible to wear, Unity needs a makintosh, her's lets the rain through, & she has outgrown almost all her shoes, & shoes too small are bad for her feet. Also you paid Unity's school fees for this term & another bill for me. How am I going to pay Unity's school next term? . . .

I am utterly worn out, both physically & mentally, by so many difficulties & cruel situations arising from you, & also about Shirin. . . .

This is the last effort I can make *for you*, if this fails I will have to think only for myself & Unity.

So DON'T let it fail. I am worth keeping as a friend & ally. You will never have a more loyal or faithful one, or one who could weather so many rebuffs or

[deleted by Hilda] cruelties or lack of recognition & so little personal gratification or reward. . . .

You will be throwing away, the one real true, thing in your life. . . .

Though no doubt if the children & I were living with you, you would think
it natural to keep us, & if you had wanted us we would have been with you, ...

. . . you feel that you were really coerced into marrying me; . . . I had no
idea or thought of marrying you, not the least shadow of such, until you talked
of marriage.

Take the case of Jas, which is a very clear example . . . he KNEW without a
shadow of doubt, that he had no intention of marrying me, & consequently I
knew it too. . . . [Therefore we were able to be] friends after that with perfect
immunity . . . I have *now*, what I had then, an enduring love & devotion for
you only I have a bit more now than then.

Hilda to Stanley's brother Percy
(16 March 1935/36?)

My decision is, to have some legal basis for the money, either without, or if
necessary with, a divorce.

If however Stanley does not wish for a legal arrangement, the only alternative
is if he comes up personally to discuss with me about it. Letter writing merely
means negotiating with Patricia, & I have no intention of negotiating with her.
I realize now, that I have in this affair merely been carrying on a correspondence with Patricia, about Stanley's money!! . . .

Stanley knows that if he trusts me, & is open with me, that he can get *any*
thing out of me. (The reason being that I then understand his point of view,
his difficulties, his needs) . . . .

Lindworth (28 March 1936)

I have received your last card & both when I saw you & when I rang you up,
I was sincere in what ever I said. Your reply to my proposal on the 'phone
showed me that what I was trying to do was no use. Your card was pretty awful.

I have written to the bank telling them to stop your allowance.

I shall not see you if you come here.

Hilda to her solicitor
47 Downshire Hill (4 April 1936)
[Someone has suggested to Hilda that Stanley really hasn't the money to pay
her. She enquiries if this is so, as this will influence her actions.]

But as I have nothing to live on after about 2 weeks, I cannot wait about
making enquiries for very long. [If Stanley really is in financial difficulty,
Hilda will try to get one of her pictures into the Royal Academy & sell it rather
than take action against him.]

Stanley to P.A. (1936–37)

I don't know if being divorced is colouring my outlook & that I am becoming
a libertine (I am sure that what ever I am it is good) but I can never quite
understand why the conventions (except for state reasons, namely that a man
could only maintain the expence of one woman) decreed only one each. I am
divorced but I am as much Hildas as ever I was, possibly more. I still see

Patricia every day & I hope I always shall have her. I notice that the feeling I have for one woman never cuts across the path of the feeling I have for another. I cannot understand this possesive business. I was *never* possessive. To anyone like myself all sorts of descriptions are given to my mode of outlook & behaviour & they are always used in a derogatory sense thus they will say I am poligamus & I say if you mean that I wish to change about with women or several wives I say yes I do but without admitting to one ounce of any thing derogatory in my doing so. I consider it a sign of intelegence in me that I should notice that with many women I can reach the most intence state of being & awareness (which is life) & in each case it is utterly sincere. Imperfections one is aware of but it does not prevent meeting. I dont understand love but I do understand the utter fusion & extacy that can be between myself & —, or myself & Hilda. . . . As soon as you aspire to some human contact you will soon see & feel the *importance* of intimacy. One is utterly handicapped if THAT has to be left out like an expurgated edition of a book. I think this letter is rather amusing: I would be such a 'dangerous fellow dont you know' 'Not safe to go about at night' sort of thing.

It is damnable that the only great things of life are put into a blasphemous category. In the gross way of life being interfered with by the law (over this divorce I mean) it is as if in depriving me (as it is at present) of Hilda & of Patricia it was depriving me of canvas & paint brushes & more than that of my own important life. Life which as you once so clearly put it is only *life* when there is human contact is my art & my art is being interfered with. I have yet another about four months to wait before my decree, which Hilda has brought against me will be made absolute, that is supposing they grant it. I *hate* the *mistress* atmosphere. I would like about half a dozen homes in which I was 'father' in each one. If I had the money I am sure I could live in absolute happiness with *each* wife if I had a dozen & I often think the irritableness that men so often experience in themselves in there homes is because they are wanting a change of wife, it may be only for a short time. It isnt just a change it is the fact that a new experience helps one to come to a greater understanding & realization of the old experience. I know more *now* how to deal with the Hilda difficulties & if I lived with her again now for a time I should have a grand time & be able to please her more than ever I was able to do before. Only the sickening thing is that if after you have left your wife you show signs of wanting to see her again (I have *never* not wanted her, *never*) that 'Ah he is coming to his senses at last, he realizes that marriage is right after all etc etc & on remarriage the registrar congratulates you. What ever one does it is always represented in some disgusting way . . . When we used to meet I was afraid of the business of leaving Hilda as I had not then found any one sufficiently strong to make me able to break away. Patricia made it possible because I felt a sort of religious fervour towards her & asperation & being a sneak & coward I wanted an excuse. Also I hoped for great things as a result. But the only great thing I can at the moment see is that it *has* broken that ghastley spell that being married to Hilda cast upon me & also it has greatly facilitated me in arriving at what I *do* want & in clarifying my mind. . . . She [Patricia] approves absolutely in my having as many women as I want. She is not herself like that & has not such inclination but sees no reason why I should not gratify any such feeling & that if I did, it would certainly make no difference to her feeling for me.

It is really agonizing when I think of the marvellous experiences I might have had in the past (when at Burghclere for instance) & how I allowed them to slip through my fingers. My life has been mainly 'day dreams'. . . .

I think the whole of my life especially the art manifestations of it has been a slow realization of the mystery of sex. . . . What you once said that you felt you had had some personal experience with a person when you had drawn them dont you think that experience was a wonderful *sexual* experience?

Stanley to P.A. (undated 1937)

I shall I presume be finally freed from Mrs Spencer in April & then I hope I shall be allowed to see her again. . . . There is nothing the least particle 'wrong' in wishing to have a union with several people one knows. To me human relationship which *perforce* exclude any sex feelings are like expurgated books. You are trying to do something which demands every ounce of your being with only one part of it like trying to write without using your hands, or always standing on one leg.

It is like the way people will have my pictures 'as long as there are no figures in it'. . . .

After their wedding Patricia returned to Moor Thatch and Stanley to Lindworth and they never occupied the same house, although she insisted on his making Lindworth – apart from his paintings his sole material asset – over to her, on the ground that it would reduce his liability for alimony.

Patricia promptly and effectively put an end to the marriage in any but a legal sense. The day after it, she and Miss Hepworth left for St Ives, Cornwall, having invited Hilda, who was aggrieved over amounts of alimony, to come to Cookham and discuss the matter with Stanley; Stanley had to remain there for a few days to finish a painting, before he joined them in St Ives, but Hilda was welcome to accompany him if she cared to.

In the suggestions Patricia Preece made to Hilda for the bizarre arrangements for the three of them she was not acting on impulse. Her plan had been carefully conceived. In a letter postmarked 17 May 1937 she had written to Hilda:

Stanley asks you very sincerely *not* to write to him, he says he has undertaken to hold no communication with you whatsoever until the decree absolute is made and he must keep to it, therefore he has not read your letter, he further asks me to tell you he is trying through Tooth to get your money paid up, he had no idea you were owed anything.

I received your letter this morning and I will do what I can to follow your instructions re the furniture, nothing in the house has been moved or altered, it is being left for you to arrange when you come here.

I am very sorry that Tooth should have to know anything, it is not my wish, if you knew how much I had suffered, having been aluded to everywhere as Stanley's mistress, may be you would be surprised.

I do hope you will instruct your solicitors to proceed at once as otherwise all our plans must be lost, we have been told by my solicitor the case would be down for hearing on May 25th and we could therefore fix our marriage for 29th which we accordingly did, furthermore I have taken a cottage in Cornwall from June 1st as a surprise, having got it for that month as I know the people it belongs to slightly, it is a charming place St Ives and Stanley is so sick of painting landscapes here, also he has had no holiday for 2 years and needs one very much, he did not know of this, I had kept it as a surprise but if you stop the decree going through it must be given up, my plan was to go there first and you come to Cookham and arrange things with Stanley and both come on after if you liked. If you will do this for us now Hilda so that it goes through as we have arranged for we shall both remember it in the future and you shall not lose by it. Stanley can not change his solicitor now, it is quite impossible as no other would take the case from Evill, Mr Pyke (mine) will not and he says no one would do so, therefore we must put up with Evill 'till the end of this anyway. Stanley wrote direct to your solicitors proposing that you should have one third of his income you will get much more this way he says. Please Hilda do this for us, you can if you wish it because your solicitor cannot go against what you say must be, it is in your hands, Mr Pyke has told us, and we shall on our side see you have not cause to regret what you have done.

Please do not write to Stanley as he cannot read your letters, I have put this one in a box so that he can have it as soon as the decree is made absolute.

I hope all will come right and I believe things will plan out to be better for you than you know of.

Her position secured, Patricia became Mrs Spencer without living with her husband. Hilda had come to Cookham as invited and had slept with Stanley. Stanley had told Patricia about it. With Miss Hepworth, then, she returned to Cookham to live at their old house, Moor Thatch, Stanley returning to Lindworth. The marriage was never consummated and they never lived in the same house.

For at least three years his financial situation had been desperate. He had already spent an immense amount of money on Patricia – more than £2,000, he thought – in clothing and jewellery. He was in arrears for several years of income tax. He had the legal costs of his divorce to carry. He now had both a new wife legally entitled to his support and an old one entitled to alimony – which for many months he was unable to pay in full. There were also two children. Lindworth itself (Spencer's only possession) had been made over to Patricia.

In his work he had the expenses of paints and canvas. It is small wonder that he had to borrow continually from his dealer, Dudley Tooth, who made himself his friend and adviser. Tooth, while making it clear to Stanley that he wanted his figure paintings as well, had to underline that these sold slowly, whereas there was a ready public for his landscapes. Stanley, therefore, found himself pushing his pramful of painting materials in and around Cookham, in every sort of weather, at all times of year. He was encouraged by Patricia to bring his day's work to show her in her kitchen at Moor Thatch; if she approved, she would reward him with tea and allow him to kiss her hand.

As if this were not enough, he did a longish series of figure paintings of a character that to him was erotic.

In the evenings he returned home. In lieu of the sexual gratification that he desired, he spent his solitude not only drawing but also – and compulsively – writing. This compulsion, one of the delights of his life and an expression of his profound egoism – 'I am so fascinated by myself,' he once said, 'I don't want to lose sight of myself for an instant' – dominated his leisure moments and is responsible for the millions of words he left behind. But as well as a compulsion it was also a peopling of a solitude with a delineation of an imaginary world whose contacts with the real world were tenuous.

Between imagination and reality, for a few years, Stanley nourished a vision of a natural polygamy, or at any rate of a *ménage* in which he would be happily married to Hilda as well as to Patricia. Behind this fantasy was his conviction that marriage was not in essence a legal affair and that in spite of legal divorce he remained married to Hilda. It did not last long. By October, 1938, all thought of living with Patricia was alien to him.

For more than a year after his marriage he lived alone at Lindworth, using its large garden shed as a studio for the figure paintings he did, his landscapes being painted on the spot. Around August of 1938 Lindworth, which now belonged to Mrs Spencer, was rented. In a letter to Tooth of 6 October 1939 he wrote from Leonard Stanley, Gloucestershire, that:

as I have no room of my own I am cut off from my work as I have been for just over a year. It's a great scandalous shame that I was turned out of Lindworth and the Studio that I had all my stuff in and did many of my big pictures in. . . .

In 1932 he had returned to his beloved Cookham, as he had always dreamed of doing, after twelve years of absence – years, however, in which Cookham had been the inspiration of paintings that had made his name illustrious. He had left as a humble, unknown village boy; he returned a national figure, covered in glory from his *Cookham Resurrection*, now in the national collection, and from his Burghclere murals. He was also not without financial resources, and from the sale of his *Cookham Resurrection* (bought from his first exhibition in 1927) he was able to buy Lindhurst off Cookham High Street, a very substantial early Victorian house. He returned, however, in poor physical shape and remained so until surgery at the end of 1934.

Six years later his life was in ruins. He had no home. He was saddled with huge debts; his financial affairs were desperate and there was a risk of his being sent to prison.

On the verge of serious nervous collapse he left Cookham in October 1938 without premeditation. He drifted away and did not come back again for over three years. He left for an evening party at our house in London and then, unable to face any more of his Cookham life, begged to be allowed to stay.

He stayed six weeks. Thereupon Malcolm MacDonald found him a room in nearby Adelaide Road and after some weeks there, he lived for many months, also in Adelaide Road, in the house of Constance Oliver, a Slade School friend of Hilda's, Malcolm Macdonald paying his rents.

Pencil note by Hilda: 'Stanley married again Sat May 29th 1937'.

Lindworth (Monday 31 May 1937)
I am longing to see you. I rang you up on Saturday evening (the day of my marrying Patricia) & wanted then to talk to you but you had gone to Mrs. Harters & were due back on Sunday (yesterday) Mrs. Carline said. I want to show you the composition I have done (there are a lot). If you should come tomorrow (Tuesday) I shall be up at Rowborough painting all the morning unless I hear that you are coming. If you come and would like to find me in the morning, you will find me in the same place where I painted that Barley or Wheat you remember . . . [directions where to find him]. I am doing a view looking down towards Cookham Bridge. Mrs. Carline sounded very well & it was rather good to think I was once again in contact with 47. There are many things which cannot be explained until & unless we meet, so do write or come.

Hilda to Stanley
Downshire Hill (8 June 1937)
I feel I must try to establish some clear idea, & yet as I am not clear myself it is rather difficult to do so. . . . I don't think you have visualised the matter from my point of view quite. For one thing, why, do you think, in the beginning I wanted so much to MARRY you? Why wouldn't I then have been content to LIVE with you only, if you had been willing to do that. . . . And if that was so then, why should it be different now?

It is not due to any conventionality. It is just that I am not that kind of person, that kind of thing does not enter into my vision.

The difference between now & then, is that having lived with you so long as your wife, it is rather puzzling to feel it is wrong to do so now: (the reason to me, why it seems wrong is that it is unaccompanied by any kind of consecutive life). Then the other point that I certainly think you have not visualized about me is this: that during these years away I have only known what you have shown me, what you have let me know. . . . I have had to reconstruct my life & my thoughts on the basis of being completely cut off from you, of your having no pleasure or interest in me & more or less hating me. These thoughts have therefore been built into my life; & in the same way as if you tear a branch from a tree you cannot join it *livingly* on again, except by an elaborate process of grafting, in such manner I have forcibly torn myself off from you (feeling that your thoughts about me pushed me to it). And though I feel that tree is my home, my husband, yet I cannot livingly join with it again, except by grafting.

I think your attitude towards me may be different because you had the cards in your hand in this respect. You *knew* all the time that I did not hate you, & that I wanted to do anything for you, that I left you *hardly*; therefore you may have thought all the time that I would always be yours. I on the contrary have had a *certain conviction* that though I might feel that you would always seem to me to be my husband, that actually you did not feel so & that you were most definitely & irretrievably cut off from me.

As there have been no such drastic reason forced on you for thinking so of me, I don't suppose you have been *forced* to wean yourself of me, in the way I have been forced to wean myself of you. . . .

. . . all the same I don't need you: that is the thing I have had to achieve & I have achieved it.

And here, you must not misunderstand me, & it may be a bit difficult not to: . . . I would I am sure enjoy it, as I did the other day; but I would not need it, & if there was only myself to consider I would definitely resist it, if it did become a temptation. It is only the thought that you might think differently about it, that would, & *did* have any power.

And yet Stanley I don't want you to think I am belittling that visit, far from it. . . .

But if you understand what I have said already, if you are *sure* you understand it; then I can go on, to say that I loved my visit, & *everything* about it. [This resulted from the suggestion in Patricia Preece's letter of 7 May 1937 to Hilda, already quoted, that she should visit Lindworth and 'arrange things with Stanley & both come on after if you and he liked', she and Dorothy Hepworth having left for St Ives on the previous day.] I love to think that you feel nicely about me, & the same as I feel for you. I returned to London, with rosy cheeks & sparkling eyes, & happy with everyone, friendly & kindly disposed to everyone, in fact in an ideal state. But, all the same even all that does not provide a *motive*, also it might not be the same again, that was a surprise, a *complete* surprise to me. Then there is another point. I wonder really whether such an arrangement, or even such an affair, would really benefit your marriage.

If you RELIED on it at all, it must have a detracting effect. Surely your marriage with Patricia cannot be perfect, without that side is perfectly achieved too; & if you know there is nothing else, you will make more effort to bring that to perfection.

Stanley do take her to the very best gynocologist (is that the word?) And then you will at least know, what to expect, & also possibly something might be done.

Lindworth [undated]

There seems to be a risk of our being together again & if it should ever be so the basis of our being together or married again would not have to have the nonsense in it that was in our former one.

The reasons if any of my wanting to be with you would be –

1. Because I seem to have started something with you.
2. Because I seem to have a conception of some sort of you & I being together to the end. I mean that I have no vision of being with some one else when I am 60 or older. But I might be & should be surprised.
3. . . . there is the feeling that we are both making something that no one else

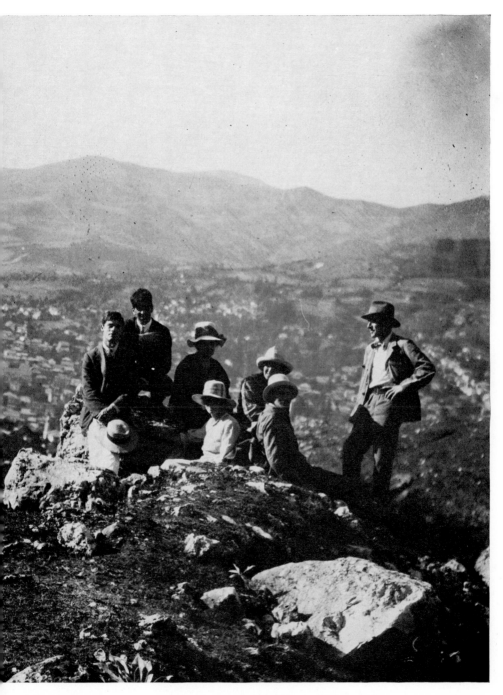

5   Photograph taken of the Carlines and Stanley Spencer on their expedition
in 1922 to Bosnia. Sarajevo is in the background. Stanley is second
from the left and on his right is Richard Carline.

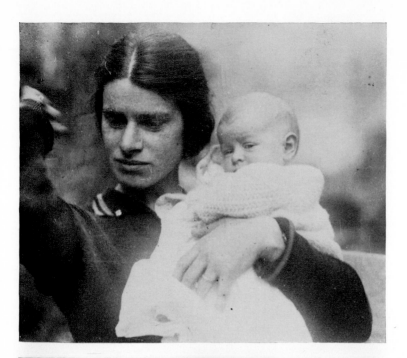

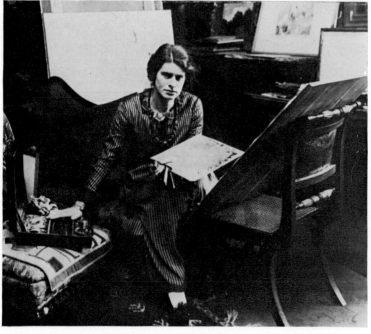

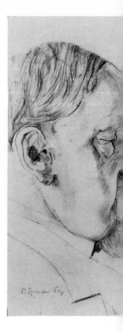

6 Photograph of Hilda and Unity

7 Photograph of Hilda painting

8 *William Spencer*, by Gilbert Spencer, pencil, 1914.
   Reproduction by permission of the artist.

excepting you & I would want to make, or could make.

4. But I should still wish for & desire other women & I should have no promises or undertakings to you respecting them. I am sure there are some women about with whom I would be very good.

St. Ives (June 1937)

I am returning on Tuesday & I would like to see you on Wednesday. *If* I am to have what *I* want then what ever the basis was & what ever you thought of it, it would have to be a basis where I could have both Patricia & you. To have only the one or the other of you was never in my mind. When you said that you would under this condition be really my mistress I wondered if you would actually consent to be so. If it is adultery it will have to be so & we might be able to bear the feeling of doing something wrong. As far as I am concerned I don't mean to bare it.

Lindworth (undated)

You see the difference between you & me & P & me is this:– I know that no degree of love that I or any one would be capable of feeling for her would be in excess of her worth. I am so far unable to love her but my inability is due to my own imperfections. . . .

Hilda to Stanley
17 Pond St. (16 May 1938)

I just thought I would like to send you a word of encouragment for to morrow. . . .

I have been so worried about this case [which she felt compelled to bring against him for alimony], knowing that I could not bear for you to lose it, or at any rate to lose it in a disasterous way that could injure you. I have known that I would rather, it were to injure *me* than you.

I hope too that you would not be willing to injure the children. It is no good pretending that children can live on air, as you always seem to do. . . . Both Shireen & Unity are so faithful in their love to you (& I would be so practically if you ever needed it & they were able). I hope you would not be willing to injure them & above all by *trickery*. . . .

Either I love you or I don't, & if I love you I cannot hurt you.

But I cannot be certain that you are equally single minded about me. I think, because I bear things without recriminations or complaining, that you think it is right to make me suffer & compatible with loving me. . . .

Hilda to Stanley
17 Pond St. (5 July 1938)

I miss not having your weekly letters, for though they were so brief, they were at least a message. I also miss the £3 a week, as you must realize, for I cannot live on air. . . . I feel very cross for instance to think of the waste of money on solicitors, money only incurred *for* you or *due* to you, so it is quite unfair that I personally should have to pay any of it. . . .

And the divorce only took place in order that *you* could marry again. I ought not to have to find £50 *myself*, BECAUSE I did you the good turn of setting you free. . . .

Why should I ever have had a divorce? I wish now that I had not done it. You are not grateful for it one bit. And I wish I had delayed the completion of the divorce till you had payed every farthing of what you owed.

It seems to me that whatever kindnesses I do are just merely *used*, & then laughed at; such as, 'look at that silly: she is trusting to my promises & to Patricia's promises! . . .'

Since the case I personally have received only £5.10.0. All the money goes to the solicitor . . . in the meanwhile I am mounting up a new debt equally large in order to live, so then when the solicitor is paid, I will have a new debt to pay off, & at the present rate I will never be solvent. . . .

In 1930 Stanley Spencer had been a painter not so much of brilliant promise as of achievement; he enjoyed a measure of domestic happiness and was established in his beloved Cookham.

Although the breaking of two marriages, its resulting financial and legal difficulties, and exile from Cookham combined with the absence of any prospect of what he must have longed for, another Burghclere, to bring him, by October 1938, near breaking point, such were his resilience, his courage and irresistible creativity as an artist that in an extraordinarily short time he was on his way to recovery.

There is one fact about Spencer to be borne constantly in mind, namely that in spite of the complexity, even the fantasy, of his intimate human relations, he delighted in solitude. And in Adelaide Road, yet not far from Hilda, and ourselves in Fellows Road, ready to give him such help as was in our power, he was by himself. Not only happiness but creativity, for several months virtually extinct, returned renewed. Yet his delight in solitude did not prevent his welcoming visits from his friends, just as, years later when he had returned to Cookham, any child who called was welcome and often the subject of a drawing as a gift.

From July 1939 he lived, for over a year, with two friends at Leonard Stanley in Gloucestershire when, in May 1940, he paid the first of his several visits to Port Glasgow to paint shipbuilding pictures for the Ministry of Information. Then in May 1941 he moved to Epsom to stay with Mrs Harter, a relative (Sydney Carlines' mother-in-law) with whom Shirin had gone to stay at the time of Unity's birth in 1930. Shirin's visits multiplied and for many years Mrs Harter was her *de facto* guardian. At the beginning of the war and with the threat of air-raids on London, Unity also went to stay. Here they were joined by Hilda, who remained for several weeks.

Nothing could have differed more radically from his feelings – involving emotional confusion, cruel letters and quarrels – toward Hilda and Patricia in the middle 'thirties when he planned to 'be married' to them both, and those of five years later when he was married to neither, nor likely ever to be. Hilda he came to adore; towards Patricia, though he saw her less often and eventually scarcely at all, he came to entertain a detached benevolence.

In January 1942 he returned to Cookham, staying with his cousins in the High Street at Quinneys, and working in the Lindworth studio: he was enchanted to be back and by himself. Deeply as he was involved with other people his imagination was so powerful that they were almost as positively present to him in his evocation of them in solitude as they were in reality. To Hilda he wrote constantly; occasionally he visited her at Hampstead and she him at Cookham. In spite of his difficulty in meeting his financial obligations his relations with both his wives appear to have been serene.

Hilda, however, was entirely without Stanley's resilience: she had never been strong; she was also extremely sensitive and the disruption of her marriage and its attendant circumstances brought about her collapse in June 1942 and she was taken first to St Pancras Hospital and then to the Banstead Mental Hospital.

Deeply distressed, Stanley called on Mrs Carline and Richard, who had seen him only occasionally since the divorce. They were greatly surprised by his concern over Hilda's mental collapse. Stanley, according to Richard Carline, blamed his own conduct towards Hilda and offered to help her in any way in his power and expressed his wish – often to be repeated – to remarry her; one result of his visit was that Stanley was reunited with the Carlines and invited to visit them, whenever he wished, at 17 Pond Street, where they now lived. Stanley visited Hilda regularly at Banstead (which involved about five hours of travel) spending some three hours with her. In the hospital they found themselves in unprecedented harmony, engaged in amicable arguments, and he brought her, as he often had before, innumerable letters, which he read out and they discussed. Early the following year she spent a month in a private nursing home, then moved into a psychiatrist's house in Finchley Road, Hampstead, where he often called.

They continued to correspond, Stanley again often not posting but bringing his letters. Both his letters and hers at times show the effects of the ordeals they had experienced. The effects of the distress that each had suffered communicated itself to the other. On his side the correspondence expressed love of her company, but also of solitude – sometimes even a preference for it. Such sentiments as:

When I see you and feel in your presence the same gladness as when I find myself back in my empty room, I do not really need your presence because it does not make me happier than I am without it

occur fairly frequently. It is easy to misinterpret them as evidence of an ambiguity in his feelings for Hilda, but such an interpretation neglects one of his crucial qualities: the sheer power of his imagination. Such a sentence does not, I believe, imply that he was as happy by himself as in her presence but that she was always with him, whether present or absent.

Most of us need the presence of others because we need to be reassured, entertained, informed or more commonly because we are bored. Stanley on the contrary had no such needs: he possessed a memory so vividly and profusely retentive and an intellect too – though often confused and self-contradictory – of such inexhaustible profuseness that though almost always ready to welcome and to seek the company of others, he did not need it. However long his periods of solitude, they were never long enough for the full expression or inner development of his memories and ideas, or, of course, for his drawing, painting and writing. He often asked why people needed holidays; it would have been as characteristic of him to ask why they needed the company of others. Hilda was always with him and he enjoyed her company with ever-increasing passion. This, however, did not prevent him from time to time expressing doubts, not only about his love for her but whether he had ever loved anyone at all.

In the autumn of 1945, after his last stay in Glasgow, he returned to Cookham, settling finally in Cliveden View, now vacated by his sister Annie, and there followed a virtually total relaxation of the tensions resulting from his marital affairs: Hilda visited him and they called together on Patricia. His return was warmly and widely welcomed. The strange conduct of his life was widely known (people have been ostracised for matters trifling by comparison), likewise, though less widely, his proneness occasionally to rage and suspicion. But though in villages intimate facts about neighbours' characters are apt to be no secret, and it is hardly an exaggeration to say that Stanley was liable to tell everybody everything, the affection he inspired shows clearly that he was recognized as a man exceptionally kind and likeable, and seventeen years after his death in 1959 he was affectionately so remembered (see chapter 5).

Spencer made frequent suggestions that Hilda and he re-marry though he had moments of reluctance and she reservations. There were legal and financial and other complications and though he consulted his solicitors nothing was effected, but it may well have been that his very obsession with Hilda and his loving reconciliation with her, as well as his ever-increasing need for solitude, made re-marriage superfluous: he was happy as things were. But from the summer of 1947 Hilda's health precluded this possibility: she underwent an operation for cancer and Stanley helped devotedly to nurse her. Over the next three years her condition deteriorated and in November 1950 she died. The funeral service was held in Cookham Church and she was buried in Cookham Rise cemetery. Stanley, joined by his two daughters, and Richard Carline, and a number of others, attended.

(20 January 1942) . . . if finally we decided to marry.
Quinney's, Cookham (12 February 1944)
[Stanley copied out a letter just received from Hilda (9 February).]
However I was thinking also that some of my most wonderful memories are

of those visits of yours to me in my little cell at Banstead. I used to be spending my entire time talking with God & contemplating & so it was as though I came straight from Heaven to enjoy you when you came. Actually I never feel that I quite reach Heaven, nevertheless it was like that. [Stanley interjects: I am loving writing it out & speaking your words & your thoughts with my mouth, it is like writing a letter together with you. . . .

. . . And paradoxicle though it seems, the outside appearance of Banstead could serve as a perfect model of my notion of the outside of Heaven. . . .]

Quinney's, Cookham (2 March 1944) to 224 Finchley Road [where Hilda had moved]
. . . the loss of Eden is all part of a great catastrophy which occurred in my life as long ago as 1920 or 21 when my wish & need for a woman became so imperative & absorbed my thought & took my vital energy to such an extent that I saw my interest was becoming *divided* that my love for a woman & my wish to marry was becoming so urgent that it was no longer able to bare the slow sure speed of the chariot of art that then took me along with it, but these desire urges & wonderful marriage wishes slipped from that controlling influence & *tore* along on its own, taking me & the chariot with it, just as if the horse of the chariot had run amok. . . .
. . . And now you say what is to be done? It looks very much as if *all* sex feeling will have to be given up; not hated but given up until it is in line with & under the controle of my still just living true belief in God. I cant [see?] how this is to be done.

Quinney's, Cookham (17 March 1944)
. . . I picture for instance that . . . possibly we could after more 'examinations' of our thought & feeling marry again, . . .

Quinney's, Cookham (17 March 1944)
[Referring to a letter from Hilda (15 March).] I liked it to the extent that because you wanted it back I copied it all out. I would prefer you to have the copy but as you might prefer to see your own hand writing which is so much the character of it I am keeping my copy & unselfishly returning your letter. I did also write a reply but as I did not use the carbon I want to hang on to it. I will bring it when I come up. . . . I wrote two answers not sent because of carbon absence and they are both interesting.

c/o. Mrs. Whiteford, Glencairn, Glasgow Rd. (4 June 1944)
The need I feel to be married to you is because I feel you are a furtherance & compleater of my individual self. . . . I wish that I could be released from my present marriage & that it could be dissolved or what ever it is. I wish it could be done without my having anything to do with it; I dont like dealing with the present marriage side of the thing at all. But I feel in a false position as I am. [Would like Hilda to come & stay.]

c/o. Mrs. Whiteford, Glencairn, Glasgow Rd (June 1944)
    . . . I am worried about your stipulation re condition of marrying you. . .
The *fact* you tell me namely that there never never will be any sex relationship.
The reason, allways difficult to give, you dont give . . . & my reply has to be I
most ardently & spiritually wish & want to marry you but I cannot accept the
condition. . . .

(Winter, 1944)
    Then the re-marriage to you is also somewhat worrying as even if you were
not willing to be persuaded to give me the married life I needed, I would on
my part be not wishing or feeling it would be right to attempt to persuade you,
. . . I feel I would like to leave matters until we can see each other. . . . [Wonders
if his brother, Percy, would sell the Cookham Rise cottage.] . . . then at least
there would be a house in Cookham for the children in the future.

Cliveden View, Cookham Rise (30 September 1945)
    But yet I feel more near to you now than I ever did in the marriage days
wonderful though they were. I feel because of the unsureness held off from the
possible realization of amazing things in each other. I often wish we could
have compromised accepted the difficulties & married on that basis . . .

Hilda to Stanley
17 Pond St. (15 October 1945)
[Her mother dying, Hilda hopes Stanley will come to stay for a few days, to
cheer them when they return from spending the day with her.]

Cliveden View (January 1947)
[Referring to his rushed visits to Hilda]: I have *always* felt a kind of support
from you & I don't see how I am going to reach any further realization or
recover any early innocent qualities if I am to not merely be cut off from you
in my daily life . . . but cut off in ones inmost being . . . [He prefers to] prepare
some stuff, compositions or writing, or just thoughts & then 'go through' with
them together.
[Would like Hilda, Unity & Shirin to live in Cliveden View.]

Hilda to Stanley
17 Pond Street (9 May 1947)
    I will not be in any any any way associated with Patricia; . . . . I cannot
bear to be near her I cannot bear to touch her, I cannot bear to be in her house,
I cannot bear to eat or drink out of any vessel of hers, & I could not bear to
own anything that ever had been hers. . . . I cannot bear to touch her in any
kind of way. . . .
    That is why as far as I am concerned a divorce is no use, for a divorce means
that you have supposedly had Patricia as a wife. . . .
    I won't have anything to do with Evill. . . . If he handled this annulment
case, I just could not bear it, &. . . . If Evill handles the case of annulment I
would not *personally* accept it as having been annulled. . . . I felt it very very
much that he had that case about income tax on your behalf. I felt that I ought
to have been told, that my name must have come into the case frequently, &

that is that statements have been made about me by him during the proceedings, even though not a case about me. . . .

My greatest joy in you, and you may think it a puny choice, was in the fact that you were pure, that you had not even kissed anyone but me. No matter what happened, no matter how unhappy I was at times, I always felt with the deepest deepest, strongest, and most grateful feelings that you had given me a jewel beyond price namely that you were pure. So I always felt that you were the best husband in the world, ...

I think also that you don't quite believe me, when I have told you that I would never physically be your wife again. . . .

That is why I feel sad when you put the double bed up, and I know you are putting it up in hope, & I know that it is about a hope that will never be.

Also I feel sad when you plan your cottage for us, including me. I can come and stay with you sometimes, but I will not want to live in that cottage, because I would not want to live at Cookham, in fact I will not live anywhere but in London, and anywhere I go there would be a part set apart for you if you wanted to be there, but actually I will not live in any house that is your house, but I do even want you to live with me.

With love dear Stanley. . . .

Cliveden View (20 October 1949)

About the Patricia business I think I have got to the point where I know I dont want for ever to be her husband . . . P: seems to think I am more sure of myself than I was. . . . Had this marriage been ethicle Christian Marriage (namely my first & only marriage) I would (had I never known of any thing else) have been probably sexually alright, but not being so, I find I know from that that this marriage is like a grimace.

Cliveden View (20 July 1950)

. . . I am having to pack in to landscape as I shall need more than what I have recently earnt in order to be secure enough to be able to settle to some big work as I so much want to do. It takes me ages these days to do one landscape: I believe it would pay me now to do these figure pictures I so much love doing. . . . I have so much that I want to do. . . . The Baptism The Creation (or Madonna & Mothers & children scene) The Cana And I expect the Day of Jugment idea would begin to show itself clearly the moment I really started on it. . . .

If some other than my self could do all the looking after you there is nothing in this world I want more than to see you. . . . But I cannot be taken away from my work & I sometimes fear that if I go to have one sip of that joy of seeing & talking with you I shall become involved in some task or obligation.

Had I not been in the fix I am in it would always have been my wish to remarry you. All the time I think of you ducky, and as a stay for my painting and composing I mentally have you with me.

Four months later Hilda was dead, but her death did not interrupt the correspondence, which continued throughout the next decade.

About seven years earlier Stanley Spencer had written to her one of his portentously long letters and attempted to analyze why their marriage had ended in legal divorce. Two things stood out in his memory. The one was that fear of more children and the non-use of contraceptives had maimed their sexual relationship; the other that inveterate quarrelsomeness had destroyed 'marriage feelings'. None the less he was clear that the divorce was a terrible mistake. The reasons why he thought so echoed in all his talk throughout the years; he never revised them. To quote from a letter in the Tate's archives:

If we could have *agreed* more than we did and striven to develop what we *had* got, I would have felt compensated for what ever seemed to be lacking. But when all that we shared became involved in the turmoils of rows and arguments, we had to *keep out* of what we very much shared with each other and it forced me to live mentally in worlds I had remembered before I knew you. But whatever seemed to be lacking in our marriage I have never in my attempts to marry since then been able to see and feel the marriage continuing endlessly into the future and through all the years ahead as I *was* able to feel about you and me. It gave me a wonderful joy when I used to imagine you and I at some distant future time still constructing our life together and *making* love. It was one of the tests I subjected myself to when I married you, namely, could I feel happy at the thought of being with you through all these possible changes and constantly occurring new needs, and I found that the idea I had was a permanent one. . . . I *can* only feel that *one*ness that I love, with you. I could identify myself with you utterly so that I felt like a single being that was me and you. Also you are the only being I can write to or want to. It is a wonderful thing to write and not have to be careful what I say.

. . . Nothing ever compensated me for the loss of you.

Chapter 4

Dudley Tooth

After leaving the Army in 1918 Spencer had spent fourteen richly creative years; he finished, in 1919, *Swan Upping*; painted *Travoys* and other works, culminating in the wall paintings in the Oratory of All Souls, Burghclere, Berkshire, the most impressive works of their kind made in England in the present century.

As his life and achievements during these years are already well known I propose merely to recall the principal facts. After spending most of 1919 in Cookham he went to stay with Sir Henry and Lady Slesser at their house Cornerways at Bourne End, Buckinghamshire, with whom he spent more than a year; the year following he went on to stay with the Muirhead Bones, who lived in a village near Petersfield, Hampshire, later moving into lodgings first in the village and later over a teashop in Petersfield. Through Henry Lamb, a friend of his brother Sydney from their Slade School days, he was introduced to the Carlines, the close-knit family of painters with whom he spent, in 1922, three months travelling in Yugoslavia, afterwards returning to Petersfield. In 1923 he stayed with Lamb at Hill Street, Poole, Dorset, who lent him his studio above the Vale Hotel, Hampstead. In 1933 and 1937 he visited Switzerland.

At the Slessers Spencer painted one of his most memorable works, *Christ Carrying the Cross* (1920), now in the Tate. The house in the background is Fernlea and the cottage on the right is The Nest, his grandmother's. When thinking about this painting, he saw builder's men carrying ladders and this seemed to him one part of the 'fact' of Christ carrying the Cross. 'It was joy and all the common occurrences in the village were re-assuring, comforting occurrences of that joy . . . I had as a child no thought than that Christ had made everything wonderful and glorious and that I might be able later on to share in that glory' (information supplied by the artist to the Tate Gallery staff for the catalogue of his retrospective exhibition held there in 1955.)

Another important work painted at the Slessers was a *Last Supper* (1920, now in Cookham Church), *St. Veronica unveiling Christ* and *Christ overthrowing the Money Changers' Tables* (1921, now in the Stanley Spencer Gallery, Cookham). *The Last Supper* is set in a malt-house in Cookham – a building that evoked in Spencer a special affection – the red wall being the side of a grain bin. The composition had been long in his mind, the earliest study dating from 1915. At the Bones in 1922, he painted *Unveiling the War Memorial, Cookham*, a less memorable work than its major predecessors. It was during his year's stay with Henry Lamb at Poole in 1923 that a momentous event occurred. Even though there seemed not the remotest chance of its being realized he had made designs the previous year based on his wartime experiences in both England and Macedonia, in the hope that some time they might be carried out in a building on a grand scale.

These were seen that year on a visit to Poole by Mary Behrend, and a little later by her husband Louis, friends of Lamb's, who had already shown them examples of Spencer's work, to which they immediately responded. Spencer himself they had met briefly some years before at a party in London. 'In my father's words,' wrote their son, 'we felt at once that we would like to do something about this castle in the air, partly because we had admired so many frescoes in various churches and chapels in Europe; but mainly because the designs struck us as bold, original & deserving of any encouragement we could give.' Stanley's reaction was short and to the point: 'What Ho, Giotto!' (*Stanley Spencer at Burghclere*, by George Behrend, 1965, p. 6).

Overjoyed as Spencer was, some four years passed before work could be begun. At Burghclere, in Berkshire, where the Behrends had settled in 1918 at the Grey House, there was no suitable building, nor even the land available to erect one. Their offer of a temporary shack to work in was declined; Spencer wrote to Mrs. Behrend, 'Thank you, very much, Mary, but your offer is not good enough.' (*Ibid.*) By 1923, when land had been bought and the decision to build taken, he was engaged on one of his finest paintings, *The Resurrection. Cookham* (1923–27). It is a sign of Spencer's dedication and courage that although no one had shown interest in acquiring this large – 108in × 116in – and complex work he was determined to let nothing delay its completion (the Behrends paid his rent during the job). He also wished to show it and it was the principal feature of his first exhibition (held at the Goupil Gallery in February–March 1927) when it was bought by Lord Duveen, who gave it to the Tate Gallery. Directly, however, it was completed he wished ardently to begin work at Burghclere, but as the chapel, designed by Lionel Pearson in close consultation with the artist, was not completed, work was begun at 3 Vale Studios. It was not until May 1927 that he settled in Burghclere, the Behrends building him a house (Chapel View) in which he lived until early 1932, when he returned to Cookham and completed the last panels. The Oratory of All Souls was dedicated on 25 March 1932, and was accepted by the National Trust in 1947.

The exhibition at the Goupil Gallery, his first, established his reputation, but William Marchant, its proprietor, had died suddenly in 1925 and his business had been carried on by Cecily his widow. After complex but amicable negotiations with her he placed his affairs, in February 1933, in the hands of Dudley Tooth, chairman of Arthur Tooth, who had shown interest in his work, and on 5 November 1932 had visited him at Lindworth (from which all his letters to Tooth, unless otherwise indicated, were written).

Spencer was sensible and fortunate in entering into this agreement, for Tooth, confident in his talent, promoted his interests for the rest of his life with energy, skill, constancy and tact, becoming a warm and understanding friend, adept at dealing with Spencer's moods of aggressiveness, suspiciousness or sheer perversity. For instance, Spencer oddly concluded his letter placing his affairs in Tooth's hands: 'If I had my choice I would give up painting' – oddly at least for a passionately dedicated painter who used to say that he didn't know what a holiday was, and in another (received on 23 March):

Please do not send any picture of mine to the Royal Academy [of which he had accepted election as an Associate only the year before]. I am not wishing to exhibit at present at all. I think if you can you had better sell what you can of mine privately without my having an exhibition in November. I can no longer guarantee the number of works you will require for a show . . . is there no possibility of my being relieved from this business of doing pictures when I am not wanting to do them. Its very unpleasant to make this degrading admission, I have not the habit of prostituting the meagre ability I have and it is only in the last few efforts of the Memorial at Burghclere and what I have done since that I have been forced to do so, in other words to hurry my work. But this has been such a painful experience that I feel that come what may I can't bare it any more.

So please don't expect anything from me but give me what ever advice and help you feel you can, as you have so vividly done before.]

 . . . I quite understand [Tooth replied (23 March 1933),] how you feel about hurrying your work in order to be ready for an exhibition in November. . . . I do not want you to worry any more, and just paint when you are in the mood, and I am quite prepared to consider the November Exhibition as cancelled, or, at least, unlikely to take place. I think, however, that you will agree that it is very important for you to have a show eventually, if you can arrange it.

In the meanwhile, I will go ahead with the framing of the canvases which are here, and will do my best to get you some money. . . . In the meantime do not bother yourself about being ready for the Exhibition and if you get into any serious financial difficulties, let me know and I will see if I can do anything to help you.

In response to Tooth's request (31 March) to write him a clear description of *The Visit* [*Sarah Tubb and the Heavenly Visitors* (1933)], one of the paintings he hoped to sell, Spencer replied (13 April):

 . . . I cannot make a very clear statement as to what the picture is about. Usually in order to describe any one picture of mine it means taking a seat and preparing to hear the story of my life. There are several matters which directly or indirectly influenced this production. In the village many years ago lived an old couple (brother and sister) Tommy Tub and Sarah Tub I remember them very well & seeing them going in & out of the gate in the picture. I remember my father describing how when one evening the 'Northern Lights (Aurorer Borealis) was very clear villagers wondered what it was, that 'Grannie Tub' Sarah Tubs mother had knelt down in her gate & prayed. As I dont clearly remember the 'Gran' I have given Sarah the part. But as I did not like the idea of alarm & of praying for that reason I have changed the state of her praying to one of *extacy* a sort of apotheosis of the old lady & visited by heavenly visitors of some sort either angels or diciples. She is surrounded & presented with emblems of what she is like & what she would love. The Grocer on the left is sharing in the peaceful atmosphere that it is the intention of the picture to convey. On the right is a woman taking down a post card rack which she usually places daily outside her shop. One of the visitors is selecting a card from the rack to present to the old woman. This is I am aware not a satisfactory or very explanatory explanation and I should think you might feel like Byron did about Coleridge.

'Explaining Metaphisics to the Nation I wish he would explain his explanation'.

But if I see an old grandmother in black kneeling in her gateway and texts lying about & green grocers shopkeepers adoring I must paint it because I like it very much indeed and see it all very clearly.

[P.S. to a letter received by Tooth on 4 May] . . . a lot of the stuff I do now is really what I should do if I had some commission such as Burghclere and it therefore means that when I do get some such job that what I do now may have to be done all over again. I am making no Benvenuto Cellini boast when I say I am now ready & equipped to almost every spark of detail to carry out the entire decoration of a church containing three 15 or 20 foot altarpiece walls, two trancept large walls & a 'run of wall' frieze going from these pictures and I could do it in about 15 years.

In response to this often expressed ambition to decorate a church or some other large building Tooth replied (4 May) with his usual sympathetic sense of the practical: 'Commissions for the decoration of churches are very few & far between; if I hear of anything I will always recommend you . . . but it would be better to continue painting quietly rather than anticipating any such project turning up again in the near future.'

Stanley's ambition, cherished until the end of his life, was never realized, his own lack of good sense – his refusal to submit preliminary sketches – preventing the realization of the only other possibility that presented itself, namely the decoration in 1939 of the Lady Chapel at Campion Hall, the Jesuit College at Oxford.

Tooth wrote (9 May 1933): 'have today sold your picture, *White Lilac*, to Mr. Kenneth M. Clark, Curator of the Ashmolean Museum, Oxford, for £45 for his private collection. He wishes to buy a more important example than this for the Ashmolean and I also have an enquiry from Mr. John Rothenstein of the Leeds Art Gallery (received 6 May) for a new picture by you.'

Spencer wrote to Tooth a description (received 16 May) of *Saints watching Boys Playing Marbles* (1933):

The incident arose in my mind in this manner. The kitchen is being cleaned & the mats have been thrown out into the garden; they are in a heap in the centre of the picture. Two boys are playing marbles. The rag & bone man has arrived & got his bag full of bottles & rags. At this moment a number of disciples come round the corner from the right & while one of them talks to the ragbone man, the others group themselves round the boys and watch them playing. They are dressed in white mainly but some apparently have got some pants from the ragbone man, taking no thought as to wherewithal they shall be clothed. There is nothing pointless in the notion of diciples watching boys playing marbles. Saints or similar species of individuals have a way of being able to contemplate some quite simple thing in such a way as to make one feel one could contemplate the same thing to the end of time without being bored for one second.

This letter illustrates two characteristics of Spencer's own attitude. One, that for him his imaginative paintings were not so much 'my creations' but real events, which he contemplated and portrayed, as he would any day-to-day event. The other, that he had little sense of hierarchy: everything was a creation of God, whether rag & bone men, boys, disciples, saints – even marbles.

In a letter (June 1933) he expressed – as he often did – the irritability and sense of frustration at the preferences of the purchasers of his work for his landscapes:

As I feared everyone as usual want my landscapes & no one wants the more imaginative work I do. I am very sorry that public galleries are taking my landscapes as being representative works of mine. Except the Tate [which had accepted *The Resurrection, Cookham*]. There is only one Public Gallery, Belfast [*The Betrayal* (1922)] which owns a representative work of mine full of the qualities which I know are the only things I have truly felt & meant.

Spencer wrote to Tooth a letter (received June 28) which shows how difficult he could be: 'I have recieved two commissions but neither of them say they will have anything to do with you . . . another client . . . says "When can you sever your connection with Tooths" . . . there will have to be no commissions on anything I sell to a client I have procured. . . .'

To this Tooth wrote by return reminding him of the terms of their agreement & that commissions represent: 'payment for the work we do on your behalf in the form of advertising, publicity for your work . . . & generally looking after your interests. . . . Above all things I want you to be contented; I want you to accept these commissions, which no doubt you have set your heart on, but I also want you to be fair & businesslike & fix prices which include our commission. . . .'

Tooth wrote to Spencer (26 July 1933) to tell him that the City Art Gallery, Leeds, had bought his *Separating fighting Swans* (1933). Spencer told me of the pleasure this gave him, but I doubt whether it was as intense as mine, for I happened to be the Gallery's Director, and had persuaded a reluctant Committee to acquire it, one member saying that he would not have it in his house, another that *somebody* must be pulling the Committee's leg, and a third that *somebody* seemed to be under the erroneous impression that the Committee was *made* of *Brass* – the required 'brass' amounted to £100. A sentence in a letter to Tooth (received on 12 October 1933) underlines the suspicious strain in Spencer's character. About a *Self-Portrait* in which he had heard the Tate was interested he wrote: 'You should let me know (as you no doubt do) the *moment* there is any enquiry of this kind as *I* also am dealing with my works. . . .'

An expression of a combination of his pride and inexperience emerges in a letter received on 11 April 1934: 'I did not know that pictures were ever sent on approval. I never have myself ever submitted or subjected any of my work for committees etc for approval. It would be injurious to me if a buyer or Gallery thought that a picture of mine was sent on approval at my request & suggestion,' but he does not object if pictures are sent on his behalf as 'a business matter between yourselves and your clients'.

Spencer's increasing confidence in Tooth as well as their increasing friendship did not prevent recurrent difficulties. For instance, Spencer proposed (in a letter received on 4 June 1934) 'a small room show of my drawings of heads sometime within the next six weeks.' Tooth readily agreed (4 June), and in a further letter, in which he said the exhibition would open on July 5, referring to various practical details mentioned that the 'charges for postage, invitation cards, catalogues, etc., will amount to about £20'. On 11 June he received an overnight telegram: 'Cancel show', followed by a letter written on the 10th: 'I am sorry to put off the show . . . but I am never eager to have a show. About the charge for catalogues, etc: it may be usual for you to charge this to the Artist & it may nowadays be a usual thing with Dealers, if this is so I see no possibility of my ever showing in London or anywhere else.'

This irritability persisted. On July 17 1934 he wrote complaining that provincial galleries borrowed his paintings but '*very* few have bought any'; that 'the Royal Academy made a great deal of gate money as the result of my work; that only *one* Gallery other than the Tate possess a *non*-landscape . . . The Belfast Gallery having "The Betrayal" . . . only because Eddie Marsh selected it . . . They are quite prepared to *show* my "queer" [i.e. imaginative] pictures, but that is all. Well, they are not going to have either . . . No pictures of mine are to be sent to any public provincial Gallery what ever. . . .'

The following month I myself experienced a consequence of this mood. Tooth assured him that he had cancelled all loans to public galleries but assumed that he would except *Souvenir of Switzerland*, writing (9 August

1934) that I 'was one of your great supporters' and (as Director of the Sheffield Art Galleries) was particularly anxious to have this painting; 'I took it for granted you would have no objection to his showing it.' The following day he received a telegram: 'Do not send a picture to Sheffield.' Even by the autumn his mood was still unchanged, and in a letter received on 11 October he wrote '. . . my pictures are to go nowhere.'

He was in fact very ill and in great pain, his kidney trouble having reached a crisis. On 11 October he records that he had just gone into hospital in Reading. He returned early the next month and was there on 21 November. This time the stone was located and crushed and he emerged cured.

The entry of Patricia Preece into his life is sharply reflected in his increasing anxieties about money. By 19 December 1935 he tells Dudley Tooth to sell landscapes at any price, since he needs the money by Christmas. On 21 April 1936 he asks for a loan (by advance) of yet another £50. In June he had a very successful exhibition, which earned him about £1115. But of this £700 had already been advanced.

There is a further loan of £200 in September and of £100 in October, and Tooth is begging Spencer to live on income. (By this time Patricia was also handling his affairs with Tooth.) On 19 February 1937 Spencer writes that despite yet another loan 'my bank has cut me off and I am disallowed from writing another cheque until my overdraft, now £65, is paid off'. Tooth copes with this, but on 24 March Spencer still complains that he cannot make ends meet. On 28 April he begs for £10 and receives it at once. On 1 November he cannot meet his demand for income tax. On 10 March 1938 Tooth writes to say that he has sold twelve drawings for £50: 'this is not a very good deal, but I understand you would rather have the money.' Moreover, in 1937, unknown to Tooth, Spencer had a loan of £200 from another dealer (at £5 a week) and Tooth eventually had to extricate him.

The figures make a dramatic commentary on the follies into which had been inveigled a man whose own demands in living expenses were minimal, indeed somewhat below what the majority would regard as subsistence level.

The correspondence of the three following years is almost entirely concerned with business affairs, but that of 1937 was more personal: 'I have the remainder of my divorce proceedings to pay', he wrote on 4 February, 'and I have just received the Court Order to pay within 7 days (that is £29), and also I have an urgent request from my bank to pay an overdraft of £54.'

Tooth responded with increasing efforts to sell his work. 'I very much hope', he wrote (21 May 1937), 'that you will not put off your holiday in Cornwall, about which Miss Preece spoke to me the other day &, as I think it would be an excellent thing for you to get away & find some new subjects & enjoy yourselves, I am prepared to advance you the necessary cash to take this holiday, and I feel quite certain that you will find enough inspiration down there to produce new canvases which will very shortly liquidate the account. As soon as you have your plans settled, please let me know how much you will need'. To this offer Spencer replied (22 May 1937) giving his travel requirements: '. . . and I must before I go pay off the remainder of the local accounts which will come to £15. The return fair will be about £10 (£5 my return & £5 Miss Preece). I don't know what the visit will cost but I should think £40 . . . so that I shall need £65. . . .' Tooth advanced him £86. (On 2 June 1937 Spencer wrote of delay in going to Cornwall as being caused by having nearly finished a landscape & 'also getting married'.)

The letters exchanged during the second half of 1937 are also mostly related to the sale and exhibition of his work. On 4 April 1938 Spencer wrote, as so often: 'I would be glad if also you would let me have a cheque of £10.'

On 22 April Tooth telegraphed to Patricia Spencer that he had 'wired her ten pounds'. On 20 May 1938 Richard Smart of Tooth's received a letter in which Spencer emphasized the high importance that he attached to the correct titling of his paintings, which is most understandable in view of the significance, from the point of conveying its meaning as a whole, of every feature down to the apparently least significant:

... I note that the landscape [exhibited at the Venice Biennale] I called 'Tree and Chicken coops' goes by the affected title 'Lonely Tree'. If my pictures are to be known by the titles that some owners give them they will be known for something that is certainly not me. I called and was careful to call the picture named on the list as 'Christ bearing the Cross', 'Christ carrying the cross'. But the Tate never called it that & another alteration of my title which they made or some have made is 'Christ bearing the Cross' which both from the point of view of what he bears and the alteration of the title is more than I can bear. I said *carrying*, & not bearing because apart from giving a sense of suffering which was not my intention . . . I particularly wished to convey the relationship between the carpenters behind him carrying the ladders & Christ in front carrying the cross, each doing their job of work & doing it just like workmen. As to my objection to the second 'his cross' instead of '*the* cross' I would point out that there may be many burdens to bear that there was never more than one cross & that was the one Christ carried & is properly therefore referred to as *the* cross & not merely *his* cross as though there were other crosses. This is in accordance with the Gospel. He was not doing *a* job or *his* job, but *the* job. . . .

The correspondence with Tooth – voluminous on Spencer's side – during May and June 1938, moved on to another issue, one with which I became concerned. I had long wished to write a book on Spencer and Tooth, aware of my admiration, suggested that I should do so. He mentioned the desirability of such a book to Patricia, but in general terms,

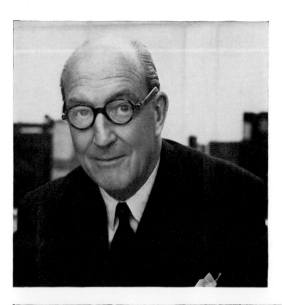

9 Photograph of Dudley Tooth

10 Photograph of Stanley Spencer
in Cookham pushing a pram
carrying his painting materials.
Keystone Press Agency Ltd

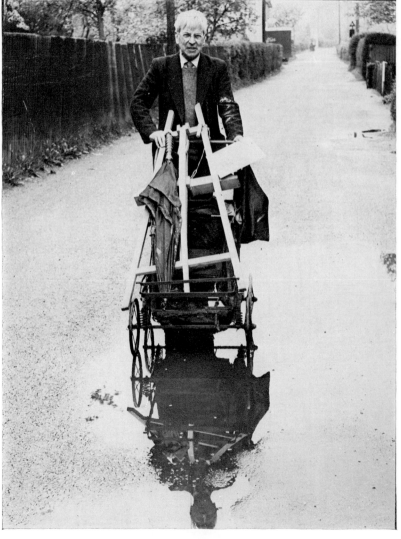

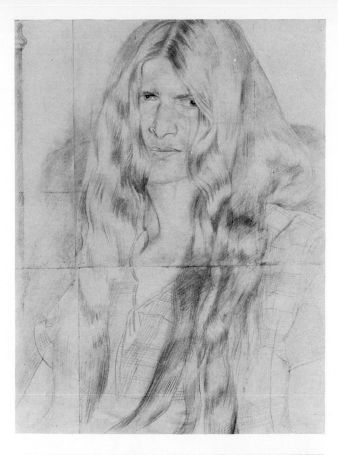

11 *Hilda with her hair down*, by Stanley Spencer, pencil, 1931.
Collection Richard Carline

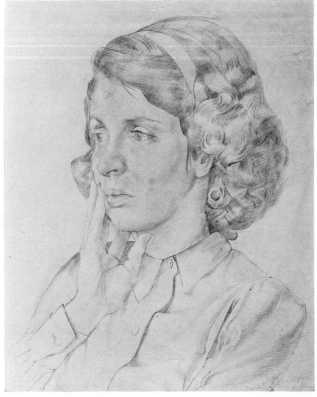

12 *Shirin* by Stanley Spencer, pencil, 1947.
Southampton Art Gallery

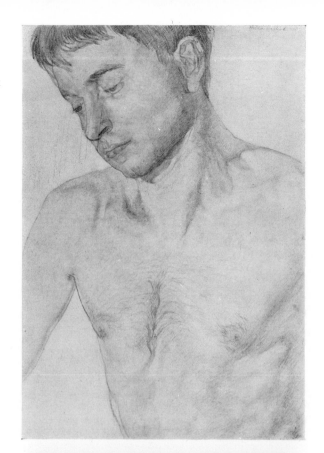

13   *Stanley Spencer*, by
Hilda Spencer, pencil, 1931
Private Collection

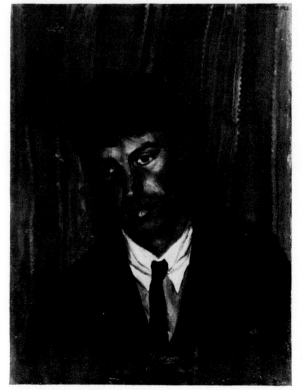

14   *Stanley Spencer*, by
Hilda Carline, oil, 1923.
*Collection Shirin and
Unity Spencer*

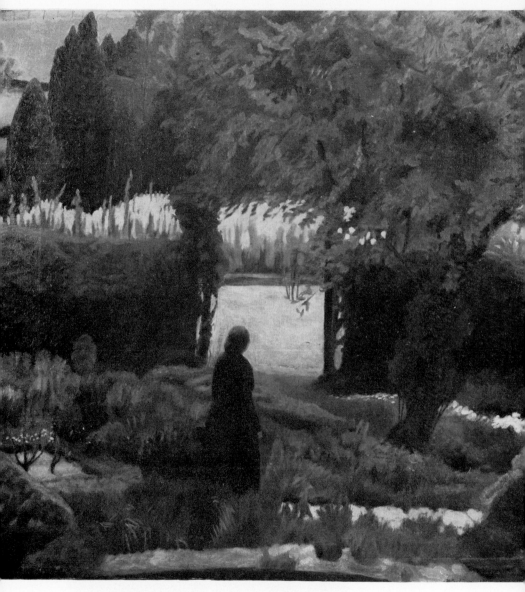

15   *Melancholy in a Country Garden*, by Hilda Spencer, oil, 1921
Collection Richard Carline

without reference to an author. Sometime that month Spencer wrote to Tooth: 'I was very interested to receive the report from my wife that you propose we meet & have a talk about this book question and its possibilities etc. My wife repeated all you had said to her on the matter and I thought that perhaps what you suggest would be the best & only way for such a thing to be done. . . .'

Spencer sent to Tooth a document (received in May 1938) setting forth his ideas about the project. The salient points are these:

I think the 'neat' 'tastefully' got up books that one understands are popular in this country but which I think are not popular are horrible. I would rather a book on myself & my work were a confused heap & mass of matter from which much could be gathered than risk something of me being left out in the interests of conciseness & briefness. No matter how I put it people *very much* want to know what I think, & would be prepared to wade through a thousand badly written pages by me for the sake of finding some of the things I have to say, rather than read one page of what anyone else had to say about me. . . . The offer I had from Gollancz [the publishers] was not to me a possible proposal. I could not possibly have presented the work I have in mind . . . (he could only offer 48 repros). It is clear to me that in future I cannot consider any proposal which makes some stipulation respecting the cost. . . . If this is necessary then it is clear to me that there is insufficient evidence to show that there is the interest in my work that is so often pretended. In this case I prefer to publish nothing at all. I am not interested in anyone else doing it any more than I would be if it were proposed that they should paint my pictures.

The idea I have as far as my share in the book is this: [There follow seven numbered paragraphs, some of a purely technical character but others that clarify his conception of the character of the book.]
(2) That these inclusions [of 'repros'] will not necessarily be for any merit but possibly because they form an important part of what I am talking about. They might be included as a part of some period I was referring to where I felt very uninspired or did not quite know what I was up to.
(6) I think in a sense a long book in which there was no hurry and in which I would, in tracing my development from earliest times, not simply keep to a middle course but wander up the by-paths both the ones that led somewhere and the ones that led nowhere, would be so interesting as not to be dull at all.

I should think it proper matter for a book if I re-experienced so to speak some boring period and expected the reader to settle down comfortably to agonizing with me for several pages. . . . The 'speed' or 'tempo' . . . will be rather that of someone out walking with someone who has a passion for blackberrying in the blackberry season.
(7) Many seemingly trivial things might be mentioned and which I think are important as being very like me. . . .

Stanley Spencer's paintings are extremely definite, as regards their subjects, but their meaning is not always easy to understand in the detail he desired, and he believed that they were fully explicable by nobody but himself. So in his document for Tooth he continued:

It *is* possible that as Mr. Tooth said from what he observed when artists had written about their own works that it might if I did so detract from the interest in my work. But apart from the fact that I am not primarily interested in my reputation, I wish to assure myself that whatever notion there may be as to my work other than what the painting conveys, shall emanate from my own expressed interpretation than in the interpretation of other people. If this should lessen the paintings' importance in peoples minds in any way I rather it did, and that they should feel some disappointment or disillusionment, than that they should base their understanding on the fake interpretation etc. that they listen to so reverently. I can say this that I should have thought that if my repute as a painter can (as it has done) survive the vulgar interpretation which some have published as coming from me and as being what I myself have said of my work, then it could survive anything.

He then goes on to describe the proper meaning of *The Centurion's Servant* and criticized what R. H. Wilenski and Frank Rutter had written about it. '. . . Well,' he wrote about Wilenski's essay, 'I would . . . prefer to destroy the picture itself than paint a picture of such a subject: *children frightened by an air raid*'. [The reference is to *Stanley Spencer* in the series *Contemporary British Artists* (1924), pp. 17,18.]

On 14 June 1938 Tooth replied.
. . . You are an artist first & foremost, and the shoemaker should stick to his last. . . . Personally I think that a book written by you alone about yourself would appear a sort of self-advertisement, & would not be in the best interests of your reputation or career. Nor do I think that a plain statement of your ideas would be as interesting to readers as they would be if accompanied by the sympathetic criticism and comment of Dr. Rothenstein's experience & official position. . . . In this case, I am certain that I am a better judge of what is in your best interests than you are &, as a business man, I can only repeat that you are being offered a chance which you would be absolutely crazy to turn down. It is for you to decide. At least two-thirds of the book is to be yours entirely. If you finally turn the suggestion down, it would be absolutely against my advice, & I think by now that you ought to have some confidence in my judgement.

Stanley, however, remained obdurate: 'I am sorry but I shall not be able to do the book under the conditions you have proposed.'
The strain imposed upon Spencer by the failure of his second marriage following the breakup of his first, with several tragic consequences, and his virtual expulsion from his Lindworth studio brought about a near collapse. The following chapter includes an account of his six-week visit – from mid-October until the end of November, 1938 – to our house in 5 Fellows Road, Primrose Hill, when his normally unremitting creative urge had dwindled: he attempted to paint a portrait of my wife but could do little more than make a beginning; a piece of his writing there is literally incoherent.

82

Malcolm MacDonald proved a benevolent friend, with whom he stayed for a fortnight and who paid the rent of a room at 188 Adelaide Road, a few minutes walk from our house. We saw him fairly frequently. Malcolm Macdonald delighted in his company and in his torrential talk, which sometimes continued until long after midnight. 'I would like', he said, 'to be Spencer's Boswell'.

At Adelaide Road was particularly apparent one of the several contradictory aspects of his character. Visitors he welcomed with the utmost warmth, yet about it he wrote '. . . Alone I would sort myself out. After sweeping the floor & dusting a bit . . . I could sink down on one of the two chairs & think & look at the floor. Oh, the joy of just that!' 'When you are by yourself & I am by myself', he later wrote to Hilda, 'as I was in 188 Adelaide Road, I have a wonderful feeling of being able to realize myself.' It was in fact at Adelaide Road that he fully discovered the joys of solitude. There he painted the first four of his *Christ in the Wilderness* series of eight, the last being completed in 1953.

The earliest Tooth letter of 1939 relates, like many others throughout the correspondence, to his financial affairs. A statement from Tooth of 5 January shows that of seven paintings sold none commanded a price higher than £80 and one went as low as £43, which is strange (even though Spencer needed cash urgently) in view of the high reputation he had achieved.

Nothing illustrates so precisely and so poignantly the poverty to which Stanley Spencer had been reduced than the many appeals to his dealer for advances of tiny sums of money, usually to pay debts of board and lodging. In 1939 he asked for £2 in April and in June for £1.14.0 and also £1 for himself; in May 1941 for £1.10.0, to cite a few instances out of many. It was about the end of 1938 that my wife had suggested Tooth's taking over Spencer's financial affairs. He readily agreed, and on 8 February 1939 wrote to Spencer to suggest that he allow him to manage his financial affairs, attend to his income tax, pay off debts and meet his bills, sending him £10 a week. In letters of 29 July and 7 August 1939 Hilda Spencer wrote to him (from 17 Pond Street) expressing her relief at the arrangement.

She went on to comment that:

it is in the practical ways that I think Stanley comes a cropper; he does not always realise the practical import of things. And he is too imaginative to be able to describe things, or even to see things, accurately. He is so easily taken in – he so readily takes all the blame himself in cases where he feels quixotic; and if, in such a case, he feels *all* to blame, then he takes the entire blame and does not see that the other person is to blame too and perhaps almost entirely to blame. At any rate he had a completely disproportionate idea of the other person's conduct so that what he says usually needs sorting and deciphering. He is incapable of protecting himself or realizing his interests or seeing faults in those in whom he is specially interested.

I don't think it is very easy for any of us to believe in evils that are very far from our comprehensions, and I think that is why Patricia achieved so much, because both of us were too credulous and because it takes a good deal of banging at one before one can accept as possible deliberate evil in somebody one knows.

The rest of Hilda Spencer's remarkable letter to Dudley Tooth of August 1939 – or at any rate of what has survived of it – is printed in chapter 3, pp. 48-51. Shortly afterwards, on 24 September, she sent him a letter touchingly expressive of the depth of her own and Stanley's affection for each other:

I am feeling very much that I want to have all Stanley's early letters to me, returned to me. . . . But when I went to Cookham to bring away my belongings, when Stanley was newly married and in Cornwall with Patricia and the girl friend, his letters were one of the items I was expecting to bring back. But I found that he had arranged them so beautifully, in order, his and my corresponding ones, all numbered and tied in lots and so on, and I had not the heart to separate his from mine and undo his work and take half away (the ones *he* had written). They all seemed to belong together and as I knew that he often reread those early letters of mine and sometimes of his, I decided to leave them there untouched.

In a letter to Tooth, written from The White Hart, Leonard Stanley, Stroud, Gloucestershire (6 October 1939), after expressing his gratitude for his regular cheques, Stanley continued:

I wish there was some way in which under the existing circumstances [i.e. the war] I could earn a little *without* having to in any way curtail my work as an artist. It would have to be something [he characteristically added] in which I had a completely free hand and was under no supervision and of course to do with art,
in view of the suspension of the actual trading of my work I could 1. Have some sort of official art employment (not painting) that would give me a small income. . . . 2. Spend the main bulk of my time in doing something of these big pictures I so often wanted to do. . . . I do not feel myself [illegible] called upon to do anything other than painting. In the last war I wasted a great deal of time in the Army, became very longing for any responsible work such as painting. I am quite willing to serve this country but on this occasion I shall decide in what capacity and way I do so. I should have thought that in view of the fitness for the work I do and my unfitness for any other work, I should be in no hurry to do other than continue my painting. . . . I am not able to work here . . . as I have no room of my own. I am cut off from my work as I have been for just over a year. It's a great scandalous shame that I was turned out of Lindworth [the house in Cookham that he had made over to Patricia Preece as a condition of marriage] and The Studio that I had all my stuff in and did many of my big pictures in. . . . [He concludes with a plea for an extra 5s. a week.] The £1.15s.0d. I receive from you every Saturday morning is the

exact amount I am charged here for my board and lodging, so that I am, or have been, dependent on the £4 or £5 that you paid me when I came here on 30 July. I need either a small extra cheque or £2 a week instead of £1.15s.od.

Tooth's reply to this letter appears to have been lost, but there is a reference to it in a letter from Spencer (Leonard Stanley, 21 December 1939):

I do not know whether you heard from [Smart], but I gave him a full account of myself. Mr. Smart was in favour of my continuing painting here ... but after I saw your letter I felt you might be wishing me to get some extra work as I suggested. I wish you were able to find out what is happening to this War Artists employment scheme as I understand that Sir Kenneth Clark is Chairman (if I am to believe my informant) I am left out of the list altogether. Also Sir Muirhead Bone is on this Committee and have recently heard the most astonishing statements about myself, from that quarter ... but I would be glad if, without my having to appear in the matter, you or Mr. Smart could find out what that body are going or intending to do for me. I carried out a £200 war picture [*Travoys*] at the close of the last war and it did receive a great deal of notice.

Tooth wrote on Christmas Day 1939 to Sir Kenneth Clark, Chairman of the newly formed War Artists' Advisory Committee: 'I very much hope that you will be able to use Spencer in some official capacity in the official war artists scheme: these eventful days will certainly bring out the best in him and I am sure he will prove amenable to work with as he is terribly in debt all round.'

As a result Spencer received in 1940 an official commission to paint a ship-building subject in Port Glasgow for £50. This eventually led also to his painting a series of *Resurrection* pictures completed in 1950.

He was still living at Leonard Stanley when in May he made the first of his several Glasgow visits. But his work there was not without grave discomfort. A letter to Tooth and Smart (undated but probably October) concludes: 'My shoes are worn out and I could do with a small cheque to cover this and other possible items of Winter wear.'

The letters of 1940 are also largely concerned with financial matters and show how seriously the war affected his sales. Tooth was in arrears with maintenance payments to Patricia and her lawyers started proceedings. On 9 March he wrote to them: 'the sale of his pictures is not sufficient to pay for his board and lodging and alimony due to his wives, and he is heavily in our debt. He is entirely without funds except what we advance him from time to time. The only way to pay off his debts is to sell his pictures. Until that is possible, we must ask you to be patient.' Proceedings were called off, but Spencer was saddled with £35 in solicitors' fees. In a letter of 4 November Tooth informed Patricia that 'I am forced to reduce your weekly allowance from £3 to £2 per week.'

In his letter to Tooth and Smart Spencer refers to a 'cheque from the Ministry of Information for £50 being half the payment for the work I am doing for them,' and in another (13 October) he told Smart of completing '3 sections of the Min. of Inf. work . . . which are now apparently on show at the Nat. Gall. . . .' In another undated letter to Smart (received on 4 March 1941) Spencer wrote: 'I have at last finished the second lot of 3 panels for the Ministry of Information. I hope they will let me continue the scheme. So far I have in length done 36ft 8 inches of the scheme which is about a third of the picture or scheme of pictures. . . .' And in an undated letter evidently written later: 'I have had a letter from the Ministry of Information approving my last 3 paintings for them and commissioning me to carry out another £300 worth. I find it necessary to go to Scotland again (to the Clyde bank) to refresh my memory and felt I must have a new suit to go in. . . . Mrs. Charlton is at my elbow in the Stroud Post Office trying to make me misspell my words; a thing I can usually do unaided.'

Smart wrote (1 April 1941):
It is good news that the MOI have bought the second series of your big project and better still that they want you to proceed with it. I am looking forward to seeing the last three canvases as I was much impressed with the first ones, and so were a great many other people. Enclosed is a cheque for £5 which I hope will provide you with what you need for your second expedition to Clyde-bank. . . .

Spencer wrote from Epsom (7 November 1941): '. . . I heard this morning that the Min. of Inf: are allowing me £35 for 14 pencil studies and sketches I made for the 'Riveter' painting. . . . It isn't much I know but I shall have to agree. . . .'
In a letter received on 7 January 1942 Spencer wrote to E. J. Ledger, at Tooths:

I am moving from above address (6 Downs Road, Epsom) to Cookham to-morrow Wednesday so please send this weeks £2 to me at c/o Bernard Smithers Esq 'Quinneys' High Street, Cookham-on-Thames, Berks. I am trying to get Mrs. Spencers' stuff removed out of the Studio so that I can work in it. Mrs. Harter [who had looked after his daughter Shirin] asked me to leave some time ago.

On 29 January 1942 he wrote bitterly to Ledger about:
an account [from Bourlets for frames] not particularized for £60 odd . . . [and rang] them up to see what in the name of goodness they were up to. . . .I told them to send me a detailed account . . . I was utterly flabbergasted; no account *I* had ever had with any Art Materials firm had ever exceeded more than about £10. No detailed account *was* sent & Mrs. Patricia was doing all this secretly . . . she never allowed me to know *any* thing of what *she* did. . . . Then about a

year afterwards . . . I got an account from them [Bourlets] no details £60 odd. The first time I saw what that was all for was when you [illegible] out of these people a detailed and full account. . . . When I once dared to ask Mrs P Spencer how she was going on over frames for her show, . . . she made some vague statement to the effect that the Gallery and others were lending . . . frames. NOT ONE WORD that she was buying them. . . . I have just discovered [where] these frames live. If I am to be held responsible for this outrageous buying . . . these frames are most certainly *not* the property of Mrs. Patricia S . . . if [Bourlets] would care to come to Cookham & take any of these frames . . . they can. Personally I do not think that should be done, as I am utterly *innocent* of that account (I make no plea about any of my other accounts . . .) & Mrs. P.S. have had an amusing time & they present *me* with a bill of £164 for it. Could you tell Mr. Tooth . . .

Another letter to Ledger also from Quinneys (received on 11 May, 1942) reveals the misery of Spencer's situation. The first paragraph deals with heating problems in his studio, solved eventually by the acquisition of an oil stove. The second begins with a suggestion that:

after my talk with Mr. Tooth [who had been released from the Army the previous month] *a cut down in weekly payments* all round might be possible. Even if it was only temporary say for 4 months it would make a difference in the years outgoing payment. It need (if Mr. Tooth thought it unwise) only be a small sum off each due, say to begin with 10/– off self, 10/– off Mrs. Hilda Spencer & £1 off Mrs. Patricia Spencer, & if he thought fit, 5/– off each of the children though with there necessary expences it might not in the case of the children be possible. Having my liabilities scattered about & not all under one roof (and that should have been Lindworth where I would have had no rent only rates to pay) makes it very awkward and expencive and this fact should be made clear. I would say that my outgoing expences ought not really be more than £6 a week all told (or if possible less) and if anyone has to suffer real inconveniences for this it is to be Mrs Patricia Spencer, as she is better provided for (by me) and the House ('Lindworth') & rent and about £1200 worth of jewelry to fall back upon & the others have nothing. I must leave Mr. Tooth to decide whether Mrs P. Spencer should be paid for this studio I am partly using & if so 'how much. When she first said to me she would require a little rent I thought she might have some & not realizing what the conditions were & these other works of mine she had been selling & getting money for I said I might be able to manage 10/– a week. Then she said she would be willing for me to have it for 5/– a week. When I said 10/– I was thinking of the whole studio & full use of all its amenities but I only have half the use of the studio (a 'slice' I have managed to squeeze for myself out of the center of the room the rest being piled high with her & her sisters & and part of Miss Hepworths belongings & furniture). I have as you know 10/– a week at present from the MoI.

He then goes on to explain that the house has a garage which Mrs. Patricia has let, which was large enough to store her furniture and his, for the storage of which he had to pay; also that one of her accounts (sent as agreed through Tooths) from Fortnum & Mason was

for items I did not recognize at all. There were several 'rugs' I never bought rugs, I never bought tables, expencive 'Sherries'. I have never bought a drink in my life & I strongly object to pay for any alcoholic drinks whatever. Mr. Tooth seemed to think that I knew of these items so I looked at the date it was all late in 1939 I was turned out of my place in Cookham in *Oct–Nov 1938* & that was the end of my having any vestige of knowledge as to what Mrs P. Spencer did. I knew nothing whatever of her activities from late autumn of 1938. I was living in my attick (rent paid for by Malcolm MacDonald) at 188 Adelaide Road. Towards the end of my stay in Cookham I used to notice . . . 'bottles of whiskey' on the grocers account every four or five days . . . This was going on for a considerable period without any sanction from me & when I remonstrated with her about it she said it was good for her etc. *It was not* & is well known to be bad for a person with her complaint, I think £8 should be deducted from any allowance made to her for rent, in order to pay us towards this past and paid for item.

At this time Hilda Spencer, following a breakdown, was very ill and in hospital at Banstead, and her condition further deepened his devotion to her, stimulated his desire for reunion with her and to care for her. An intimate friend of Stanley's, concerned at the consequences of such a course, in view of their occasionally stormy relations, wrote in June several letters to Tooth with a view to his opposing it.

There exists a draft reply by Tooth probably written in the same month.

I had a long discussion with Stanley and Richard Carline as to what best can be done about Hilda Spencer. Stanley is naturally very anxious about her but I am quite confident . . . that he will do nothing quixotic or unexpected and will consult me first. I personally favour their getting fixed up again one day, if Hilda gets alright and provided that such a domestic situation could be arranged as would keep them from upsetting each other through being constantly in the same house. I would like, too . . . to get the children more under Hilda's and Stanley's control and supervision. This is the healthy solution . . . it is a great pity that the first marriage was ever broken up. I look forward to a time when Stanley can devote his time wholeheartedly to his family and his painting and is free of all other distracting influences. . . . I quite understand your fears of Hilda's probable reactions on Stanley if they come together and I will certainly see that any influence she may have on him will bring him no harm. . . . I am confident that his decision will not be precipitated by Patricia.

And to Spencer (3 July 1942):
. . . I think it important that we should have a talk as it seems at present that we are rather at cross purposes in our dealings with Patricia Spencer. I am convinced she is out to help the situation if we do not upset her unnecessarily. . . .

Spencer wrote to Tooth a letter from Quinneys (undated but probably in July):

... I went yesterday where she was sent suffering from a nervous breakdown to Banstead [hospital] and saw Mrs. Hilda S. who seemed to me considerably better. We sat at a little table & chatted the whole afternoon about Chopin, Schumann and Wagner ...

In a letter to Tooth from Quinneys (12 February 1943) Spencer wrote with reference to a conversation:

I was saying I had done so little *painting* in these last few months ... & you *jokingly* said what do you do with yourself all day ... since Jan 1st 1943 I have done 18 compositions (16 inches by 11 inches) ... whether my activities are wise or work good is a matter for criticism; this is so that you can inform those who think otherwise that 1. I am always busy and active. 2. That I love my work, and 3. that on the contrary of being at all neurotic I am always merry and bright. ... I and Mr. Carline [brought] Mrs. Hilda S. comfortably from Camberwell to Westminster Hospital.

To which Tooth replied (13 February): 'I am not worrying at all. ... All I want is to feel that you are cheerful and the inspiration will come along in time. ....' He told Spencer that his debts were now paid and his financial affairs in order.

From Quinneys (26 May 1943) Spencer wrote a letter to Tooth which shows his absence of facility and how hard he had to work to realise his ideas, but also his basic confidence:

... My time is chiefly taken up with the long ship painting [for the Ministry of Information] but at long last I have broken the back of it. In spite of the great difficulties I have had with it – it is I think going to be a worthy associate of the others I have already done. Anyway, I am getting a lot of pleasure from it now. Having been such an age doing this, I may have given the impression that this represents my average speed of doing these things, but it does not. I was *never* at all happy about it and for several months did not touch it. ... I wish I could get going as well on the religious track. Anyway I have the material and notions for something good and when I fail its only a momentary lapse, and the permanent title of all my works is 'Excelsior'.

On 17 July Tooth was able to tell him that his account was just over £900 in credit, and that his paintings in stock should realise about £1500. 'At present they are not saleable, but they will be in time. You should have no financial worries.'

But the situation was unstable. In August, for example, bills had to be met for Hilda's stay and treatment at the Banstead Mental Hospital and the Westminster, and Tooth represented to the Ministry of Information that Spencer was working for them at a loss. They promised £100 a picture more. Much of this correspondence is naturaly concerned with the exhibition and sale of his work as well as Tooth's benevolent concern with his business affairs in general. It includes an annual statement (for 1943) that gives some indication of Spencer's financial precariousness. His credits for the year amounted to £450: £400 from the Ministry of Information for two of his canvases, and £50 from occasional commissions for portrait drawings in pencil. His debits were £611, itemised at £104 for living expenses for himself at £2 a week, £182 for living expenses of Hilda at £3.10s.0d. a week, £117 for living expenses of two children at 22s.6d. a week, part of children's education £50 (the rest was paid by a relative), £104 for Patricia's living expenses at £2 a week, and £54 income tax on £450.

Hilda Spencer's letters reveal her magnanimity. In one to Tooth (about 20 September 1943) from 224 Finchley Road, NW3, she wrote:

... I am very troubled with regard to the money I have saved arising from returned income. ... I wanted Stanley to take what money I had saved in this way at a time when he was so badly in debt but he wouldn't do so. ... [But she also expressed anxiety on her own account]:
With regard to my savings I wonder whether you have realized that if Stanley died (which he won't do) that there would be nothing whatever for me and the children. ... Patricia on the other hand would be well off for everything Stanley died possessed of would automatically go to her and he has hundreds of drawings. ... Patricia would be well off; and yet she has been saving constantly and also she has the house, which really could bring in £100 apart from the garage. ... I am really fond of Patricia, so I am very glad for her to be alright, but I feel it is odd there should be a down on me for having saved something. ... Of course I feel that it would be a good thing if he left his pictures and drawings to the children ...

To which Tooth replied (20 September 1943):
... I have noted all you say about your savings, about Stanley leaving his drawings to the children. The main thing is for you to get fit and not to worry too much about Stanley and his possessions: I will keep the ship on an even keel. ...

Spencer's attitude towards his wife was less sympathetic than Hilda's:
... I felt so uncomfortable [he wrote (18 December 1943) from the studio beside Lindworth] that I had to secure myself a bed from my store [Webbers at Maidenhead] because the one I was using belonged to Mrs P. Spencer; she might be taking it from me any moment and I preferred to sleep on one of my own. It meant taking down and putting back most of the store. I recovered a lot of drawings. ... I trust that Mrs Spencer and Miss Hepworth are not allowed to go to my store. ... I cannot and will not do anything if I am only using the Studio because Mrs P.S. *permits* me to. If I have no legal right to be and work in that Studio I will not remain in it and the rent from M of I must stop.

An even higher proportion of Spencer's correspondence with Tooth in

1944 concerned his continuing financial difficulties. Most of it is addressed from Glencairn, Glasgow Road, Port Glasgow. A letter from Tooth (15 April) notes 'that you are planning a prolonged stay of 3 to 5 months in Glasgow; I think it may prove a very wise decision. . . .'

In Port Glasgow, however, in spite of the kindness of the people with whom he lodged, he suffered acutely and in an undated letter written from Quinneys on one of his occasional visits to Cookham, probably in April, 1944, to Tooth, he described the discomforts of his life there:

The atmosphere is more conducive for my work here which is chiefly the ship building work and I got more done. . . . Although for this I need no other status than I allways have, I *do* need some of the personal needs that are readily given and supplied to any member of the services. In my work up there I am *far* more exposed to the weather than a great many people whether soldiers or sailors or any of the civil defence services. I have to rough it I can tell you. I have three miles to walk *daily* (mile and half each way to and from my work) in the rain. I dont go by bus because they are all packed and one can stand in the rain for as long as the walk would take. Not on *one* of my five visits to Scotland have I known what it was to walk in boots that did *not* let the water in. The Doctor up there told me they had two days out of the year when there was no rain, so that it is a very wet sopping place. Also for some of the views I have drawn I have had to, and still have to, stand where the tide comes in and I have found myself standing in water once or twice. If there is any possibility of personal equipment being provided I should have it. If this cant be done because I am not in the services then they should provide me with the extra coupons I would need and the cost of extra clothing. To go to Scotland I need.

> Strong pair of boots
> A pair of webbing leggings
> Waders
> New suit of clothes of some sort
> Good strong waterproof mackintosh
> Good thick shoes
> Mackintosh hat of some kind.

I have no one looking after me up there and a soldier having the rough work I do and no quartermasters stores or means of renewing things when quickly worn out, would suffer some of the discomforts I have had up there. So something must be done to make it easy for me to renew boots or socks etc. . . . I dont wish to be an official war artist but I must have *that* much at least of official war artists comforts. . . . It was only through the great kindness of the Scotch people at Port Glasgow that I had a comfortable time. My absence of personal needs was allways a concern of theirs and a surprise. They could not understand how I coming on this work could be so poorly provided for and not provided for at all . . . I am to be on the same basis as a private soldier as far as supplies are concerned and I will hear no stories from M of I or Admiralty that things are scarce and cant be got nowadays. P.S. Could you keep this letter private. I will come up and take it to the M of I and the Admiralty and see if something can be done. . . . I shall only do work that such personal equipment as I have allows me to do in comfort. Let me know what you think. . . .

In another undated letter also written from Cookham he described the misery of his circumstances there also:
. . . I would prefer to be home at Cookham but I have no place there at all now. I had you remember to leave [Quinneys]. . . . The last three weeks in Cookham I tried to manage in my studio but there was no lavatory or wash place. . . . I had been invited to stay . . . at a charming cottage occupied by the Griersons who were hoping I would stay as long as I liked, but I was hiked out by the interfering individual [the woman with a jealous passion for him previously referred to] and forbidden to stay there. As I wished to avoid scenes I had most reluctantly to come away having stayed there about 4 days while the inter-ference [the name he often used for the woman in question] was away from Cookham. I must therefore stay here [Port Glasgow] indefinitely until some-thing can be done to control the interference. I can only work when out of reach of that person. There are others matters I should mention as they seriously affect my work. . . . There is the problem of Mrs. Hilda Spencer and the difficulty about my eyesight. About Mrs Hilda a month or so . . . I wrote about our re-marriage and she agreed to re-marry me on the strict under-standing that there would be no sexual life whatever. As one of the chief hold ups of me in my work and also a cause of my work containing elements in it that puts people off it is the lack of balance in this matter in my life, I felt her offer was not much good to me and at least the matter must go into abeyance. So for the time being that hope is dropped.

On 22 November 1944 Spencer wrote from Glencairn asking for Tooth's advice. His brother Percy had told him that he was worried about their elder sister, who lived in a cottage [Cliveden View] belonging to him but was permitted by the authorities to remain only if a relative lived there also, and offered it to him at a nominal rent:
I, knowing how next to impossible it is to get a place in Cookham wrote . . . . asking him to hold [it] for me with a view to discussing the pros and cons. If and providing the interference could be . . . eliminated this . . . would suit me better than anything I could think of. . . . If some legal measure could be found preventing her from 1. Coming to the house, 2. waylaying me in the road and 3. in any way communicating with me . . . I would like to rent the cottage. I do not want to return immediately from here and in any case I am making sure of a 'bunk hole' for myself up here in case if I came to this Cookham cottage and found it did not do.
As far as my association with Cookham is concerned it *is* only the interference that is a difficulty. Where ever I go there is the possibility of her turning up on the doorstep.
But I wish it was possible to have a small house like this. My wish simply put would be this. 1. To be remarried to Mrs Hilda Spencer. 2. To have this cottage, to buy it if possible by small weekly payments. 3. So that I could have somewhere to have Hilda and the children if and when they wished. 4. So also that I could have a place to put all my furniture and belongings. . . .

P.S. If you have any alternative suggestion to this offer of a cottage . . . I would be glad to know what you think. For instance for some reason Mrs. Hilda Spencer seems very averse from coming to Cookham. I have not yet told her of this cottage.

Tooth replied (27 November 1944):
. . . it is not clear whether you wanted me to write to your brother [about the cottage]. . . . I would like to see you installed there providing we can not only restrain, but get rid of [the interference]. I have gone into the matter with [a solicitor] and he is writing to her, if strong measures are to be taken, you must not weaken at the last moment; after due warning, if she continues to approach you, as no doubt she will, it will be necessary to imprison her. If you will send me her address, we will try to get her to a meeting here and give her a good fright. If she remains in Cookham, Mrs Hilda Spencer will certainly not go there; she does not appear to like the idea of going there anyway. It will be time enough to arrange your divorce and re-marriage when your living quarters are settled and you have tried out a period of living there with Mrs Hilda Spencer and seen whether then . . . a re-marriage is likely to prove a success. Personally, I think it would be better if you could settle down together elsewhere, say at Burghclere if a cottage could be found.
Resurrection Picture. . . . one large picture 3 ft high and 40ft long, & 5 separate pictures, unless you can eliminate the 'elements which people object to' in your recent work, I can see little hope of the picture or pictures helping to reduce your debts. May I see the compositions before you start to paint? If you could paint religious pictures without any element of sex creeping in, I would rather have them than landscape. There was nothing to offend people in the 'Christ in the Wilderness' series. However, you must do what your inner feelings indicate.

The last letter of 1944 (29 December) in the year's correspondence from Tooth informed him that he had received a 20-page letter which he enclosed, to which was attached from Hilda a cheque for £1700 for him, and he urged Stanley to wire immediately 'Tooth, 31 Bruton Street, accept cheque. Am writing'.
This will put her mind at rest; she is obviously distracted and we can always pay the cheque back into her account. . . . Perhaps you would also like to wire her . . . at the same time I am certain you will be doing a big thing for her and specially for her sanity if you sent these wires *at once*.

Tooth, who obviously thought that the possession of such a sum was a hallucination and made wise suggestions how it should be dealt with, concludes: 'the great thing and the only thing that matters is to set her mind at rest. . . . PLEASE WIRE AT ONCE.' To Hilda Spencer he wrote a letter at once tactful and humane.
On 10 October 1946 a letter from Cliveden View shows, in spite of their alienation, Spencer's solicitude for Patricia's health:
I saw Mrs. Patricia Spencer about a week ago. She was concerned at the

expence of Doctors regarding herself and the need she has of them. I said that as long as I and you could be satisfied that the expence *was* a needed medicle one and as long as we saw and were satisfied with the Doctors I and you would always see to these Doctors expences if she was not able to do so. . . . I think I must see Dr. Mercer (who is my Doctor) about her state of health. She is so thin it is terrible to see. She can get about a little bit but not far. I am wondering if there is any taking of these sleep daughts or drugs and of their effect and so on. . . . I do not know *why* she seems not to have the means to pay these smallish doctors bills, but I dont want her health and what can be done to preserve it, to be neglected.

With some relaxation in the grim consequences of the break-up of Spencer's marriages and some distancing from the two other women with whom he had had close emotional relations, and with the establishment of a more secure reputation bringing him a less insubstantial income – though his regular allowances remained at £3 a week – his need to confide in Tooth diminished. His friendship remained as warm as ever, but their correspondence from late 1946 onwards was largely confined to business affairs.

With Spencer working hard on his Glasgow *Resurrections*, Tooth wanted to help his peace of mind. On 7 June 1946 he wrote to him: 'Don't worry. Will keep you alive. Don't feel you have to paint landscape.' None the less, despite Spencer's personal austerity of life, it was not easy to keep him solvent. In 1948, to take one example, his weekly pay packet was £3 (he was living by himself at Cliveden View) for food, heating, etc., though he could call on Tooth for cheques to cover unforeseen expenses like the increasing bills for his children. But in April Patricia's weekly cheque had to be reduced to £2.15s.0d. On 8 December he told Tooth that he had bought a new suit, a pullover, some socks, a shirt and tie – he itemises the expenditure – 'so that I am a bit short'. A friend had paid for the suit in return for an Inverness cape, and he asked for an extra £2.

By August 1956, however, he was becoming comfortably off. But he increased his own weekly cheque only to £3.10s.0d., still asking Tooth to send cheques for such extras as arose. It was an arrangement on which he had come to rely and he enjoyed the freedom from preoccupations alien to him. By 27 November 1957 Tooth was able to report that his account now showed a credit of £2,500, with £1,000 put aside for income tax due on 1957, 1958 and 1959.

Lively sentences occur in a few letters, two for instance in those to Peter Cochrane, a member of the firm. In one from 176 Melville Garden Village, Whitehouse near Belfast, where he stayed with a brother, (13 October 1953), referring to our proposal to hold a retrospective exhibition of his work at the Tate: 'I enclose the letter I had from John Rothenstein (which I have answered saying I would like to cooperate) which I do not remember if I told you about. It looks as if I shall be queen of the May next year; hardly a suitable epithet for me but you know my meaning. . . .'

In another from Cliveden View (29 November 1953):
I dont know whether if ever the Tate show comes off but it [illegible] and might be a nuisance if that picture was tied up anywhere at the time though on the other hand if it was at the Cartright [Hall, Bradford] when the Tate show came off it might buck the Cartright up no end; they might say 'this fellow Spencer you know' and then they might buy it, you never know. . . .

Among the few letters of 1959 – the last year of his life – are a few which show that Spencer, for so long the victim of matrimonial tragedies, financial insecurity and at times poverty, physical hardship and ill-health, enjoyed towards the end of his life a modest balance at his Maidenhead bank, honours (CBE and Knighthood), and above all a house of his own. He was still alone. But he was popular in Cookham, asked out for many meals to the houses of friends, and always welcome. In a letter to a friend he wrote from the Vicarage, Cookham (February 1959):

Between Peter [Cochrane], David [Gibbs] and you and me I think Jack [Martineau] and his Lordship [Viscount Astor] have found[ed] a trust (just those two) and have bought my old home in Cookham (Fernlea) to be renamed the White House to be handed to me to live in all my days and to be held in trust by them and then on my ceasing to need it to be given to the children.

Tooth's last letter to Spencer, who was in the Canadian War Memorial Hospital (19 November 1959), said: 'Let me know whenever you want anything: anything you ask shall be yours'. Spencer had less than a month to live.

Without Dudley Tooth's sensitive friendship and his tactful solicitude Stanley Spencer could never have survived his financially desperate straits of 1935 to 1945, the years during which, in spite of his abject personal poverty, he had to be rescued time and again by loans from this most understanding of bankers.

Chapter 5

Friends and Neighbours

The preceding four chapters rest on the evidence of the private letters cited in them. There is now not enough other evidence available. With only one or two exceptions all those closely involved are dead. In telling the story by the evidence of the letters and in hoping that the telling will disclose the man, I am none the less acutely aware of the many pitfalls and fallacies that evidence of this kind can generate.

An implicit reliance on documents, especially private documents, as affording a privileged access to the truth of things is, I believe, a methodological fallacy that has already distorted much biography in recent years. In the general introduction to this book I noted how transitory were some of the (usually disagreeable) emotions violently expressed in Stanley Spencer's letters. His moods could indeed shift like quick-silver into their opposites, but a letter puts on permanent record only the dominating mood of a fleeting moment. And, as has also been noted in the same place, it may put similarly on permanent record what are in fact fantasies to people his solitude or to compensate for a reluctant celibacy or for the tribulations that Stanley's follies brought so abundantly on him. Their interpretation and evaluation postulate a delicate and scrupulous scholarship and even so will remain a difficult and complicated business.

There is no doubt that between about 1930 and 1940 Stanley Spencer could be in many respects an extremely disagreeable man, unlike either his earlier or his later self. Why and how this came about should now be clearer. In 1945 he returned to Cookham and remained there for the rest of his life.

The present chapter gathers together the impressions and reminiscences of friends and neighbours who, for the most part, knew him only in those years. They have not been assembled as character witnesses for the defence, but in a belief that neglect of oral evidence is just as fallacious in biography as is exclusive attention to personal documents.

This is not, of course, a biography but an attempt to show what manner of human being Stanley Spencer was. What anybody is really like is known only to God. The nearest we can approach this knowledge is by collation of how he appeared to those – as many as possible – who in one way or another were well acquainted with him, met him frequently, were involved in his work or his life. The present chapter attempts to make possible such a collation. I am aware that already it is late in the day and that within the last decade many have died who would have made

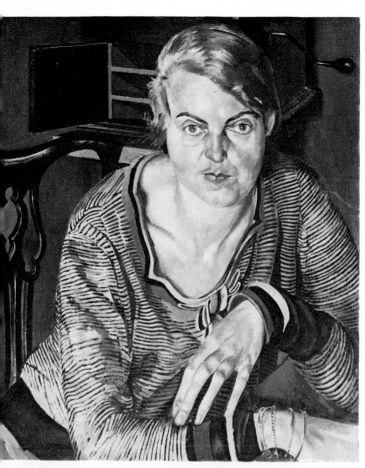

16 *Portrait of Patricia Preece*, by Stanley Spencer, oil, 1933. *Southampton Art Gallery*

17 *Self-portrait with Patricia*, by Stanley Spencer, oil, 1936. *Fitzwilliam Museum, Cambridge*

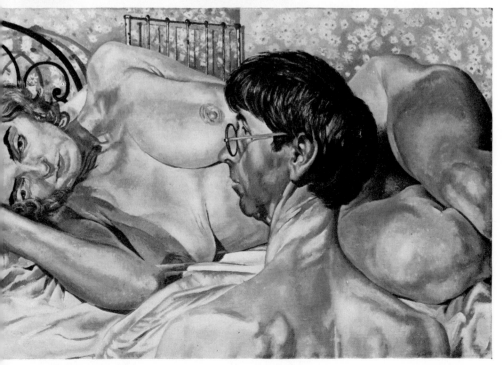

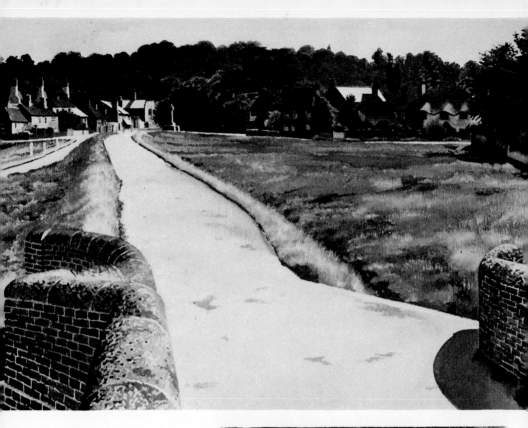

18 *Cookham Moor*, by
Stanley Spencer, 1937.
City Art Gallery,
Manchester

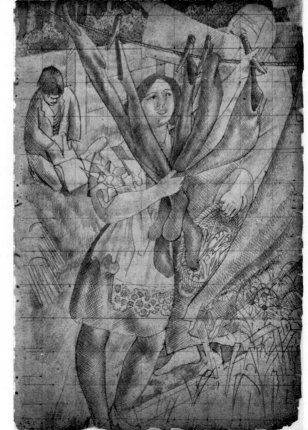

19 *Elsie taking in*
washing.
Drawing from a
scrapbook begun in 1943.
Private Collection.

informative contributions. But if only before it was too late somebody had collected contemporary impressions of Turner, for example, he would not have suffered for so long from his Thornbury.

I have said my own say, in several books, on Stanley Spencer as man as well as painter, and there is no point in repetition. For the years covered by the present chapter may I, therefore, refer the curious to the chapter devoted to him in *Time's Thievish Progress* (1970)?

The reminiscences that follow are arranged in alphabetical order except for the first four, which are from friends who first knew Stanley Spencer before the Second World War, and two of whom are concerned with a period before it. They end with Canon Michael Westropp's account of his death.

ELSIE BECKFORD
(Born Elsie Munday)

When working at Selbourne in 1928 a friend who worked for Mrs Behrend informed me that the Spencer family needed a maid at their house in Burghclere. I applied and had an interview with Hilda and Stanley. I took a reference and they engaged me. This was at the time Stanley was painting in the Sandham Memorial Chapel which was built in 1927. I found Hilda and Stanley to be an extremely nice couple and loved their little daughter, Shirin, whom I took for walks and to the Chapel to see her daddy. Stanley explained his work to me in great detail. I was with them at Hampstead when their second daughter (Unity) was born. In October 1931 we moved to Lindworth in Cookham Village. (It was here I met the young man who became my husband.)

It was obvious to me that Hilda was a sick woman. She seemed very tired and lacked energy, but I was fond of her and did all I could to keep the household going. Unity was a sweet child and one of my most enjoyable tasks was to care for her. Stanley often talked to me about his pictures but I found it difficult to understand. I loved his landscapes. In the picture *Workmen in the House* Unity is seen playing with one of my gaiters which I wore when using my motorbike. Stanley was not fussy over personal appearance, but he kept himself clean and I washed his clothes. He didn't do his hair. An artist he said thought more about using a paintbrush than a hair brush. He appreciated the work I did and enjoyed the meals I prepared.

ELIZABETH ROTHENSTEIN

In mid October 1938 we gave a house-warming party at Fellows Road, Hampstead, and invited Stanley Spencer. The curtains for the drawing-room had arrived only on the afternoon of the party, which was to begin between nine and nine-thirty. I had finished arranging the rooms at about seven and was on my way upstairs to rest when the front door bell rang. The timid Viennese maid opened the door and I turned to see her shutting it with a look of alarm on her face. I had never met Stanley Spencer but had often heard him described and instantly guessed it was he. I called out for the door to be opened and through the crack allowed by the frightened girl appeared a tiny figure resembling a chimney sweep.

Later in life Stanley became comparatively tidy and conventional in dress, but at that time, living alone with no wife or maid to care for him, working out of doors in all weathers on his saleable landscapes, self-forgetful, very poor, he had become almost sordid. There were no buttons on his grimy overcoat, which was fastened by a huge safety-pin. He wore a battered Tyrolean hat that appeared to have melted into folds over his steel-rimmed glasses. His hands were dirty, nails black, and his hair was obviously uncombed for days.

He apologised for being early but said that he had caught a convenient train from Cookham and come straight from the station. He asked that we should let him find a book for himself. He did not want to interrupt preparations for the evening. When I came down later I thought for a moment that he had gone, but when my eyes had become adjusted to the half-lit room I discovered him crouching on the floor absorbed in a book on medieval sculpture, small and fragile as a dried leaf. At the next moment, however, he stood up rubbing his eyes, talking in the squeaky voice he used when beginning a conversation. 'When you think of these old boys who did these marvellous carvings on cathedrals or village churches that mostly they were just village boys. . . .' and Stanley was off on one of his conversational flights which might lead anywhere and go on for hours, be delivered at times in the magnificent language of the Bible, at other times in local Cookham dialect or in rough and crude school-boy slang. All these ways of expressing himself were jumbled together and all of them revealed an essential part of Stanley's nature, which had in it something of the saint, something of the seer, majestic and formidable, but also something mean and quarrelsome, bitter and nasty, reminding one of a sparrow fighting in the dust.

Observing Stanley's need of some preparation for our guests I asked if he would like to wash before our light supper. Thanking me he did retire, but reappeared in about two minutes with his hands unwashed and nails inky black, hair untouched. He was the success of the party and his gaiety and vivid conversation drew around him a large group of people. In fact everyone wanted at one time or another to become part of his audience. Owing to his fascination guests were unaware of the flight of time; at about 12 o'clock someone thought to ask Stanley where he was spending the night. He replied that he would go to Paddington and if no train was available he would sleep in the waiting room. John said 'Nonsense' and I went to prepare the spare room. Stanley stayed with us for six weeks.

I was a reluctant hostess because we had not entirely settled in our new home. But I was eager to talk to Stanley, whom I had heard described as a religious painter, as a visionary, a mystic. I was deeply intrigued and hoped that in talk with him I might resolve some of my own doubts which made it still impossible to regain my Christian belief.

For this reason, the following morning, and because I so admired his earliest religious paintings we studied reproductions of them. Stanley, at first, seemed irritated at my candidly expressed dislike of his later 'religious' paintings. We returned to the carvings on and in medieval churches and thought about the simple lives of these unknown craftsmen and their obvious joy in their works. Stanley became radiant in response and expressed the belief that all his own painting was an attempt to express religious joy and, as it were, to lift up the smallest and even the ugliest objects to give each and everything a part in heavenly glory. This was his objective throughout his life and he voiced it unceasingly.

On that morning in Hampstead, however, this joy reminded him of his own lost vision. He jumped to his feet and began pacing the room accusing himself of wrecking his life and Hilda's by forsaking her. He had treated her with cruelty, was not even able to maintain her. He could no longer paint his religious pictures but was compelled to grind out landscapes and flower paintings which he hated doing, but they sold and money was imperative. This theme was repeated endlessly. He described, however, his second wife with some pride. He had acquired a beautiful and aristo-cratic, expensive wife. It was as if he were bragging about owning a Rolls Royce. But there was no money left over for Hilda, himself or the children.

I tried often to bring the conversation back to religious belief. Back in his childhood, in memory, he could recapture his joy. In the evenings his father, he told me, read aloud from the Bible – preferably the Old Testament – to some of his children. Stanley would paint in the corner. From the backroom the elder brothers would be playing Bach or Beet-hoven. Impelled by these happy memories, Stanley could often render a whole movement from Bach, managing somehow to indicate the several instruments. At such times an expression of rapt peace and gentleness would illuminate his face. He would conduct his performance with a finger.

His mother was a Methodist and it was at her little chapel that he and Gilbert attended church. His father played the organ at Hedsor, Cookham, and even in Whitechapel. But Stanley thought his father read the Bible to convey the magnificence of the language rather than the religious message; in short he thought his father was probably an agnostic. It was difficult, however, to get Spencer to commit himself about his own beliefs. One could only discover them obliquely. He was obsessed by his lost vision. All his visionary work had been done in what could be called a state of innocence. He described the Cookham life that led him into these visionary conditions: home, the security of a gifted and warm family, great music; reading his Bible, walking about Cookham and meditating alone in his room, his spirit becoming imbued with the feeling that

Christ, that God walked the streets of Cookham. He would sense that the vision was imminent. As he was falling to sleep he would say to himself: 'Tomorrow I will see God'. When he awoke he knew that he could paint.

Stanley was a genius. What exactly that means I doubt if anyone knows. His sensibility and imagination were beyond, far beyond the normal. But his intellect was quite ordinary. He had never had to measure it against his peers, since he received only the barest rudiments of an education. He had an unerring response to great literature and the great masters of painting. I think this led him to believe that his mind was as great as his other gifts. Had he remained a village boy and led the life of the craftsmen he so admired he might have retained the intensity, the simplicity and rapture of the early years. But contact with the sophisticated society of London had implanted within him a distrust of simple faith. He lacked the intellectual courage to fight his way back to the point where, as C. S. Lewis described in *Pilgrim's Regress*, the seeker at last must make the blind leap required by faith. But although Stanley resisted committing himself in words I am convinced that the inner 'subconscious' man was God-centred.

At the time I am speaking of Stanley and I were both in more or less the same situation; both strongly impelled towards acknowledged Christianity, both unable to commit ourselves. Stanley replied to one of my questions, 'Of course Hilda is a Christian Scientist and I have tried hard, but I can't get on'. A few minutes afterward he asked me if I knew a man called Desmond Chute. He went on to say that Chute had been the person who had helped him most; he had had a long friendship – mostly by letter – during the war years. 'After the war he appeared in the barn where I was finishing *Travoys bringing in the Wounded*. He saw a painting by Gil [Gilbert Spencer] there, a crucifixion. He only looked at Gil's painting, didn't look at mine. Since then he dropped out of my life.'

Many years later I was to learn a little more – from Robert Speaight's biography of Eric Gill (1966) – of the reasons for the lost friendship. Both Chute and Stanley knew Eric Gill. A group of Dominican Tertiaries came to feel that Stanley's powerful Christian imagination needed some granite and foundations built into it. It was thought that a visit to Gill and his small community would offer the opportunity of administering the 'hard tack' Spencer needed. Stanley was invited to Hawksyard (the Dominican house of studies in Staffordshire) where he witnessed the clothing of Gill as a Dominican Tertiary. Father Vincent McNabb was present and was entrusted with hardening the muscles of Stanley's mind. These encounters could have but one consequence. The emphases of Dominican teaching current at the time would have repelled and infuriated Stanley. These apart, the Dominicans cultivated an intellectual clarity alien to his temperament. It was the same with Eric Gill. But not only did Gill pursue a hard and unsubtle clarity; he had also an abrasively opinionated and aggressive intellect, and was more inclined to talk than to listen. But

Stanley was no less aggressive and opinionated and loquacious. He was also a man for whom precise religious dogma was a narrow-minded pedantry, whose mind lived and moved in muddle. So, as Stanley described the encounters to his brother, 'we fought like hell'. On such occasions he could be outrageous and even blasphemous. The gentle Chute was unacquainted with such violence.

There was one area of their religious thought, however, in which Spencer and Gill were at one. Both had the keenest interest in the place of sexuality in religion, and indeed mixed the two. But Gill had the capacity to put his belief into a language of some distinction. One of his texts he borrowed from a letter of Desmond Chute's. 'If naked bodies can arouse a hell-hunger lust, they can and do kindle a hunger for Heaven'. Gill described the image of the naked man or woman as an ikon, and developed the theme that great art has 'had the effect of deepening our respect and admiration and love for the natural world, the world God created – its infinite beauty – even its comicality and, so to say, its Rabelaisian buffoonery and pig-style coarseness'. Both painted erotic and even pornographic works. But Stanley had not the eloquence or the elegance of style to represent his paintings in such dignified words.

There has been a strange contrast in the reputations of these two men in this respect. For his erotic paintings and drawings Stanley has been vilified. I have seen only a few of them. They struck me as juvenilia: works of a man sexually unfulfilled. I was once shown a portfolio of Gill's drawings, which he produced after lunch at Count Harry Kessler's house in Weimar for the entertainment of the guests. In it were erotic drawings that stunned me and outraged his host. Yet Gill, in his semi-monkish smock, managed to keep intact a reputation for the higher pieties. But times change, and a painting of Stanley's that in 1939 Dudley Tooth kept behind locked doors upstairs has recently been acquired by the Tate and would shock nobody.

To return to Fellows Road and the morning after our party, Stanley broke off the long conversation to ask me if he might stay with us for a few days. He told me that he was so tired that he could no longer paint. Unless he could leave Cookham he would get no rest. Patricia, his second wife, expected him to produce a painting every week or ten days. He put his painting materials in a big pram and with an umbrella went out each day whatever the weather, sometimes walking as much as two miles to find a subject. When the day's work was finished he had to take his canvas to Patricia's house, where he was received in the kitchen so she might assess the work he had done. If she was pleased she would allow him to kiss her hand. 'I am a princess,' she would say. And Stanley said, 'And you know she *is* a princess!' Patricia would give him tea in the kitchen – after the marriage ceremony he was not allowed into the house.

One night during Stanley's visit John and I dined at Harriet Cohen's house, where I sat by Duncan McDonald of Reid and Lefevre. I spoke jokingly of the talk-exhaustion I was suffering from, mentioning our voluble guest. Duncan told me that he had a deep sympathy for Stanley. 'About eighteen months ago,' he said, 'Patricia Preece brought her paintings for us to look through. She told me that if we would give her a show she hoped to go and live in Paris, if not she would be compelled to marry "that dirty little Stanley Spencer".'

As the weeks went by I was depressed to see that Stanley seemed more rather than less disturbed. Physically he was a burnt out ember, shrivelled and spent. Occasionally the spirit flared up in response to people or ideas or memories such as his home life during his early Cookham years. But currently he was absorbed by his misery and self-accusation; mourning the loss of Hilda for which he blamed himself: insisting that he was still married to her and yearning to win her back and make reparation. I was amazed and puzzled how this great misfortune had come upon him; how he had lost the wife he loved, how so famous and successful a painter should be homeless and abandoned; why he was not living with his second wife – had never lived with her.

It was clear why he was so poor. But how had this peculiar and terrible situation come about in the first place? From odd fragments of his talk I began to have a shrewd idea, but Stanley was the least self-pitying of men and the least likely to blame other people for his misfortunes.

He did indeed once casually speak of having only one kidney, but it was not until years later I read Maurice Collis's biography of him that I came to appreciate how very ill he was in the crucial years when his marriage broke up. His health had been impaired by malaria caught in Macedonia. Working on the Burghclere murals he had severe attacks of renal colic. He once had to crawl in agony to the Behrends' house. He went into hospital and his illness was diagnosed as stone in the kidney. But the stone could not be removed and for the next four years he had recurrent attacks, and it was not until November of 1934 that the stone was crushed and he was delivered from agonies of pain that in the toughest of men can be prostrating for weeks. Yet in spite of all this he worked without stopping and by the middle of 1932 completed the colossal enterprise of painting the Burghclere Chapel, nineteen enormous canvasses. In addition, as Collis enumerates, he painted ten landscapes during this period, a portrait of Elsie, and five large figure paintings for the Empire Marketing Board.

Every evening at Burghclere and sometimes during the day as well, when Hilda was away, as she often was, he was writing endless letters to her. Love letters though these were, it is not surprising if his pain and exhaustion could bring on his fits of carping and critical irascibility. (Even when well he was subject to short bursts of spleen.)

Patricia Preece's advent into his life is recorded in these letters. She flattered and courted him and gradually intoxicated him; she also, as time went on, seduced him but left him tantalized by withholding the final satisfactions, all at a time when under the strains of uninterrupted work and severe physical pain he could hardly have been mentally stable.

From these letters and also from Maurice Collis's account of the sequence of events in these years I have been able to confirm the fleeting glimpses and moral certainties that I had from fragments of his tumultuous talk, mostly about other things, during his six weeks with us in Fellows Road.

He was profoundly disturbed in mind. The immediate cause turned out to be that he had been summoned to court, having fallen into arrears in payment of alimony. He was often near so tears because of his treatment of Hilda, whom he loved so dearly. And the money situation not only grieved but frightened him. I asked him bluntly why it was that he had failed to pay Hilda. He shook his head sadly and in a kind of bewilderment himself. He didn't deal with the money side of his life, he told me. When he finished a painting he handed it over to Patricia, who took it to Tooth's and received payment. Patricia kept the money and gave him just enough for his meagre needs. (I had marvelled that he never had more than a few shillings and was grateful if I paid even a 2d bus fare for him.)

Little by little I pieced together the strange story of his disastrous second marriage. When Stanley was working on the Burghclere chapel Hilda was very often away. She was pregnant and unwell. She was also often needed at home when there was illness in her family. He needed a wife in every natural sense. It was the usual story. Stanley was becoming famous, he was alone, women began to pursue him. Patricia Preece played on his loneliness, his physical needs, which she excited and exacerbated while giving nothing. Stanley became infatuated. He was intoxicated at having a beautiful woman as a nude subject, or dressed in the expensive black lace underclothes which they bought together in Maidenhead. After buying fur coats, glamorous clothing of all kinds for a year, Patricia wrote him a letter to say that she preferred jewels. Stanley bought her £1,200 worth of jewels during the year before their marriage, she having persuaded Stanley that Hilda was neglecting him and was no more than a millstone around his neck.

She needed the financial support that Stanley could give her, but physically she could neither take nor reciprocate a man's love. On the fringes of the Bloomsbury circle she could assure Stanley that its illustrious homes housed marriages that often allowed a partner to enjoy two or more spouses. Stanley was a village boy, easily impressed by glamour and easily gulled. He came to believe that it could be respectable in high intellectual circles and what he called 'the swells' to live thus, and he was mesmerized into thinking that he could have Hilda as well as Patricia. For Patricia it was absolutely essential that Hilda remain the sexual partner, this side of marriage being impossible for her. But since money was the object she needs must become his legal wife. So she gulled him into a divorce. He was required by his solicitors (or rather her solicitors) to write bitter and critical letters to Hilda. This came so hard for him to do that in the end, as it emerged, Patricia took over the correspondence. She wrote to Hilda to ask that she no longer write to Stanley before the divorce came through, telling her that it was Stanley's wish.

Being at the time so over-worked and ill that he was hardly of sound mind, Stanley was a tragically easy victim. Patricia gained an income but never admitted him as a husband. They never spent a night together. By the autumn of 1938 he had enormous debts and all his earnings were in Patricia's keeping. Stanley was so terrified and overawed at the necessity of presenting his tiny self before a bewigged and censorious Judge that his health grew worse and worse. But it was not only the majesty of the law that overshadowed him; it was also his grief at once again having failed Hilda.

I went straight to Dudley Tooth about this matter as soon as I understood it. Dudley Tooth's handling of Stanley was paternal, sensitive and courageous. He had not realised, when he handed over payment to Patricia on delivering her husband's canvasses, that the new wife simply pocketed the money. She did not pay the income tax. She allowed her husband insufficient to provide for Hilda and her children – or indeed for himself (not that he had any interest in money for himself), for he could not afford any clothes.

DudleyTooth thereupon took on himself the management of Stanley's financial affairs and divided the money between all parties concerned. (He was sometimes tricked. Letters in his archives disclose that Patricia sold at least two of Stanley's paintings, without Stanley's knowledge, to other dealers, claiming that they were her own property.) He negotiated with the Income Tax inspectors and paid a lump sum to free Stanley from this also frightening burden. It must have taken many years before Tooth could have recompensed himself for so instantly taking over this and many other debts still owing to Maidenhead shops where Stanley had spent money so lavishly on Patricia's clothes, furs, and jewels.

So much for his misfortunes. He blamed himself for everything and seemed genuinely unaware of the enormity of the trick played on him. He had what Chesterton once described as the vast patience and forbearance of the very poor, laced with abundant humour; very tolerant, without a trace of self-pity, he grieved for Hilda and said not a word in disparagement of his second wife. Rather the contrary. Nor did he ever explain the trap sprung on him.

His enduring love of Hilda had suffered from the accident of the times they lived in. As I came to see when I read, in 1976, some of his letters to her, birth control was outside their ken, and the only way they knew to control unlimited conceptions was withdrawal. But this wrecked Hilda's already delicately strung nerves. Her fragile health again kept them apart. And Stanley's virility was as strong as that of any healthy countryman – no more, no less. Many of his drawings and writings were a substitute for the normal life he was denied. It is ironic that this man, who has been presented as a sexual fanatic, had less of sexual life than most unmarried men. In comparison with many of the artists of his day, such as the Bloomsberries or Augustus John, he was sexually on the level of a gifted school-boy. But the puerile and pathetic drawings and writings with which Spencer filled his long and lonely evenings are now 'documents' for posterity.

It is a pity that it has become relevant to dwell on Stanley's almost non-existent sexual life, since to those who knew him well this side of him was so little apparent. With women friends he was scrupulously delicate in his speech, and his delicacy was a matter of comment when they exchanged memories of him.

Our own memories of Stanley at that time are by no means exclusively of a man suffering and almost broken; he had a unique and uproarious sense of humour. Nor did his weakened physical condition stem his torrential vitality in talk. His sojourn with us became a strain because of his volubility and a stamina that left his listener limp, or burnt out. I found myself laughing aloud when recently I read a letter of his to Hilda in which he complains of her tired expression when he was talking to her, comparing her unfavourably with other women who glowed with appreciation of his elucidation of ideas. How often have we fallen back exhausted, facial muscles sagging with weariness, from the effects of Stanley's high-voltage personality and torrential talk; and this after only a weekend visit and when, as in the late 'fifties, he was just out of hospital. But these visits were always delightful and often hilarious.

I regret that I destroyed the diary I kept of his talk when he was with us in 1938. I was experiencing the revelation of a personality so unique that I wanted to make notes of his conversation. The characters of Cookham became persons so vivid to me that they occupy a place in my memory perhaps clearer than my own experience. When, many years later, John and I walked about Cookham Stanley pointed out where these boyhood friends lived; where such and such an incident had taken place, picking up our Fellows Road discussions as if years had not intervened.

Having him as a guest during the socially over-crowded months before the war made our dinner-parties memorable for our guests: so vivid was his talk and so irrepressible his humour. He laughed at himself more than at anyone else. He described Horace, his magician brother, who appeared on the music halls during his better days and at the curb-side when he had imbibed too freely. He felt that Horace had gone to heaven in a truly personal and delightful way, when deep in a glorious booze-up he rode his bicycle into the Thames.

Maurice Collis rightly recorded that most of Stanley's friends were women but went on to suggest that he chose women in order to excite sympathy and even pity. In fact he was the least self-pitying person I have ever known. He liked women as a continuation of his devotion to his mother. He said that as a child he sought security in his mother's skirts when together they walked the village streets. Being small, the village bully boys liked to chase and scare him. He timed his walks alone to avoid them. He could always feel slightly threatened by large or self-important male personalities. He was quite simply more at ease with women. With men he felt he must hold his end up.

His relationship with our daughter Lucy, who had her fourth birthday that same October, was one between equals. I found that Lucy's audacious life could take him out of his tortured meditations, though they filled him with a different sort of anguish. Lucy used the walls which divided all the gardens of a very large number of houses as highways along which she travelled on hands and knees. Overhanging branches caused difficulties and fits of rage when her long curly mane caught in the twiggery. Pain was no impediment, but she fell off from time to time roaring with tears and frustration. Stanley and I watched her from the window; Stanley grave and tense with anxiety. He remonstrated with me about the dangers of Lucy's way of life. He took a critical view of me as a mother: his own had been so unlike. Mothers should be islands of safety and peace, protective above all.

The time came when we decided that Stanley must return to normal life and begin painting again. He told me that he could not bring himself to return to Cookham and the pain of being a wifeless man in a place where he had so longed to live a fulfilled married life. Malcolm MacDonald, therefore, found him a room in Adelaide Road near at hand where we could see that he was contented. In fact this little room became a joyous place of peace, and he learned how satisfying it could be to live alone. He began his series of *Christ in the Wilderness*, showing the saviour in deep and intense meditation of even the least of God's creation. The first was of Christ cradling lovingly a scorpion in his hands.

It was to be expected that a man who had been so pulled out of his orbit by social vanity and the lure of a more gratifying sexual life and had found that he had lost everything in this alien gamble should, in the realization of his total loss of everything he loved and longed for, seek for a sexual booze-up of the sort that brother Horace had had on alcohol. It was perhaps unfortunate for him that instead of a purgative, transient orgy that would relieve his frustrations he found himself with a woman who loved him intensely. When his need was over he was planning to unite himself once more with Hilda. He had never accepted that his marriage with her had been ended. He felt profoundly and eternally married to Hilda, he constantly told me, during the weeks he was with us. One reason he was happy to be in Hampstead was because he knew that Hilda was near. He used to walk the street where she lived and look longingly at the house where she was.

His violent love affair lasted long after he had any wish or need for it. He became a man on the run. But he described his persecutions and altercations with zest and hilarity; how she stoned him and he stoned her in return; how he sought refuge with Cookham's friendly policemen. But even during his most hectic efforts of escape he had immense admiration and respect for the huntress.

To me, however, the saddest thing about Stanley was that because he so increasingly needed cosiness in his life – cósy was the word most frequently on his lips when describing his paintings – his religious paintings, those he most wanted to get on with, became happy resurrection stories, happy marriage stories, in which the mystery and majesty of God disappeared. He never quite matured, I think, as a personality, and his loneliness was dispelled by his telling himself (and his friends) stories about his amusing imaginings.

I remember one occasion when he telephoned us that he was going to come over to show us his drawings for *Christ at Cookham Regatta*. He came in carrying a heavy bag. The contents were drawings roughly foolscap size. He asked that all the furniture should be moved back and on hands and knees he put together the enormous study of the projected painting of that subject. All the while he was piecing the bits together he was telling us about the identity and habits of the characters he had drawn, the girls in swimming-suits, the competing boats, the onlookers on the banks. Finally he rocked back on his heels, and I said, 'Well, Stanley, where is Christ?' Stanley shouted with laughter at the realization. 'Poor old Jesus,' he said, 'he's got pushed right up in the top corner.' At that stage Christ and the Apostles were minute figures I had failed to recognize. 'Poor old Jesus, I've got to find a better place for him!'

For the greater part Stanley was indulgent to those who had done him injury. But on occasion he would work himself into a passion about imaginary enemies, such as the War Office, which at one time he blamed for the destruction of his early 'vision', or about, say, his bullying by students at the Slade (his tiny stature, in my own experience, could elicit male aggressiveness) or even about John, on whom he might turn some momentary grievance and accuse of damaging his reputation as a painter.

But these passions would evaporate. During the war I had written a book on Stanley for the Phaidon press. Into it there had crept some small errors of detail. They concerned matters of family origin, and when I met him again after the war he intimated that his family had been irritated at my confusions – it was his grandfather and not his father who had been a builder, and such like. He had a more general grievance about method. But when on a visit to him in 1950 we talked it out he was honest and candid. He referred to a remark he had made to me the first time we had met after the book's publication, which was that he had liked the book enormously until it occurred to him that I had been supervised by the Jesuits. He developed this by saying that he had only meant that his paintings could not be contained in a Catholic mould; that there were Chapel elements in them, even pagan elements. 'I'm not a Catholic, you see'. I told him that I had observed the fact, adding that the parts he thought were Catholic were simply attempts at clear thinking and definition. That the term 'mystical' was used with the utmost looseness to mean anything from vaguely elevated feeling to the contemplation of God by a Saint John of the Cross; that when I tried to distinguish between my use of imagination and intuition I was trying to show the difference between his early work, which seemed to have the simplicity of a lived experience of 'celestial things' (in the Wordsworthian sense), and his later work, which had anything but this kind of simple conviction and seemed rather to be Stanley trying to remember back and imagine himself among celestial scenes. Stanley then said that, alas, this was true. That a man was the sum of his experiences; that the war had done him terrible damage; that his sexual imaginings were now part of himself; that his marital difficulties added their dead weight on his mind and were a part of himself, so that it was as if he had later in life left heaven with all this baggage for ever afterwards around his neck, and that he was impeded by it from returning to the simple intuitive insights of youth. He ended up with the words of a popular song of a few years earlier, 'That's my weakness now'. Then he began saying that he thought that the reason why people objected to his distortions, objected in a rather particular way, when, for instance, they were ready to accept more happily the distortions of Henry Moore, was that he was painting things that people find disturbing and important; things they care about. They become angry because his *Resurrections* don't look like their ideas about the *Resurrection*. A friend of his when visiting the Academy had seen a man and his wife looking at the big *Resurrection* picture, and the husband had said, 'Come away from that and don't look at it; its too materialistic'. Later in the day Stanley showed us some drawings and he pointed out one in particular, 'You see, it is a flower show in heaven and the angel there is judging gardens, you know, the way they judge village gardens sometimes'. I wanted to draw him out, there being something odd and childish about the way he always seemed to make heaven exactly like earth. But when I probed he only looked puzzled, saying, 'Oh no, its just gardens - judging gardens in heaven'.

I asked him to explain why he used certain shapes in his pictures such as the exaggeratedly round faces he so often used. As I suspected, he said that certain shapes delighted him for reasons that probably went right back into his earliest childhood, which he couldn't dig out. He thought that the round shape business had probably been confirmed in him by seeing it used in the old masters and he cited as an example the face of one of Fra Angelico's baby Christs. His distortions he linked to his intuitions about things, in that they partly arose, he said, through trying to capture a feeling about a scene he was trying to paint. He would probably draw the thing in a state of very deep absorption and all at once – it being very difficult to get the impression down before the feeling cooled. Looking at it afterwards he might see that he had made an arm too long, but to draw the arm in correct proportion would mean changing the whole, and that would simply be a different picture, and for good or ill he had to paint that picture as he had first conceived it, including in it any faults which were accidents in the first inward seeing and recording.

In his many conversations about family history and religion there was an overlapping of categories. He distrusted clarity. Of this distrust we had a vivid illustration. Among the visitors to the Cookham Festival of 1958, when a big exhibition of his work was on view at the church, was Penelope Betjeman. Stanley had spoken of his work to a group of 'pilgrims' in her presence and she had been enchanted by his talk. During one of his visits to us at Newington, therefore, I invited the Betjemans to lunch, knowing that Stanley would relish Penelope's splendid originality and her religious passion.

He was in a particularly forthright mood. When I was seating our guests, 'May I have my back to the window?' he asked; 'landscape makes me ill' – a reference to the years when he had to grind out landscapes to pay Patricia's bills. During lunch the talk was of his religious paintings and his *Resurrections*, and it turned to religious belief. 'Do you,' asked Penelope, 'believe in the resurrection of the body?' Stanley turned the question by a joke of some sort and I had no idea that her perfectly legitimate query had upset him. But when the Betjemans had gone, 'That bloody woman!' he burst out, 'asking me if I believe in the resurrection of the body!' He was so inflamed that we dropped the subject. Why he was so furious I did not know. I think it was primarily anger at the introduction of a clear concept into his imagination and of an invitation to commit himself. What was abundantly clear was the depth of his feeling and his lack of detachment from religious beliefs. If he became an agnostic, as he sometimes said he was, he was an uncomfortable one.

Throughout his life, in good times and in bad, one of Stanley Spencer's most engaging characteristics was that he treated everybody in exactly the same way. He would speak with the same immediacy of spirit to spirit to a Cookham child as he would to Lady Astor, to a maid as to a chairman of the Tate. The subject matter of his conversation would probably have been the same as well, for he rarely liked to talk about things other than his paintings and the imaginations that, in figure and episode, peopled them. He had a reason, for he felt that everything of importance about himself had been put into his drawing and painting.

He was substantially right, I think, and this is why his painting and drawing are more elucidatory of his self and his writings than his writings are of his graphic work. For he could paint and draw, and was entirely mistaken in thinking he could write. In writing so many millions of words and preserving them for some immense autobiography he was, once again, his own worst enemy.

In what precedes, knowing well how often in recent years the written word has misled biographers, I have tried to give some indication of what Stanley Spencer was like, especially during the crucial phase of his life when, by accident, I saw him every day for many hours and had him in our house. Evidence from these years is now rare. I have, therefore, been allowed to write at greater length than other contributors. Even so, what I have recorded has of necessity been severely abbreviated and pruned.

STANLEY GOULD
[Stanley Gould was a Cookham cabinet maker who knew Stanley Spencer from the 1920s. He preferred to talk rather than write, and what follows is taken from a tape-recording made in June 1976.]
Mind you, when Stanley was a boy Cookham was a very different place from what it is today – a bit wild and strange and promiscuous, you know. The Spencers were an integral part of it and for years Stanley was looked on as just another village boy. In those days villages were far more different from one another than they've become – each one had an accent of its own, easily recognisable.

Cookham was full of 'characters' though the Spencers *were* a bit special, but far less noticeable than they would be now. For instance Stanley's father used to walk about in his pyjamas and a trilby hat and he always wore bedroom slippers. Then there was Horace, such a wonderful conjurer that he could have become an international figure if he hadn't been so drunk. He was in prison for a bit but his brilliance as a conjuror somehow got him out. Stanley's sister Annie dug her own grave. His brother Percy would have been a fine architect or builder, if he'd wanted, instead of an accomplished cellist. But Stanley really was very special. Once I met him on the path to the church just standing in front of his canvas. 'Why aren't you working?' I asked. 'I'm waiting for light on that puddle', he said, 'so that I can begin exactly where I left off yesterday.' His *Crucifixion*, now at Aldenham, was based on the reconstruction of Cookham's main drainage.

Patricia and Dorothy Hepworth I didn't like at all. 'Patricia's always turning the screw on me for money', Stanley used to complain. A new porter, seeing these two ladies together for the first time – Miss Hepworth in her masculine style clothing – exclaimed: 'Fancy courting at their age!'

Stanley had no sense of time whatever; he turned up at any time and stayed on and on – and never stopped talking. He turned up the night after he returned from his Chinese visit [he had been a member of a cultural delegation in 1954] calling out, 'This is Peking Spencer!' One night he addressed The Cookham Dean Arts Club and reminisced for hours; most of the audience was bored but I was fascinated. He often spoke of his fear of Hell – 'and just think of the adulterers all over the place!'

HENRY TRIVICK
I first met Stanley Spencer in 1937.

After that I saw him frequently, and over the years we developed a very happy, fairly close friendship, which lasted up to the time of his death. On looking back I have never been able to understand fully why he should have been so friendly and kind to me. It was I who gained much, there was nothing I could offer in return, not that he would expect anything – he did not think like that. I had been told that he could be easily offended, but in spite of my rather abrupt manner I never found him take offence from any remark I made. Not once over the years, and we met many, many times, did he say or do anything to which I could object.

When I called to see him he never turned me away, even when he was busy painting. It was always 'Come in, Henry' or 'Come up, Henry'. He would then show me the work on which he was engaged and explain his ideas (or 'notions' as he called them).

When Stanley made an arrangement he would enter it up in his diary and I could be sure he would keep it. A more reliable and kindly person it would be difficult to find.

He said that if it were not for lesser artists like myself there would be no Stanley Spencer, we helped to hold him up! It was always so; there were periods of great artists coming together and barren periods too. He said he wished he had more 'fire' in his work, he always had to be precise and deliberate when working; he found it impossible to produce a very quick spontaneous work.

He had no qualms about looking closely and using certain methods and ways employed by great masters. On more than one occasion when I called on him I noticed a book of coloured reproductions on the floor beside him as he worked. He made no attempt to conceal it and once he explained why and what he was using from the reproductions to suit his requirements.

When he was painting the large 1927 *Resurrection* he was troubled about the top left-hand part, where a considerable landscape is shown. 'I went to have a good look at some Constables and then after that I put in a tremendous effort in painting it – it's as good as a Constable, I know, because I put my everything into it', said Stanley. I asked if he had not looked at Rubens' great 'Chateau landscape' in the National Gallery – one of my favourite landscapes. Of course he knew it – 'a great painting – but it's not England or English and Constable's are', explained Stan.

He was very insular; he told me he had often been asked if he had painted in Paris. 'No, what is wrong in painting in Cookham?' was his reply.

He also had trouble with the composition of the large 1945–50 *Resurrection* painting. He pointed out to me what bothered him but he did not see how he could put it right without painting part of it again, and this was against his principles. The part that troubled him was that to the right of the table tomb. It did not respond to the pronounced movement on the left of the composition, where the hands of the people hold up the granite lid, and is continued by the girl's arm and finishes by the hand of the bald man. I think he tried to give more emphasis to the right side by lightening the stocking legs of the kneeling woman with the hair bun, but he was not happy about it. He said he found these very large compositions the most difficult of all to hold together.

It has often been stated that he had a habit of painting his compositions by starting at the top left hand and working his way across and then down and across until he reached the bottom of his canvas. As a fairly regular 'dropper-in' to Stan's bedroom studio at Cliveden View I had the opportunity of observing his methods. He would sometimes start at top left, another time middle left, and sometimes in the centre. As he said, wherever he was working his mind's eye was taking in the whole area of the canvas. All his compositions that I saw were carefully worked-out in pencil prior to painting.

I noticed that when he made a drawing he held the pencil in a much more perpendicular position than that employed by the majority of artists. He had a way, too, of making a few fine pencil strokes on the corner of his paper 'to get the feel of it,' he said.

He liked, when he could manage it, to paint his compositions in the open air, which was rarely. It was usually too cold for him, even with his overcoat on. He would get himself in the shelter of a house or of a tree. He felt better and said he could concentrate more. Little wonder, time and time again I found him at work in his little bedroom, much overheated by two paraffin stoves.

I showed Stanley the Penguin book on Pasmore. He liked his early works but found his abstracts and constructions dull and boring. 'He has not the vision or strength to develop his early works and has been caught up in the tide and cannot swim against it', was Stan's comment.

Augustus John he knew well from his student days at the Slade. He had great respect for John's power as a draughtsman. 'The best draughtsman of the bunch,' he once said to me, 'but his compositions could not bear comparison with mine!'

Stanley was always a great champion of 'brother Gil'. He said that Gil's drawings were better than his, and to prove the point he produced some of his own and Gil's drawings mixed together and picking out his brother's work showed me why he considered Gil's the better! These were executed in the 1920s.

I have always been a collector of books and I would often show them to Stan. He enjoyed this and his sharp, shrewd eye often spotted interesting

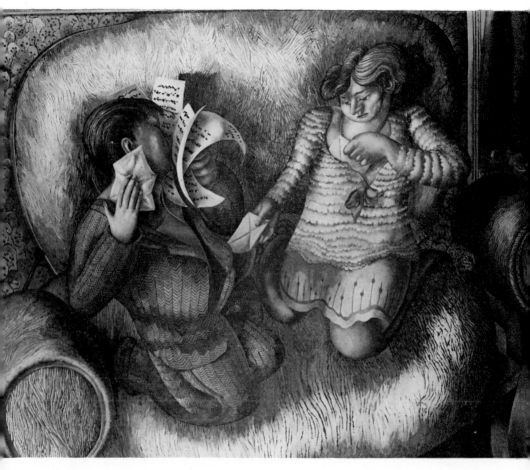

20   *Love Letters*, by Stanley Spencer, oil, 1950.
Photo: A. C. Cooper. *Private Collection*

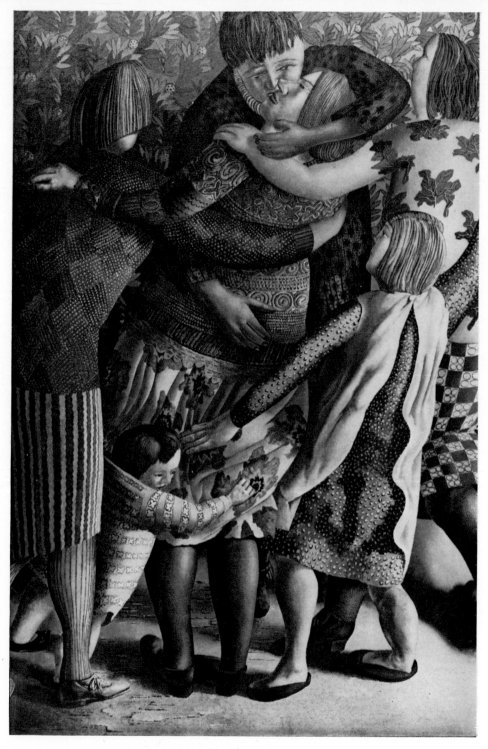

21 *Hilda Welcomed*, by Stanley Spencer, oil, 1953.
The Art Gallery of South Australia

points in the illustrations that escaped me. After thirty or more years I can still remember some of the reproductions which he specially liked. One was Vermeer's *The Artist's Studio*. He thought the composition to be one of Vermeer's best and he explained in considerable detail his reasons for thinking that way about it.

Among others on which he had special comments to make which I remember was Giotto's *The Kiss of Judas*. This artist was always a great favourite of his. He drew my attention to the part where Christ is embraced by Judas – their noses almost touching and seen between them are two figures, with their noses close together, the four noses making a very important part of the composition. 'This painting was the result of Giotto's great belief in what he did; it was divine inspiration of a very great artist, it could not be achieved in any other way', was Stan's comment.

Another time we were looking through a book of Hieronymus Bosch's works with colour plates. When we came to the illustration of Christ carrying the cross Stan paused and pointing to the faces of the mob mocking Christ, said that today we have exactly the same type of man, those who attend Saturday afternoon football matches and who cause so much hooliganism and smash things up.

A friend of mine, Dr Elliott, then living in Bourne End, had constructed his own telescopic camera enabling him to take excellent coloured slides of medieval stained-glass windows from inside the churches. Stan enjoyed them and from time to time passed interesting or amusing comments. One I remember well. The slide shown was taken at Milton Church, Oxon, and showed the corpse of St Lazarus being wrapped up in a shroud by two young women. 'Ha!' said Stan, 'see those two young women? I bet they've done that kind of job many times before, you can see by their expressions as they work that one is saying to the other "say, Jane, did you have a good time last night when you were with your boy friend?" '

When he was going out 'special' he would wear an 'arty' shirt and a yellow necktie – he had a passion for these – and he nearly always wore the inevitable grey woollen pullover.

Stanley liked to tell low stories. One evening driving home from London, we exchanged low stories, jokes and limericks for most of the journey. I recited a naughty limerick, but Stanley said that I had got it wrong! 'It goes like this . . .', and he recited it correctly to me.

He was a great devotee of Charlie Chaplin. He regarded him as one of the great geniuses of the music hall, stage and screen world. Whenever a Chaplin film was on at one of the Maidenhead cinemas Stan would go off to see it.

I once showed Stanley some of my black and white lithographs. Stan was impressed with the possibilities of the medium and said he would like to try it when time permitted. I kept him up to it and he agreed to come with me to the Regent Street Polytechnic every Thursday for a period. I was then a visiting instructor for two days a week in charge of the lithographic class. In October 1952 Stanley made his first visit to the Poly ('Polly' Stan spelt it). There was a two-hour gap between the day and evening classes. Stan agreed to stop for the evenings. He worked on his lithos. At 9 p.m. we finished and I took him back to Cookham.

One afternoon Stanley did take a few hours off from the Poly. He went to see Siegfried Charoux in Bayswater. When he came back he said with a grin 'Old Siegfried has the finest collection of Charoux's works in London! Aren't I lucky. I sell everything I produce.' I asked him if he visited London art exhibitions. No, he didn't – only those of friends. His 'war-cry' was always 'I am interested in Stanley Spencer!'

We visited Kettle's in New Oxford Street, to purchase some tinted papers for Stan's lithograph *Marriage at Cana*. One could purchase all kinds of coloured fancy papers. He bought some quiet coloured papers large enough for me to print his *Marriage at Cana*. This is why a number of lithographs of this subject are found on different coloured papers.

Towards the end of the summer term in 1954 he gave a talk at the Poly. Stan had brought along some slides, reproductions and original drawings. The latter were pinned up for all to see. But Stan would not have the official operator to work the projectors. 'No. I want Henry to do that.' So do it I did. He liked the personal touch of someone he knew – it gave him a comfortable feeling, he said.

It was a brilliant talk to about two hundred people. Little Stanley standing in front of this large number of students and staff carried all before him. His command of English was surprising, the logical sequence of his comments could not have been bettered. He was on top of the world that afternoon, full of confidence, full of fun and full of the brilliance of Stanley Spencer's works.

He made a small pencil sketch on the back of an envelope for his first litho. He showed it to me and decided he would enlarge it to fit onto a plate I offered him.

The subject was the *Marriage at Cana*. The bride and bridegroom and guests about to sit down to the eating of the wedding cake. I gave him some litho chalks and he sat down in the front of the room to draw. A few minutes later he came to me to say he had made a mistake, could it be deleted? I said it could not at that stage and suggested that he turn the plate upside down and start again. This he did and got on with the drawing. He used no scaling method but drew quite freely on the plate, without any guide-lines or tracing. (The few lines Stanley made before he turned the plate upside down can be seen on all the proofs of this lithograph.)

When Stan finished the drawing he showed it to me and in his usual modest way asked me what I thought of it. For a while I said nothing but studied what he had drawn. The longer I looked the more puzzled I became. Then I quietly pointed out that the two very prominent chairs in the foreground had no supporting struts at all – just the legs coming from the chairs' seats (they were the wooden kitchen type of chair). 'My word – I overlooked them.' He then drew them in.

As the proofs came off Stanley was rather pleased with them. Fishing for compliments he explained that he had left out the chair leg supports but had put them in later and he thought they now looked good. One young student looking at the lithograph said, 'Oh, you'll learn.'

There was an interesting sequence to the litho of Stanley's *Marriage at Cana*. A year or two after Stan had died it was decided to open a Stanley Spencer Gallery at Cookham. I thought it would be a good idea to print a posthumous edition off the plate. I printed the edition of 75 on grey paper – all numbered and stamped 'Friary Studio'. This enables collectors to distinguish the posthumous edition from the original edition of about 30 on various papers, signed by Stanley Spencer.

It was only in the last few years of his life that Stanley knew Lord Astor – 'Bill Astor'. They got on well together and Stan was proud to associate with a 'Real Lord' as he put it. He told me the following with considerable glee. When he was painting Astor's portrait at Cliveden he was asked if he would stop for dinner that evening. Astor was expecting some guests and he thought that Stanley might like to meet them. He refused. He told me that he had old clothes on, and would have felt embarrassed, but he did not like to tell Astor, so he pleaded that he was very tired and wanted to go home to get a rest. Astor insisted that Stan should have something to eat before his chauffeur drove him back to Cookham. A small table was laid for one person, food was placed on the table and Lord Astor proceeded to wait on Stanley as he ate his meal. It pleased him no end to find himself being waited on by so distinguished a person as Lord Astor.

Stanley loved publicity. He broadcast and appeared in films on his own work and was often photographed. He was 'news'. He once warned me not to be photographed or give information to people I did not know. 'Somewhere they will have a little file on you and could produce it as evidence against you to suit their purposes.' He must have had some unfortunate experience, though he never told me what it was – perhaps it was the 'Munnings affair' that frightened him. [In 1950 Sir Alfred Munnings had tried to have Spencer prosecuted for obscene pictures, a move defeated by Sir Gerald Kelly, then President of the Royal Academy.]

Stanley had that rare faculty of being able to throw off any thoughts or worries and concentrate on his immediate surroundings. A few weeks after Hilda had died he was at my home, laughing and joking apparently without a trouble in the world. His conscience must have pricked him, he turned to me and suddenly said, 'Henry, you must think me very callous. Here I am laughing and joking and my Hilda only gone these few weeks.'

I heard Stanley repeat to me time and time again details of his love affairs. I became rather bored with listening to them so often. It is not for me to repeat details of his private life. He spoke of them when driving by car up to or down from London. When two people are alone talking of such matters one gets a clear picture of what it is all about. I feel it sufficient for me to state that Stanley above all was open and honest; he was not licentious, lustful or vulgar, and bore no malice.

I would not for a moment suggest that he was an ideal man. Far from it – though I got on extremely well with him I suspect he could be a difficult person to live with. He could be dogmatic and selfish, as most people are who are dedicated to their work, suspicious of certain people – probably not without reason. He was not tolerant of artists who held widely different opinions from his own and he was very much a villager. He was not a good father, he left relatives to bring up his two daughters Shirin and Unity. They were not aware of their father's importance as an artist – that is what Stanley told me.

Nature bestowed on Stanley a body small in build and stature, not worthy of the mind it held. He tried to compensate for this by showing a considerable attitude of aggression. He would chat so brightly that he gave the impression that he was contented with his lot, but there is no doubt that though aware of his ability he suffered from a feeling of partial failure. He had a high conception of what he wanted to achieve but was disappointed with his achievement. His self-portrait painted during the last few months of his life tells us much about him. It has the force of characterisation which he himself felt and understood, gazing wistfully into the future, not knowing what it held in store for him.

We can look at the genius of Turner as a possible comparison with Stanley in certain respects. Turner, too, small in stature, eccentric and dogmatic, had a high conception of what he wanted to achieve. Achieve it he did, he rarely tasted the experience of failure. Both had ideas of writing (both spelt badly), both made 'sexy' drawings, both were interested in music – Turner played the flute, Stanley the piano – both came from humble stock, both had two daughters – though Turner's were illegitimate.

But Turner was more dedicated to his art than Stanley, who wasted a considerable amount of time by drifting from place to place in quest of companionship.

ALFRED and MURIEL BOXER
We live at the Rise, only a few minutes walk away from Cliveden View, and Stanley Spencer often dropped in for his 'evening cocoa'. His talk sparkled, and it was frequently half past one next morning when we said goodnight. He would bring down an art book, or take one of ours and go through it, commenting, and admiring. I never heard him say an unkind remark about other men's work.

Of his kindness I can give a fine example. He had 'popped in' one morning for a cup of tea, and while my wife was out of the room my baby son pulled the tablecloth and upset the teapot. Some of the boiling water scalded him. A neighbour took them to Maidenhead Hospital; Stanley insisted on coming, and as they all knew him at the hospital we had immediate attention.

I visited his little house in Worster Road frequently, and was very privileged to see the Aldenham *Crucifixion* on the wall, and watch its progress. He said that his real work was finished when he had completed his pencil drawing. The brushwork, colouring, he said, was 'knitting'. I found this fascinating and was largely responsible for persuading him to show the still unfinished *Christ Preaching*, now in the gallery, at the 1958 Exhibition. It drew crowds of people intrigued to see how he worked.

JOHN BRATBY

The first occasion on which I met Sir Stanley Spencer was in 1957 at the Beaux Arts Gallery. He had come to see my paintings, on exhibition there. I remember him as a nervous small man, scurrying around, with a blushing pink face, talking to me incessantly, as we looked at my paintings, which happily he liked. We went upstairs and something in one of them made him burst into an excited and effervescent description of a small visual incident, seen many years before, that he had always wanted to make the subject of a painting, but had never actually done so. He had seen a little girl lose her playing ball under a fence made of wire netting, and her bent figure trying to retrieve the ball at the base of the expanse of netting was an image that had stayed with him over the years. It amazed me to hear this gentleman, whom I had newly met, talking with such excitement, familiarity and at such length, about this small detail of experience. If I, ten minutes after meeting somebody for the first time, told that person for a quarter of an hour in a bubbling manner all about my excitement fifteen years earlier over the visual delights of the inside of a television set, where a butterfly fluttered, I would expect that stranger to look at me with suprise and caution. But Stanley was not inhibited. If he felt the need to express himself, he would do it, without restraint.

We crossed to the other side of the room to look at some paintings there, and suddenly he whipped out an envelope from his coat, and with a pencil hurriedly started to draw the image of the little girl searching for her ball. He used the top of an old wooden chest as a drawing table, chattering away to me about the incident as he drew with total absorption. He then gave me the drawing, which I treasured for many years. Having given me the drawing, he explained an idea he had for triptych, the subject matter to be children playing by a wire netting fence, with balls thrown into the air, with a background of the fence. That was to be the subject of the centre panel. The flanking panels were to be of children flying folded paper aeroplanes and playing with yoyos, also against the background of the wire mesh fence. The focal image of the whole triptych was to be the one drawn on the old envelope. He described this idea for a painting so elaborately, that I can see it in my mind's eye quite clearly today. I do not know if he ever did any preliminary drawings for this triptych, or executed any part of it, or even if he described his vision to anybody else. I think he must have done the painting, if only in part, because his enthusiasm was so intense. It was as if he had known me for years and very well. He confided to me all those inner feelings and private inspirations.

CECIL W. GAINS

I knew Stanley for well on twenty-five years.

One cold winter's afternoon there was a knock on the door of the Malt Barn, and there stood a huddled-up, grey, white-faced figure looking very frail, ill, and very miserable. It was Sir Stanley Spencer. He asked to come in out of the cold.

I took him into the living room, which was once the kiln of the old brewery – the room in which he had painted *The Last Supper* years before – and having asked if he might remove his shoes, he sat cross-legged in a winged chair. He was still wearing the grey waistcoat that he especially bought for his investiture at Buckingham Palace. After knowing him for over twenty years I had never before seen him look so ill. This was understandable as he had only just had his big operation.

After I had made him some tea to warm him up – he refused alcohol – he began to thaw out and his spirits to revive. He then asked to hear some music on the gramophone, and knowing his great love I played Bach. To my astonishment he suddenly informed me that he could sing Bach – anything of Bach and immediately proceeded to prove it when I tested him out. His knowledge and memory were incredible. It was then that my wife and daughter returned from shopping.

Sitting on the settee opposite them, he then slowly rose to his old animated self and in a great surge of excited reminiscence began to re-live his early childhood in the Spencer family. He told us of his brother Horace, the conjuror, how, when all the boys were in the big bed together, Horace, who had earlier secreted away objects at the foot of the bed, such as dead frogs, coloured stones, old bird feathers, and the like, had held his brothers spellbound by his weird intonations and then, diving down the bed, produced the object of his magic.

When he was making portraits of our daughters, after drawing all the morning and breaking for lunch, Stanley informed us that he would like his 'rest' afterwards, for half an hour. He then asked for an army blanket, if we had one, or a coarse blanket and proceeded to retire to a bed. Removing his shoes, he sat very upright at the head of the bed and with legs crossed put the blanket completely over his head and remained in that position for a full half hour, after which he got up and resumed work.

One day, around the period of the 'Singing Bach' episode, Stanley informed us that he had been commissioned by the University of London to paint the murals in their new building and he had made up his mind as to the subject he wished to paint. He said he had given it a lot of thought and was very keen to carry out an idea which he thought was very suitable. Unfortunately, the authorities of the University were shocked and would not hear of such a design – to Stanley's disgust and bewilderment. He then said that unless he was allowed to execute it he would drop the whole commission.

When my wife asked him what his design would be, he replied: 'Just mothers pushing their prams with babies – all around'.

JOAN GEORGE

I first met Stanley Spencer towards the end of 1954. I was trying my hand at free-lance journalism at the time. I immediately recognised the artist as a 'natural' for an article. Not only was he well-known and slightly eccentric – practical if unworthy reasons for a choice of subject – but there seemed to be an immediate *rapport* between us, which had its roots somewhere in his benevolent view of humanity, impatience with hypocrisy, sense of humour and that famous Spencer love of 'cosiness'. An unusual set of values to emerge at a party, but one with which I concurred whole-heartedly.

Finally I arranged to interview him.

I foolishly believed that the cheerful *bonhomie* of our first meeting would see me through an interview. I knew nothing of his work or background. Intuition, I told myself, was all-important, and my main interests were the character and vision of Spencer, the man.

At the appointed time, I knocked on the door of his quaintly ugly cottage at Cookham Rise. The artist answered the door himself and preceded me up the steep little staircase to his studio-bedroom. I soon realised my mistake. Spencer, the artist and Spencer, the man were indivisible. The large, unfinished canvas on the wall almost dominated the man. The small room was full of the tools of his calling – a trestle table, an easel, paints, palettes, brushes, pencils. The furniture was negligible, apart from an imposing, Victorian mirror, which hung over the mantlepiece and helped to make the room look larger and lighter.

The interview was opened with gentle questioning about my qualifications. What had I read about him? Nothing! Oh, dear. Various people had written books about him, and they were in the library. Had I seen his pictures at the Tate? No! Or his pictures anywhere else? No. Then how did I hope to write about him? We—ell, it was Spencer, the *man* I wanted to write about. The psychology of the artist, his make-up, views, opinions – I wanted to know what made him tick.

I was dispatched to the Tate without more ado and told to learn something about my subject's work before putting pen to paper. There was also an impressive little lecture on humility, which I cannot recall in detail, but it seemed entirely appropriate at the time.

Stanley was acutely sensitive about words and how they were used, particularly where he or his work was concerned. Sometimes it was as if he caught them in mid-air, scrutinised them with the skill and speed of long experience and then pronounced judgment. Anyone who knew him well, would recall the quick turn of the head, the raised eyebrow, the quizzical look over the tops of his spectacles – the professorial Stanley – questioning, not only the choice of words, but all that lay behind them; the perception, judgment, integrity and values of the speaker. What an impressive teacher he would have made! Just the right amount of panache and emotional depth-charge, to give a lecture the necessary punch to imprint it on the minds of his students for ever.

I did not immediately admire his pictures, much as I liked the man and his obvious sincerity where his work was concerned. After my visit to the Tate, I returned to his cottage, knowing that I could not lie, and determined to be cautious and tactful at all costs.

'Well, and what did you think of my pictures?' he asked. There were distant, volcanic rumblings behind the directness of the question.

'I found them interesting,' I replied carefully. Then added with genuine enthusiasm, 'I particularly admired the precision of your painting of the bricks, in *Christ Carrying the Cross*.

The volcano erupted.

'You wouldn't have noticed the bloody bricks,' he shouted, banging his small, white fist down on the table, 'if you had loved my picture!'

I was a hard case with much to learn. Clearly, nothing that I wrote would be acceptable to him unless I *loved his work*. I began to think of my article in different terms. To understand Spencer, the man, and gain his confidence and trust, I had to learn to see things his way. This was not quite so difficult as it may sound, because there was this intuitive feeling of kinship between us, which gave us a great deal of common ground. Of course, I should have done my homework; studied his paintings and read what the experts had written. But, if I had done that, and gone armed with preconceived ideas and second-hand opinions, might not his exasperation have been greater? In retrospect, it seems to me that I learned much more from Spencer, the educator, than I would have done from Spencer the misunderstood and largely misinterpreted visionary painter. With each stormy meeting (even the rows had a 'family' feeling about them), the lesson was being rammed home, that every word written about Stanley or his work was of prime importance. To trivialize either, or to be inaccurate, was an offence against human nature, and therefore against God, since the two seemed to be inextricably connected.

I learned, too, that to paint beauty was no challenge to Spencer. The drive to endow the hum-drum and the ordinary with a God-given light of love was part of his religion. The ugly people in his paintings represented the ordinary folk of life: the neglected ones, the odd ones, the unloved ones – sometimes ugly for the very reason that they had been neglected or unloved.

I remember once, asking him what he thought of Picasso whom I had always regarded as a painters' painter. 'Picasso!' Stanley spat the name out with venomous passion. 'I can draw better than Picasso! Come and look at these.' Whereupon he showed me a folio of drawings for his series of paintings, *Christ Preaching at Cookham Regatta*.

Looking back, I believe that his battles with me, during the eight or nine interviews which took place in 1955, could have been reflexions of his own inner conflicts. I am certain that he longed to be, not only a *great artist*, but also a *great human being* – a guru, a philosopher, a leader among thinkers – at the same time remaining the humble representative of Tom, Dick and Harry. To keep the balance between these very different views was a challenge to his liking, but at times it became precarious. He was particularly vulnerable if someone came along with a private vision of their own, because it jeopardised his, and Stanley wanted disciples, not rivals. I suppose that Picasso posed this threat, and until I could share his vision and get on to his wave-length, perhaps in a minor way I did too. . . .

As soon as my article was published, it was as if a barrier had been removed, and we could become friends at last. Until then there had been a certain formality in our relationship. My small daughter had accompanied me to interviews on two or three occasions, and on one, had said: 'Oh, no! We're not going to see that little man you always have rows with, are we?'

But now all that was a thing of the past. I had learned much about Stanley. There was some basis for friendship. He was fond of my mother, and once said to my daughter: 'I wish I could draw like you,' when he saw her drawing with the unselfconscious ease of a seven-year-old.

Despite all this, we met infrequently during the next three years. But, when our paths *did* cross, all the old buoyancy and fun returned. Our banter sometimes developed into personal reminiscence for Stanley. Sometimes I used to think that his constant reference to biblical subjects was less an indication of religious zeal than a prop of old memories. His knowledge of the bible seemed to be synonymous with recollections of childhood and his father. He seemed to like to keep these distillations fresh and at hand, for his spiritual comfort and reassurance. Cookham, I suspect, was another prop.

He also loved to teach, and there were conveniently yawning gaps in my artistic and musical education for the professorial Stanley to fill. Not that there was anything approaching an orthodox lecture. In a way his method anticipated the current educational trend of encouraging students to find out for themselves. He would speak with such rapturous enthusiasm about Bach, Beethoven and the piano music of Schumann that I could not get to a concert hall quickly enough to hear these composers with, so to speak, a new ear. The same thing happened in art.

In the past, I had tended to dismiss Victorian English artists as 'sentimental'. Stanley insisted that I should take a closer look, particularly at

Frederick Walker, whom he admired and, surprisingly, admitted to having been an influence on his own work. I am eternally grateful to Stanley for these paternalistic nudges to broaden the basis of my outlook and tastes. They helped to add a dimension to life, which could have been neglected, or at best delayed, if we had never met.

Stanley had a way with children and old people. If he had never touched a paintbrush in his life, his genius – as I saw it – lay in his perception and understanding of people. Despite this, he once admitted to me that he was distrustful, and a little frightened, of intellectuals. Sensing his meaning, I believe I added something like 'They can't see the wood for the trees.' When one struck the right chord for him, his reaction was immediate. Delight would animate his face, and, with youthful enthusiasm, he would say, 'Yes, that's it,' and quickly follow the train of thought along his personal line, extending and enlarging upon the theme as he went.

Once, when I was visiting him at his cottage, a student arrived. The boy had hitch-hiked from Birmingham to show some of his work to the master. Stanley invited him in with great cordiality, asked his name and agreed to look at his work. I remember thinking that it was mediocre, but Stanley found something good to say about each canvas that was shown. Only at the end did he offer constructive criticism – in the most tactful way imaginable. He then showed the student some of his own work, explaining various points to him. The lad went away delighted.

On another occasion, I visited his Cookham Exhibition in 1958, with a blind friend, Yvonne. Before she lost her sight, Yvonne, a highly intelligent, sensitive person, had read widely and painted quite a bit. She could remember some of Stanley's pictures which she had admired. We had planned to walk around the church and vicarage quietly, on the warm, June day, and I would describe the pictures to her as we went. But Stanley caught sight of us, and despite the many other demands on his time, we had the unique experience of having each picture lovingly described by the artist himself. Soon, a small group of people formed around us, and, as we progressed, the following grew and grew. Several times he took Yvonne's hand and gently drew it over the painted surface of the canvas, saying, 'Lovely and smooth, isn't it?' How Yvonne enjoyed that day!

Then, a strange thing happened. Over a cup of tea in the marquee afterwards, Stanley whispered in my ear, 'I never know what to say when people ask if I believe in God.' I was astonished. I thought I *must* have misheard him. With all the village bustle in the tent, the subject was soon and easily lost.

After my early struggles to keep the peace, I had maintained a cautious silence on the subject of my own religious beliefs – or lack of them. Perhaps he had, in his intuitive way, correctly interpreted my non-committal attitude, and the jocular, whispered confidence implied a shared scepticism. However, I firmly believed that I had imagined it all, until the subject cropped up again, a week or two later, and word for word he said exactly the same thing again. Memory plays some cruel tricks. Although I can remember those words with complete clarity, the ensuing conversation after he had said them for the second time, is completely forgotten. If it had been very startling, perhaps it would have stuck in my mind, but there were times when one became punch-drunk with Stanley's volubility. Although the opening theme seemed to be so clear and distinct, Stanley's very personal vision could easily obscure his explanation for the listener. One became a sort of eavesdropper, straining to understand the passionate torrent of words. It was tiring work listening for long, and the capacity to ask questions, or even take it in, drained away as concentration and mental energy waned.

However, by this time I had acquired some feelings of respect and understanding for this curious, lonely, original man. I realised, too, that he knew all about suffering and weakness, in spite of his buoyant and cheerful exterior. In July, 1958, he was just 67 years of age. Most of the time this was hard to believe, because he always seemed to be so young in spirit.

I believe that, in this penultimate year of his life, he was beginning to regain something of the joy of his childhood. It wasn't just people's adulation, which surged up in the wake of honours and public recognition, and which he loved, but a newly-found freedom from emotional problems and entanglements, which had dogged him for most of his adult life. It may have been this which prompted him to say to me: 'I could do with another 200 years of life to catch up with all the work I want to do.'

He was now anxious about the possibility of an operation, but did not at this stage, suspect that he had cancer.

As soon as he began to feel better, he started drawing and answering the letters of well-wishers and others. Among his letters was one which contained the following:

I possess the large volume on Frederick Walker. I possess the little book on him. I possess the 'Cornhill' engravings.

I subscribed to his name being re-cut on his grave-stone many years ago, in Hayward-Brown's days.

I love Frederick Walker *dearly* and his wit. 'The servant who broke his flute and said she didn't'.

I have always thought and *said* that he is one of England's greatest artists. Fancy asking me whether I know the plaque of F.W. in Cookham. Gilbert and I have both loved and revered F.W. and I cannot understand the vicar saying no one seems to know about him as I have spoken to the vicar often. So please attend and say, 'Stanley and Gilbert Spencer *certainly* know of this great and delightful man – a true artist'.

During his stay in hospital, two thoughtful patrons had decided that life should be made easier for Stanley in the future. Fernley, his birthplace in the village High Street, which had been built by his grandfather – a master builder – had come on to the market. A Trust was formed and the Victorian villa purchased for him. He was quick to point out to me, however, that he had been able to contribute several hundred pounds himself. The house was in good order; there was a telephone and neighbours were closer. When he was installed, an unofficial rota of village ladies arranged to keep an eye on him and do specific tasks.

He was not to be alone for long, however. Francis Davies, a friend and concert pianist, was looking for a home for himself and his grand piano. Stanley gladly rose to the occasion and agreed to share the house with him, pleased with the idea of the companionship and the music. Both meant a great deal to him, particularly at this time.

Stanley had mentioned Francis several times before I met him, and for some reason I had assumed that they were contemporaries. So I was surprised, calling at Fernley one day, to be introduced to an athletic-looking young man with a robust, casual sort of look about him. Stanley, still frail and with an almost chronic sore throat, croaked, 'It's marvellous, we have Bach in the mornings and Rachmaninov in the afternoons. It helps tremendously with my work.'

Francis needed little persuasion to play, and even less to give a piece the 'full works'. That afternoon he played *The Miller's Dance* by de Falla. It must have been heard half-way down the High Street, for it nearly blasted us through the ceiling of Fernley's small, front sitting-room. Stanley explained: 'Francis likes the romantics and plays them with fire. People are frightened of fire nowadays, but I like it.'

Before long he became ill again, and one day when I called he was in the back bedroom at Fernley, looking like a puckish skeleton propped up by pillows. He held a brown paper-backed book in his skinny, white hands. I realised, sadly, that his buoyancy was degenerating into peevishness as he croaked: 'It's no good, they're all inaccurate. I've found three mistakes here, in the first two pages of Eric Newton's book on me'. He seemed to be anxious about his place in posterity and talked of sorting out his papers with his daughter. Francis had left. People came and went, but there still seemed to be too many hours when Stanley was quite alone with his tortured body and disturbed mind.

The return to hospital was inevitable. It was becoming obvious that, following his colostomy, cancer secondaries had set up. In his last weeks he could not speak. His vocal cords had been affected, and at first we would converse in whispers, then he had to resort to a scribbled message on a piece of paper. His courage was boundless, he never invited pity, and there was a spectral shadow of the old Stanley in his smile.

RICHARD KENNEDY
Over several years I saw Stanley about once a month after 1947 until the time of his death. Sometimes he came to our house in Marlow but more

often I went to his house in Cookham.

When I arrived we usually started by looking at the work he had been doing in the day. At first it was always the *Resurrection, Port Glasgow*, which Stanley had pinned up on his bedroom wall.

Referring to his big *Resurrection* pictures like this one and the *Cookham Resurrection* Stanley observed that he thought them too loosely composed and regretted that he could not give them a central axis round which everything revolved in the manner of the great Italian masters.

'It took me a long time to think of a centre for the *Cookham Resurrection*', he told me, 'until I thought of Hilda's scarf and this gave me the clue of the big tomb.'

I thought at the time his mind worked very like that of Marcel Proust, but I forebore to tell him so. One day I arrived at his house to find him using a rag to smudge in some grass.

'I thought you painted every blade of grass', I said to Stanley.

'I am subtle, Richard, subtle!' he replied. Indeed he was. This was perhaps one of his principle characteristics.

He worked with the care and precision of a dentist. 'The trouble with me', he said, 'is that I have too much control. I can draw the works of a clock and end up in the right place'. His method was to enlarge up a small sketch or drawing by squaring it up and transferring it to a large canvass.

The meticulous pencil drawing he made on the squared canvass reminiscent of the work of some Japanese master was itself a work of art. Although he never mentioned Asian art to me he was something of a mandarin in his perfectionist and formal attitude to life.

In one of the back bedrooms of his house there was a drawing of litter on Hampstead Heath which had been left as a drawing on the canvass. The accurately drawn spiders web of lines over the ruled up grid made it extremely beautiful.

The subject evidently had some autobiographical significance for Stanley, but the mine must have run out while Stanley was working on it.

His studio was his bedroom but it was scrupulously tidy with every drawing carefully filed away.

If anything went wrong during the process of transferring the small drawing to the canvass Stanley was in serious trouble. This happened in the case of the big *Regatta* picture, which was half an inch out at the top, and this according to him affected the whole composition. Visitors to the Cookham Gallery can see in this unfinished work pencil alterations, something Stanley had never done before.

This method was to paint each shape up to the pencil outline to a point when nothing more was required to be done. 'If I know the shape', he said, 'I know the colour and the tone!' He would then move on to another shape. The result was a sort of jigsaw effect with shapes waiting to be filled in, but the skill with which those areas of blank canvass were left contributed to the composition and ensured its remaining appetizing.

Stanley liked to work slowly. He said, 'I like to press up against my subject and slowly push it forward. I enjoy feeling its weight'. He accompanied these remarks with his very characteristic hand gestures.

After spending some time talking over the work he had been engaged on, we would leave the bedroom and descend to the kitchen, where Stanley would make tea and fry some bread and bacon, and we would have a cessation, as he called it.

He would talk brilliantly about art. The fascination the Greeks showed in the human torso he thought was due to the intense curiosity they felt about what was inside.

Renoir was the only painter among the French impressionists he could tolerate, and when he was painting the pictures for the Chapel of Peace, he justified his using cobalt blue by the fact that Renoir used it.

To paint a picture of Jesus and leave out nature as Rouault did seemed to Stanley incredible. Cow parsley was as much a part of the Gospel story as the words and suffering of Jesus.

The painters he admired were Signorelli, Pinturicchio, Ucello, Piero della Francesca and Fra Angelico.

The sophisticated handling of paint in the tradition of Titian, though he respected it, did not move him. When he received a commission to paint Diana Dors, he said, 'I shall do it if they can confirm it, but it is not my sort of job; it needs a Goya'.

Stanley could not paint a dishy female. Flesh and blood seemed to evade him although he was a master of movement and a great choreographer. The voluptuous side of a woman's body was not for him; though his work did not lack tenderness the lust was missing.

Ironically Maurice Collis, in order to make a copy for his biography of Stanley, turned this excessively innocent man into the Satyr of Cookham.

One day I arrived at the house to find Stanley looking at some drawings he had made that day and very excited. He had scattered them on the floor – they were drawn with a very fine pencil line on very thin paper. (Stanley had genius for finding paper likely to rot or disintegrate in a short space of time.) They consisted of river scenes, holiday makers reclining in punts moored to the river bank.

He explained to me that they were intended for a new project he had in mind, a Chapel of Peace, which was to be a companion to the Burghclere Chapel, in which he had so poetically expressed his life as a private soldier in terms of paint. This would express his peace time journey through life from a small boy in Cookham to being a celebrated artist and friend of Lord Astor, but Stanley did not see this journey in snobbish terms but as a spiritual unfolding like that of a flower.

As a small boy he had watched the 'nobs' at Cookham Regatta, the big social event of the year; now he was proposing to recreate it in spiritual terms with Jesus preaching from a punt that contains the common little Cookham children and the twelve apostles – in between this social bracket he is surrounded by the various layers of Cookham Society.

This time Stanley was pleased to observe that he had got over the difficulty of giving a big painting an axis on which everything turned, which was of course Jesus leaning forward addressing the children.

Stanley was a great musician and devoted about a third of his waking time to playing the piano. The Chapel of Peace which never got off the ground for lack of anyone to put up the money, was musically inspired. The visitors listen to Jesus's words in silence as they are borne to them with the ripple of the water among the reeds.

This is what Stanley said about the proposed work when he visited us to draw our youngest daughter in order to get his eye in for drawing the children in the barge.

Stanley spoke a good deal about his childhood in Cookham.

As a result of his father's preoccupation with the Bible Stanley saw the social divisions in his environment in biblical terms. God could be conceived as living over above Cliveden Woods, the abode of Lord Astor, and the Regatta thought of in terms of the Feast of the Passover.

These very naive ideas seem extraordinary in such a sophisticated man as Stanley, but hearing him talk about them I realised he was translating his social environment into art and a very subtle form of art, giving it a universal quality in the same way as Rembrandt succeeded in giving the swells and the old beggars in Amsterdam a universality by translating them into high priests and publicans.

Stanley, as he frequently remarked, saw himself as a member of the small village shop-keeping community. He was scared of women as sexual objects, but delighted to talk to them. He always wore a collar and tie and shaved every day. He never took his jacket off to work, and never failed to wear a dark suit with rather crumpled trousers. He delighted in social distinctions but this pleasure was purged of all social ambition. He was in fact an intensely social person, welcoming everyone who came to his house with the same radiant smile, and he delighted in visiting his friends. He always replied to letters punctiliously.

Conversation was his great delight, especially conversation over the tea cups; he was absolutely brilliant at it. I am sure he could have won easily in competition with all the great conversationalists of the century, Bernard Shaw, Oscar Wilde, etc.; he was a master at creating pinacles of fantasy and humour.

Unfortunately the conversationalist requires an opposite number to bring out the best in him.

Stanley spoke bitterly of how his restricted life in Cookham prevented him reaching his highest peaks as conversationalist for lack of suitable protagonists, and how he had sometimes regretted he had not submitted to Roger Fry's blandishments, when the latter had tried to induce him to join the Bloomsbury Group, who were spiritually highly antipathetic to Stanley.

When I visited him a day or two before his death in Cliveden Hospital his powers as a conversationalist were undimmed though handicapped by a difficulty in speech, but they were still there. He was reading a book on Verlaine and was bubbling over to talk about it and be as brilliant and subtle, and profound as ever.

CATHERINE MARTINEAU

We are thankful to hear Sir John is planning a book on Stanley to give a better balanced picture of him. My husband and Mr G. G. Shiel, who has since died, were so distressed by Maurice Collis's biography that they insisted on a certain amount of pruning (for which he held them up to ransom all right!) but the reproach remained that they, as Trustees, had entrusted this book to the wrong man. Lord Astor over-influenced them, I'm afraid – and Dudley Tooth had an entirely different point of view about Stan, and didn't really mind. Now only my husband remains, and he will die a happier man if the record can be put straighter. It was an added shock when *Miss* Collis added fuel to the fire.

It is delightful that Sir John is asking for the recollections of friends and neighbours – Collis never came near any of us.

Tom Balston, an old friend of my family, often came to stay during the war years, and one Saturday afternoon asked me did I realise I lived within reach of one of the greatest living artists; and on the chance of finding Stanley at home we set off on dilapidated bikes down Hedsor Hill to Cookham.

Stan was to and fro from Glasgow at the time, but we were in luck. He was in his studio – a hut in the garden at Lyndhurst – shiny-eyed about his ship-building paintings. He did his parlour trick, shooting a roll of lavatory paper right across the floor, on which he had drawn in detail those astonishing designs. You can imagine the impression on *me*. So it was touching but characteristic that the last time I went to see him, three days before he died, he told me exactly what I was wearing on that first visit, and then wrote, because he was too weak to go on speaking: 'When you came with Tom Balston you gave me Hope indeed, and later when I saw Jack [Martineau], I knew I had what I so wanted, Friends!'

Sad to think now that instead of accepting this simply and gratefully, I annoyed him by somewhat pooh-poohing it, saying something like, 'But Stan, you always had friends – far more important ones – we are very ordinary', because I remember his look as he seized the paper again and scrawled, 'Your vein (and I hope it is *not* your vein) is that ordinary people are not worth much. What condescension! All that is, thank God, quite wrong. Mary Behrend said, "Stanley, those old gardener's wives, or postmen won't understand what you say". I said, "*you*, Mary, might not understand but they *will*". Round the corner of the paper he has written: "It's the more intellectual who seem to have this unredeemed and unredeemable thought about "the usual run of people".'

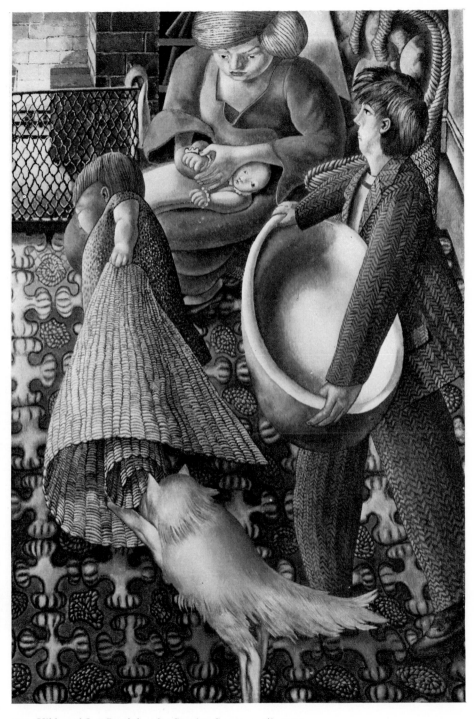

22 *Hilda and I at Burghclere*, by Stanley Spencer, oil, 1955.
Photo: A. C. Cooper. *Private Collection*

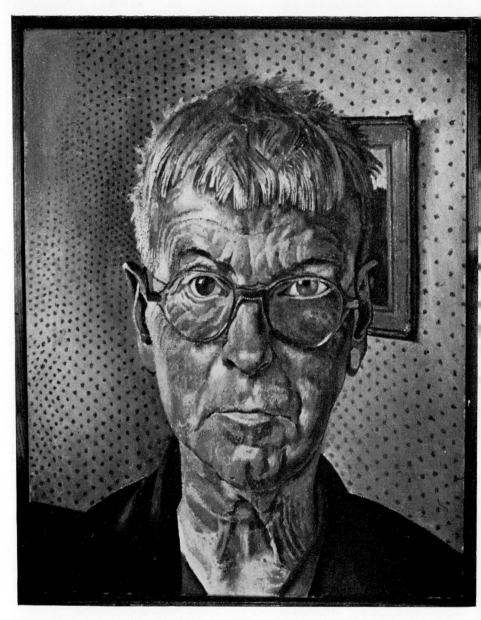

23   *Self-portrait*, by Stanley Spencer, 1959.
Photo: David Rowan. *Private Collection*

On another of one of my last visits to him I went straight to the hospital from the airport; having been out to Florence to see after a sick aunt. Stan asked me had I seen any Signorelli. I had to say 'No', so he said impatiently, 'People like you who have the chance to go to Florence like as not never have heard of Signorelli!' (Not quite fair!) Then he asked me did I look carefully at the designs at the foot of the Campanile. Again I had not! So he took up his pad and drew perfect hexagons describing in each roughly what they represented – Creation of Man, Expulsion from Eden, Noah drunk, Agriculture etc. An astonishing feat! Gilbert says the only picture he thinks Stan ever saw in Italy was a common little print hanging in a transit camp on his way home from Salonika. Yet his detailed knowledge of the work of Italian painters and sculptors from photographs and books was as vivid as if he had seen them with his own eyes.

Early in 1943 I was left £10. Being naive and youthful I wrote to Stanley saying that I heard when home from Glasgow he was stopping children in Cookham and drawing them as a relief from his painting. Would he accept my £10 and come and draw my five-year-old? I think he liked the cheek of it! Years later laughing about it he said, 'Ha! Ha! Set a sprat to catch a mackerel! Stanley knew what he was about!' Anyhow he wrote saying he was just finishing 'that long ship-building picture. I will bus to Maidenhead Bridge and walk up from the Dumb Bell!' This reminds me of the uncanny but practical way he got about – no fuss – arriving often quite unexpectedly like a fairy. Once we got home from Suffolk, and found him quietly painting in the garden.

My son Richard remembers him arriving in Suffolk and flinging himself flat on the grass; smelling it rapturously. Why do we only hear of him enjoying dirt?

By the time we knew him his constant theme was Hilda – and only Hilda. 'You can only be married once. It's a pity men don't strut about like cocks and get their vanity out of them. I married Patricia out of *vanity*!'

A Glasgow lady once arrived on my doorstep, and without preamble said indignantly, 'You have the greatest living artist, *starving* a few miles away – and you do not feed him!' I said feebly that he came on Sundays when he wanted (for his 'Blow Outs', he said; 'I get a little tired of m' fry') but I didn't think he wanted to be interrupted in the week. However from then on I fetched him more often, and we kept a room always ready for him. He liked being called in the morning by our little nursery maid. When she drew back the curtains he thought of the Angel rolling back the stone of the Tomb – and painted a picture.

We had five children, and he loved above all 'Nursery Tea'. On his birthday one year I made the awful mistake of arranging to have his cake downstairs at 6.30 with a few neighbours, and a bottle of bubbly to drink his health. He behaved himself – just! – but afterwards complained bitterly: 'No Nursery Tea – and on my *Birthday*!'

He would keep the table 'in a roar' – his imitations (like his mother, according to Gilbert) were inimitable. I remember one of Mrs Harter leaving the room in indignation stirring her cup of tea, having been accused by Stan of having more than her ration of butter. One of his favourite quotations one summer was: 'Then came still evening on – Milton never got it wrong did he? – so true, and not a word out of place!'

Which brings me to his astonishing analytical and scholarly appreciation of literature and music. I understand it better now that I came on type-script excerpts from the diary of his brother Sydney – what he read and discussed in bed with Stan. It is plain that education in the Spencer home was more advanced in many directions than in any Public School of the day. I think that is what Gilbert is getting at when he complains of Stan rather enjoying playing up the part of 'village boy made good'.

It was an incredible family – the intellectual level of the talk, the reading, the music far beyond that of ordinary educated people, let alone villagers – and Stan drinking it all in.

My daughter Jane, a little girl at the time, reminds me of the way Stan used to sit at the 'pi-ar-no', his feet not quite touching the pedals, playing Bach very slowly – as if he was the composer – understanding the reason for every change of key and the necessary sequence of the theme. And Gilbert tells me that once his brother Will played a short piece of Bach to Stan, to which he listened intently – and then, without the music, went and played it through slowly – but note for note correctly!

When he read, it was with the same concentration and perception, but his expositions or explanations of what he read were delightfully, often comically, fresh and original. My daughter wants me to say how he would 'chat up' the Bible to us, so that all those old Testament characters came to life as if they were old cronies of his. He 'chatted up' the figures in his pictures, too, telling us what each was thinking or saying. He would get down on the floor with the children with photographs (say) of the Glasgow *Resurrection* spread around, and pour out his stories, delighted to answer all their Whys. 'Why were the disciples feet all crossed?' in his *Last Supper*. Jane thinks he answered: 'They're a bit bored you see, they've heard it all before.'

He would receive special visitors at Cliveden View with natural good manners. Ordinarily we barged through the back door, through the smelly little kitchen, and clattered up the lino-covered stairs to his room to find him. But I remember when I arranged to take Eily Darwin over to see him (important to him because of Gwen Raverat – and having herself been at the Slade) he 'received' her at the front door and ushered her up to his bedroom. What though his little bed in the corner was just as he had got out of it, we might have been in the Doge's Palace – the canvas on which he was currently working stretched all along one wall, and on a table in the window a carefully selected set of drawings laid out for her inspection and discussion. At first he was hesitant, almost anxious, said he couldn't manage life, had made a mess of it – was unhappy – but perhaps she would care to look at these drawings. I remember her exclaiming 'Unhappy? Oh Stanley, you happy happy man! *Look* at these drawings!', and the quick delighted smile he gave her.

Our boys grew up, and went to Eton and persuaded Stan to come and give a talk there with lantern slides. When I took him to a school concert it was not a success – the standard was too low; Bedales, he said, was far ahead. But his own talk was a great success. The Hall was crowded – huge young giants around him – and Stan's tiny figure in complete command – first making them laugh about his once having been in the army, and presenting imaginary arms.

In the same way he stunned the boys at Aldenham School, talking of his *Crucifixion* (which Jack, a brewer, had commissioned for a Brewer's School), when he said: 'I have given the men who are nailing Christ to the Cross (and making sure that they make a good job of it) – Brewer's Caps – because it is your Governors, and you, who are still nailing Christ to the Cross.' He painted an enchanting Predella of the interior of Cookham Church as he remembered it as a little boy, to go beneath the *Crucifixion* – but it didn't look right there and it was hung on its own round the corner in a chapel. In 1958 after the service when the Bishop of St Albans dedicated the *Crucifixion*, a group of the *élite* went to look at the Predella, and one of the Governors then asked Stan why he hadn't put a Cross on the Altar. 'I don't know', said Stan. 'It wasn't given me!' The Governor, all 6ft 6ins of him, stupidly said to me, 'What does he mean "wasn't give him?"' I said, 'By God, I suppose', and Stan overhearing said, 'Yes, its like a child who feels perfectly happy and sure of himself while his hand is in Daddy's – but, my God, should Daddy take his hands away!' The Bishop was tall and beautiful, like the Governor. I remember their two grey, dignified heads bending down amazed towards the tousled, muffled-up little figure of Stan, quite silenced by his sermon.

I often told him how much better his sermons were than the ones we had in church. When he was with us at weekends he quite liked coming to Evensong – often went with the Shiels to Cookham – loathed the hymns, but gloried of course in psalms and Bible. Once he described himself going to a Quaker service looking through his fingers to see who was going to speak, no one did! 'So I saw my chance', he said gleefully. He spoke of course on the beauty of the old language of the Bible, and the iniquity of new translations.

Coming home one evening from church he said, 'I think God created Man, because he must have been so lonely!' Stan knew something of the loneliness of creation, I thought. Maurice Collis thought it mad, but it doesn't seem at all odd to me that when on his own at Cliveden View in the night he poured out his wildest thoughts and ideas to Hilda – dead or alive. In a lesser way, don't we all wish we could tell things to our nearest and dearest, whom we have perhaps long lost? We are told, too, that we all dream the most fantastic stuff – some of which might shock us if we remembered it when we woke. The pity is that the box into which Stan cast all his fantasies and midnight scribblings is now regarded as of more importance than his works. I wonder what Stan would have thought of that. His brother Percy said that Stan once pointed to the box where it stood in the corner and said 'You can burn that'. He wouldn't be likely to burn it himself and once he was dead everything he left behind became holy – and was locked away in Dudley Tooth's basement.

In the winter of 1955–56 he came each weekend to paint Jack's portrait. He wanted to do it really because it was a chance to paint *fur*. (Jack was that year's Master of the Brewers Company.) One day when working on the robe without Jack, Stan came scuttling in later than I expected, his eyes gleaming. 'I just slipped up to the National Gallery this morning', he said. 'My fur *is* as good as Tintoretto's.'

Stan obstinately resisted all advances from Cliveden until the latter half of 1957. He used to tell me, 'Who do you think has been here?' (if I had been out). 'Lord Astor! – He says why do I find things to paint in Jack's little garden, and not in his – but I've been all round Cliveden and I've told him there's *Nothing* for me there!' However when Bill told him how unhappy he was, that did it. Stan relented – and painted Bill's portrait on the terrace, looking, indeed, terribly unhappy. Stan used to come on to us after one of these Cliveden days, and say he thought it would make an awfully good Russian play – the painter on stage the whole time – and everyone, one by one, in the houseparty coming to pour out to him the same sad story from a different point of view. His sympathy was with them *all*. There was nothing he didn't know about the difficulties of marriage! He used to say about matrimonial rows, 'The worst of it is they are just about a little bit of linoleum!' Collis makes it seem that Stan was fortunate to be 'taken up' (however late on) by so important a 'Patron' as Lord A. It was rather the other way about – Stan comforting poor Bill – having nothing to do with Cliveden until, at the very end of his life, he found he was needed there to help.

His pain grew those last months in his old home, Fernley – which by now Jack and Bill had bought for him – Cliveden View being hopeless for an invalid. I drove Gilbert over to bring him back with us to tea – but I could see the smallest lurch in the car hurt him. I said something about it – and he answered sharply, 'If you haven't got used to my being in pain yet, its time you did'. After that he and Gilbert chortled away together (about the vagaries of their mother's long-ago serving girls!) as if nothing in the world was wrong – and time was young.

On one of my last visits to Fernley he was standing in the big room with *Christ Preaching* on the wall behind him, and that last terrific self-portrait blazing away at me on a chair opposite – still unframed. He waved an arm towards it, and asked me what I thought of it. I was terrified by it.

I said slowly, 'Well, its not the Stanley I know, is it?', and he said, 'No', with a smile.

After the programme on the wireless about him, 'our' Stanley hardly seems credible! Of course we knew there must be other sides to Stanley – deeper, stranger, sadder – but 'our' Stanley was invariably delightful, funny, strong, sympathetic, *brilliant* of course, lighting up our lives then, as I might say the thought of him still does – and the pictures on our walls. One, a group of snowdrops, is especially dear because of the letter he wrote about it. On getting it, I rushed straight over to Cliveden View – as of course he knew I would! – to see the tiny 'pot boiler', and he said, looking from me to it, 'I pity the poor mut who is going to buy this', knowing perfectly well who the poor mut would be! – having in fact organised the whole thing.

Dear Cash,
... I have just done my first 1955 pot-boiler; a weeny painting of some snowdrops. They were challenging me from my garden and I had to go to them. There was only one small clump but they are fearfully pleased with themselves. You could imagine them discussing it: 'He's come right to where we are and he is looking very hard at us. He has gone indoors now – no, he is coming out now with a camp stool – there's something up; he has tied a jumper round his head, for warmth, I suppose; goodness now a sort of school satchel and out comes a furry sack which opens in front, and now a hot water bottle of all things. He has put that in the sack, and now he has put himself in the sack, and he is painting: I knew there was something about us.

VAUDREY MERCER
First of all let me say that, in spite of what other people may think, he was never vulgar, and he would have been shocked even to hear a doubtful story, let alone to tell one. He was of a kind, gentle and timid nature, and, as a consequence of this, his war experiences were exceptionally vivid in his memory.

He loved to talk and would expound at great length, especially on the subjects of music and religion, so that if one invited him to one's house to have a drink at 6 p.m., he could well be with you at 2 a.m. the following morning. On the other hand he would always listen to whatever one had to say, though it was sometimes difficult to interrupt his flow of language.

I remember on one occasion being called to see him [as his doctor] late one evening when he was living at Cookham Rise. I found him busy painting one of his huge *Resurrection* pictures by the light of a single candle; I remarked to him, 'How do you manage to see what colour you are using?' To this he replied, 'Well of course I cannot see clearly what the colour is, but the effect in the morning is sometimes tremendous'. That same evening, I had the temerity to suggest that the perspective of the lid of one of the tomb stones was not quite correct. When I arrived to see him again the following morning I was amazed to find that he had altered the picture along the lines I had suggested. I said, 'But I had not thought that you would alter the picture; I am not an expert', to which he replied, 'But you were quite right.' After that I was careful to avoid making any such remark.

During the flood in 1947 I well remember seeing Stanley, in his wading boots, making his way through the flood water to Moor Thatch, in order to take provisions to his wife. This was not done to attract attention to himself, but was merely an act of kindness, because he was worried about her safety.

He had one tremendous ability, he could see. And because he could see he was able to notice everyday movements which the ordinary person would have taken for granted, and therefore would have passed them by unnoticed. For example, the carpenter looking down his saw to see if the teeth were set correctly, or the child lifting up the barbed-wire to crawl underneath it. This is, to my mind, where he excelled; he was able to create a 'picture' out of a caricature; in other words he was able to capture, in his mind's eye, the action of a moment.

MARJORIE METZ

My portrait took three weeks. Stanley painted each day and the sittings lasted for five to six hours. They were all under electric light as Stanley came in the afternoons and it was winter.

He brought a roll of canvas on the first day and he said 'Have you a flat surface where I can cut it?' He already had in mind the size and shape of the canvas he required. We showed him the kitchen floor and he found it suitable and he rolled out the canvas and cut it. Then he fixed up his easel and pinned the piece of canvas on to a large sheet of hardboard. It was not put on a stretcher until it was framed.

Then he said to me, 'Sit down'. I sat down on an armchair and he said 'Just sit like that', and that was the way he posed me and each day I would get back into position which was not difficult because it was a natural position for me to sit.

When he arrived the first day, he just said; 'I have come to start the portrait'. I asked, 'Well, what do you want me to wear?' He replied: 'Bring down your wardrobe and let me have a look'. I brought down a number of dresses and among them was an evening dress and he said, 'That's it'. And it was.

I found that it was very necessary to be with him mentally while he was working. He told me of a particular sitter who was apparently not interested in him or in conversation with him. She was thinking of other things, so he could not go on with the portrait.

When we first met Stanley he was completing the Glasgow *Resurrection* series and was preparing for the last of them, *Resurrection, Port Glasgow*. We used to go to his house at Cookham Rise and he showed us innumerable preparatory drawings. He spent about two years preparing for this painting and in the meantime these drawings were mounting up, every character and every pose.

He was very gregarious. At times he was tempted to come out when we almost felt he should not because he ought to get on with his work, but one could very easily tempt him. He loved a party and he loved coming out to dinner. He loved people.

We knew of many kind acts he did, particularly when he was in hospital. An accident case was brought in from a local research laboratory. An assistant had been involved in an explosion and was in a very critical state and his young wife was sent for. The hospital staff spent many hours trying to save this man. His wife was there all the time. In an effort to distract her Stanley did a portrait drawing of her. Unfortunately the man died. Stanley gave her the drawing and asked us to have it framed on his behalf for her. It was a remarkable drawing because it so well portrayed the look of shock and bewilderment in her eyes.

PETER MOBSBY

My first local knowledge of Stanley Spencer came from the Cookham builder, Mr Davis, who in the course of conversation said that Stanley was 'all right,' but that 'his trouble is he's secky'. I don't know how he would have spelt the word, but he pronounced it as written above.

I had known of Stanley for a long time by 'reputation', and my uncle owned one of his pictures, but the views of the middle-classes, particularly in those days, were not necessarily mine, and as I came to know him myself, I accepted him at face value and found him delightful up to the last time I saw him.

He was a complete 'natural', naive to the point of childishness at times, yet possessed of an awareness that nothing was as simple as he would wish it to be. He was unfailingly polite in an unsophisticated way, and assumed, on the briefest acquaintance, that one knew everyone he knew, and by their nicknames at that! He could meet me in Bond Street six or eight months after we had last spoken together, and carry on a conversation amid all the noises of traffic and passing people, as though we had last met the day before yesterday.

He lived for his painting and took little – if any – interest in the wider issues of the world beyond Cookham and it's immediate neighbourhood. On the latter subject he was an entertaining talker, as he was on the subject of his personal experiences, his friends and family, and his painting. He rarely talked of other painters, but his brother Gilbert he clearly looked up to. 'Oh, Gil is a much better painter than I'll ever be', I have heard him say more than once.

Nothing was ever apparent of the grisly 'inner life' revealed by Maurice Collis, though I knew of the hoard of autobiographical papers, and had even read a couple of files at Stanley's request. He had tried to find a publisher for these and asked me to read some of 'the stuff' and tell him what I thought. 'They all say it's too long; they want it cut down by half. But I can't. If I cut any of it, it won't be me. I want it published as I have written it.'

After reading the two files, I had to agree with the publishers who had already passed judgement. The content was interesting enough, but Stanley appeared so afraid of the reader missing a point, or misinterpreting his intention, that everything was written down more than once in different words, or different approaches were tried to present everything 'in the round'. Stanley was quite philosophical when I gave him my opinion. 'I was afraid so. But I won't cut anything. I want it published as it is. It won't be me if it's not.'

A remark of his which has been quoted as an example of indecent sensuousness is the one wherein he wished to be a fly to wander over human flesh and discover any minute turn of form, or wrinkle, undisclosed to the eye at a distance. But this is surely only a very graphic expression of an aim dear to every real painter, and something he was trying to do when working on his last self-portrait with a mirror held between his knees.

Very clearly I remember visiting his cottage and viewing the eighty odd (I think) drawings for his *Christ at Cookham Regatta* paintings. As we went through the sheets one by one, the Regatta was revealed visually by the drawings, and verbally by Stanley's comments and actions.

'Look at that one! That's the way old so and so' (I forget the name now, but the Bridge Hotel was under his management, or proprietorship) 'used to look at his watch when it got near closing time.' That one was a figure with it's back to the viewer, delving in it's rear trouser pocket to examine surreptitiously a large round watch. Or again, 'Look at that foot! I could never draw feet. But that one's really good.' This was a female figure in high heels seen from the rear. Page after page followed accompanied by a running commentary and the actions. The Eton boys coming up the Thames, the scene by twilight when the whole concourse of boats carried their lanterns, and boatloads of 'toffs', a word Stanley was very fond of. 'Grand' was another word of which he was making constant use when referring to people, and 'don'tcha know' slipped off the tongue without affectation.

Personally, I always enjoyed his references to Christ and the Apostles as 'J.C. & Co.', given without a trace of irreverence. 'I want to paint J.C. & Co. like a football team, don'tcha know, sitting there in two rows with their arms folded like this, and looking tough.'

More than once he expressed a desire to be able to paint more broadly, as for example in the *Christ in the Wilderness* series, but he was never able to. I have seen a canvas pinned to his wall, with the squared up drawing on it with the forms shaded in pencil. I can only assume that painting to him was a matter of colouring only, and became so automatic that without the shading he would have omitted to change his colour and the form would have been lost.

WINIFRED PULLEN

He was a fundamentally religious man and had an intimate knowledge of the Bible, especially the Old Testament prophets.

He was charming with children and was very kind to ours. He gave up an afternoon to talk to the girls of the Abbey School, Reading, to please our elder daughter Caroline (who was a pupil there) and he brought her home the carnation that Lord Astor had worn in Stanley's portrait of him.

Women ran after him, partly because of his charm and in later years because he was famous. He was always kind and courteous and had lovely manners. It was rather sweet the way he always left a little on the plate 'for manners', as people used to say. I think for him women were of two kinds. There were the 'mother' type – like Hilda, for instance, before her breakdown – and these he treated with great respect – and there were the very worldly, sophisticated and fashionable ladies (like Patricia) who flattered and dazzled him because he was fundamentally simple and honest.

He was at home in any kind of company and yet he did not seem to 'talk down' to village people. He had great feeling for poorer people but was certainly not envious of riches. I have never met a more unworldly person. He certainly did not preach, yet I think everyone who knew him must have been influenced. I certainly learned to use my eyes, and my understanding.

ADRIAN C. ROEST AND RAY LOVERY (a conversation)

Ray: When I asked him what he liked, what interested him most, he said 'Rubbish', so I said, 'What do you mean by that?' and he said, 'I love disorder'; so many things going on so that he could take an interest in Hampstead Heath because of the paper blowing about the grass. That sort of thing. The litter. It was that. I think there was one painting where he had done dustbins . . . a brick wall . . . but certainly when I went with Adrian to the house in Cookham he showed us the *Christ at Cookham Reach* and the thing that fascinated me most was the boater on Christ's head, and he loved this detail. In the other room there was this tapestry . . . well I say tapestry . . . it was an enormous canvas, it was sort of the height of the room, rolled up, and he was painting bits as though he would have a go at one bit and then he'd leave that and say, 'Oh I've got fed up with that', and he'd have a go at another bit. So the way he did his canvas, he'd sort of sketch it out and fill bits and the other picture was going on at the same time.

When he came here he'd got his hair sort of cut short in front, his sort of spectacles looked sort of . . . flashish, didn't they? A shortish chap and he had this carpet bag and he was very sensitive because he'd just had this operation and he couldn't even bear a kiddy sitting on the settee with him. This worried him most, with a kiddy he could never tell what was going to happen. He was at ease with adults because he knew they wouldn't jerk. He didn't want to have to use the contents of his carpet bag.

I found him a very interesting person to talk to because he had so much to say. I've got to be a bit careful here, about these women, because I've also read about him since. I was sitting on the settee with him, wasn't I? I got the impression, talking to him, that he was being pestered by these women.

Adrian: There has been a distorted picture of this man, possibly because he was slightly unusual physically, a small, little man, an unusual man, but they seemed to be looking for the unusual in a sexual sense. Really he was a very ordinary man, who had had an unhappy marriage, as far as I know, had disappointments but was completely balanced otherwise except that he was a man of incredible enthusiasm, whatever he was doing at the time. To some people this would be abnormal perhaps?

About Hampstead and the litter. He was almost obsessional about it. The end of his garden, at Cookham, as a child, had fascinated him. He would go round and investigate the bits and pieces of the heap at the bottom of the garden and he liked the disorder; it was the disorder. When this was all tidied up he was much less enthusiastic.

Ray: I got the impression that he liked a lot to be going on. When we went down to his house and I asked him about this boater, he painted every straw, he just enjoyed doing it. Not like the usual painter who tries to give the impression as such, he wanted to put all the detail in.

He sat in a corner and he talked, and he was fascinating to listen to, without stop, for $2\frac{1}{2}$ hours. And all the time he was in great pain. Trying to sit on an air cushion or relieve himself in some way from this awful discomfort. But he had this trémendous drive. It was subject after subject and just fascinating to listen to.

He was the most human dynamo I have ever met. Something just burned in him. He had incredible drive. This little guy. He was fascinating to listen to. He wasn't patronising, good gracious me it must have been jolly tempting to be patronising, and no question was too trite for his attention.

Ray: He was very polite, as you say, but one did feel this powerhouse of energy. He was very quick, in his thoughts.

Adrian: I have never met anyone, in the business sense or any other way, who, bearing in mind the man was really ill, in great pain, and yet had such enthusiasm for anything he had to say, immense energy, which carried him on in conversation. I thought he was stupendous. And I must say this, I thought his paintings were awful! Because I'm totally at a loss, had never seen anything like them, didn't understand them, still don't like them. But as a man, to sit there and listen to him, there just wasn't anybody like it.

Ray: What I liked was that he so enjoyed the simple things in life. He didn't look for luxuries. That was the impression I had.

ANN ROEST

There was, in 1953, a time when I showed Stanley's book of pictures to my class of 46, ten-year-olds, and they liked them and wrote to Stanley and drew pictures for him. He was so delighted that he came to meet the children and wrote to them, every child. A pity this did not find its way into the National Press????

In 1946 my Father, Clifton Reynolds, came to know Stanley Spencer via a lecture Stanley was invited to give to the Wycombe Arts Council. My Father had to make all the arrangements and very excited he was to do so, knowing, as the family did, of the great fame of this artist.

Mr Spencer came to share a meal before leaving for High Wycombe. We lived in Bourne End. I met Stanley, therefore, when I was 18. The talk was about the lecture and we learned Stanley would be describing his first *Resurrection* picture. To help himself to do this he had provided himself with a large photograph, in black and white. His Teaching Aid! Since the family were already very familiar with the picture in the Tate this photograph worried us. It sure worried Stanley. 'Will it do?' he asked. Of course we said it would. What else? It did do.

He gave his lecture then, on his first *Resurrection* picture. It was a wonderful experience for me. I learned things about that picture I had never dreamed. Stanley said he had had the devil's own job with it to achieve proper perspective of the front graves. But the outstanding story was this: 'I woke up one lovely sunny morning in Cookham and felt like a trip to town and I thought I would like to visit my picture. You see, to have a picture IN THE TATE, was a grand thing for me. I was very young. So off I went to the station and up to London. Because I am so small and because no one really knew who I was, I managed to go into the Tate quite – er – sort of – incognito. I felt most excited. I went towards my picture and saw two of, these sort of, critic type people – very posh, very knowledgeable – most frightening and they were deep in discussion of my picture. Two large men in city clothes. I crept close and listened. They did not even notice me. I listened and listened and was amazed at all the wonderful things they could see in my picture that I had never even thought myself, never even tried to do or even understood. It was great fun.'

I visited Stanley often in his little house above Cookham station [Cliveden View]. He was always pleased to see me and stopped whatever he was doing, either painting or playing the piano, and we talked. I often took my friends along. Boys and girls my own age. It was just like visiting one of my own family. I can describe that house in great detail – spotless downstairs and ghastly untidy, up. His front paint room was warm, interesting, even exciting. Unusual. Stimulating. It was a superb work-shop. Full of paints, canvas tacked to the wall, papers, drawings, cups of tea, a bed and a few bits of odd furniture.

I went to Teacher Training College and one evening when Stanley was visiting at home with us, he said to me, 'What can you teach?' I offered him a selection and he chose fractions. 'I never learned how to do fractions, I never needed to know how to do fractions; fractions are an invention of the devil to torment people like me.' We sallied forth to learn fractions, together. It was hilarious. And he never forgot. Ever after, when we were out together and we met someone he knew – be it in a Bond Street Gallery or in Cookham High Street – I was always introduced: 'This is Ann. She is the most wonderful teacher. She can do fractions.' Nor was this said humorously. It was said and meant sincerely. This was his way. He made me feel good. And it was not just in teaching he made me feel good.

One day, after I was married, he asked to see my pictures. My paintings. It was one of those happy afternoons when all was going well and, unabashed, I got my folio out. He looked through every single drawing and painting and I felt smaller and smaller. My husband sat and watched and was killing himself laughing. Stanley took no notice of either of us. Then, suddenly, he pounced. 'This one. This bit here. This pram and this woman (pointing to $1\frac{1}{2}$ square inches of picture in a paper size quarto); I wish I could paint like that. It is just natural to you. I have to work for it!' I grew 500 feet tall instantly. Again, complete sincerity.

I had a holiday at Bourne End with a girl friend and two boy friends. We invited Stanley to join a party we were giving. About twenty people were coming, all our age. He accepted at once and arrived promptly. I remember the potatoes took ages because we forgot to cut them up and started them in cold water on a slow electric heater. We had no drinks, being too poor, and yet the party remained patient. All was talk and flow. Afterwards several of us wanted to go swimming. Stanley did too. We went off down to the Spade Oak Ferry and swam. It was dark. On leaving the water Stanley caught his foot on a nail in planks. He made nothing of it and nor did we. Then he went off back to Cookham walking up the railway line. Weeks later we heard his foot had gone seriously septic and had given him immense trouble. He never told us. None of us had the grace to offer to take him home although two of the boys had large motor bikes.

Stanley, when invited to visit for the day, arrived early; sometimes about 8 am. This suited father very well. He rose at 5. He would remain with us until midnight and be driven home by my father. One great day he came to draw me. Armed with paper, etc., we set to. It was an EXPERIENCE. His face, all four eyes, was ten inches from mine, for hours. Since I was not unused to this sort of situation due to the painting interests of my family, I withstood it fairly and met with Stanley's approval. He started one and discovered my hair would have to be put onto a separate sheet of paper, so he threw that one away. He started a profile which he so disliked he threw that away. He tried another three-quarter face which went the same way and we stopped for lunch. I lay back exhausted, on this sort of aeroplane chair, and giggling, raised my hands into a position of prayer on my chest. 'Hold it. Hold it like that, Ann; I'll put those hands on a tomb.' (I held it like mad.) 'They are exactly Dürer's hands. Whoever would have thought anyone could have hands so identical. Keep perfectly still.' He drew my hands successfully.

After lunch, realising I would be disappointed with an entire day and only one pair of hands to show for it, he took up the original one with the awkward hair, and completed it.

People used to get Stanley (and 'get' is the right word) to draw them or their children. Then they would flog the work. For lolly. Gifts from Stanley flogged by mean people. This hurt him.

One day Stanley came to visit, just after he had received his knighthood. He strutted. He did this because my husband and I jolly well encouraged him to strut. We liked it. We all three laughed and played at it. So – Stanley told us all to sit down and shut up and he organised a reconstruction of his knighting. We had several friends in. He was very proud of his knighthood and so were we. We wanted to know all about it and the best way was to show us. I was the Queen. I had to sit just there. I sat. My husband was the usher person. Others had their places detailed off. So it was done. 'I arrived and lined up and waited and it was a wonderful feeling but I was nervous and afraid to do the wrong thing.' We encouraged him. 'I came in round the corner and the Queen Mother looked at me. I am perfectly sure she gave me a litte tiny wink, just to make me feel better. She is a wonderful person.'

'When I went to Buckingham Palace I had to take my little bag there, to hold my towels because I have had this operation. Why did the press have to headline that I took my shopping bag to Buckingham Palace? Is there anything wrong with my little bag, Ann? I have to take the towels because I have to keep very clean.' Why the hell can't the press just do a tiny research before they crucify? Such a deep hurt this gave him.

Upon another occasion, when Stanley was ill, he said, 'I like you coming to fetch me and take me home to spend the day with your family. It is these little social occasions which I like best. So comfortable and good food and people to talk with. I like it!' And he did so like my husband too. Then I had my first baby. Naturally my wish was to have a drawing and therefore I asked Stanley if he would. He instantly agreed but showed concern. 'I frighten children', he said. 'I have to draw so close to them and so intensely that they scream sometimes.' Therefore we waited until my son was $2\frac{1}{2}$. The day came and Stanley brought his papers and pencils. But he was too ill. He just had not the strength to draw. Of course it did not matter and he went upstairs to rest.

And, one day at school, this teacher said to me, 'Ann, I am so sorry to hear Stanley Spencer is dead'. And I ran away and cried. As I cried, away in a classroom, his voice seemed to come: 'I am sorry, Ann; I did mean to do the portrait for you. I really did.'

I loved this man. He gave all he had to give to me, my father and my family. Just as a person. A fascinating person. Never banal. Always interesting, ever natural and easy. Relaxed and so simple to please. And he took us as his friends. But he did know how we felt, so that is all right. We all felt we had been given a jewel. A special treat. Almost as though, when he described things, we had been there too. Stanley was a great actor. He loved to lead and to enjoy and to be unashamed and natural. He liked us to invite friends to meet him. He talked and talked and talked and he never bored.

One day he said, 'I see this great picture. There is God amongst all His angels, in huge and wonderful clouds, and on his left hand side sits – Bach. (He then threw me a cheeky look!) And – on His right . . . sits – STANLEY.'

FRANK SHERWIN

There are so many anecdotes and memories of Stanley, in fact everyone in the village, who knew him, seems to have some story to tell.

Two little stories come to mind. Stanley was returning from a painting session in the churchyard; he was holding his wet canvas of Cookham Church and, as I am an artist myself, we were discussing the clock just above the sundial; his face lit up as he said with enthusiasm. 'I say, wouldn't it be fun to cut a hole in the canvas and put behind a watch, then we would always know the time!'

He visited us the day after he received his knighthood at the Palace and gleefully went through the whole ceremony bit by bit. In the absence of the Queen, it was the Queen Mother who actually laid the sword on his shoulder. 'She looked down at me and remarked, "Mr Spencer, I have been wanting to do this for a very long time",' he was so pleased and he said: 'It was all so cosy, it was just as though she had said, "Stanley I have got a boiling of marmalade on in the kitchen and I would be very pleased if you would take a jar home with you just for yourself".'

D. J. STRAWBRIDGE

There was a dramatised feature about Stanley on the Third Programme which we listened to, based on somebody's book. It seemed to attribute most of Spencer's paintings to a preoccupation with sex. It went so far as to state (by putting his thoughts about it into words) that he imagined *Christ at the Regatta* (leaning forward with the 'leaning' cushions behind him) was preaching about sex! Since I remembered Stanley as a very pleasant individual, and my wife and I had heard him talk about his paintings on sundry occasions without any suggestion of this sex motivation or significance, I wrote indignantly to the BBC to protest at the misrepresentation! I received the casual postcard in reply.

We then decided to hear what *The Critics* would say, advertised as they were to discuss the Third Programme feature, about a week later. They gave what seemed to us a fair 'criticism' of the feature as such, but extended their comments to the character of the *real* Stanley. One of them said he had been 'preoccupied with dirt – I mean real dirt', and backed this up by saying that Stanley had in fact said that he was 'preoccupied with excreta'. This was all solemnly commented upon as part of the indication of how queer Stanley was supposed to be. It made my wife and me writhe! We both have a vague memory of someone saying that Stanley had replied – during his last year – to the enquiry of how he was, that he was 'preoccupied with excreta!' Of course he was, poor devil, literally, with his box clamped to his belly after his operation. It would be just like him to make a wry factual statement about it.

On the 'sex' angle. True, his *Present on the Moon* was a cheerful matter of fact comment on the girl who had obviously got the best present her boyfriend could give her and was full of phallic symbols in the form of half-peeled bananas, but it could hardly offend anyone, and when Stanley pointed out its essential features to us it was in a cheerful straightforward manner, without any of the slobbering excited attitude attributed to him in the Third Programme feature. It seemed to me that, to Stanley, it was just another picture making another point about the human scene.

My chief contact with him and his paintings was over raising money for Cookham Church in 1958. When the village exhibition of his paintings was being planned, he never thought that thousands of the ordinary public would flock to see his pictures and be impressed by them, and when it happened he was undeniably delighted. Just before the catalogue was to be printed I heard that Tooths had sold his *From up the Rise* (a painting) to a buyer who insisted on taking it abroad at once and would not leave it to be exhibited first. I went up to Cliveden View to see what he thought, being in some consternation. He beamed all over his face with delight that it was sold, saying, 'I've got to live', but he at once busied himself with arranging that the Exhibition should have the drawing for *From up the Rise*.

MICHAEL and RACHEL WESTROPP

Soon after our arrival in Cookham Stanley became a great friend and a frequent and welcome visitor at The Vicarage, calling himself one of Rachel's adopted children. When painting in the vicinity he often called in for nursery tea. Jane, aged four, when asked one day if she had any other brothers and sisters beside John answered, 'No, only Stanley,' a remark Stanley enjoyed.

In 1958 Cookham Church was faced with having to raise a large sum of money to repair the roof, ravaged by death watch beetle. Stanley was greatly concerned about how he could make a contribution and suggested that we might hold a small exhibition of some of his pictures, those he could borrow from friends and owned by local people, and in this way help to raise some money for the church. He was delighted when we suggested that it should be held in the church and at the vicarage, and a small committee was formed and it was planned to take place for two weeks in June. With great humility he left the hanging entirely to others. When this was completed Rachel called him from the churchyard where he was painting, and he came into the church obviously greatly moved at seeing his paintings at last accepted by the church. This was for him a very great moment in his life.

He saw the *Christ in the Wilderness* series hung together for the first time, and in the choir stalls under the panels in the roof which had inspired him to create them and for which he had designed them. Also *The Last Supper*, *The Visitation*, *The Nativity*, *The Odney Baptism*, *The Crucifixion*, recently completed for Aldenham School, and the unfinished *Christ Preaching at Cookham Regatta* and others all hanging in the church. Many landscapes and portraits and drawings hung in the vicarage.

It was a complete surprise to Stanley and the committee that the exhibition drew thousands from all over the country. It could have run for the remainder of the summer, but it was only possible to extend it for a further week. Stanley was always about, either painting in the churchyard or talking to visitors, and he gave two lectures in the church to crowded audiences. It was a very happy time for him, some of his paintings at last being exhibited in Cookham and in the beloved church, the setting of their inspiration. Reporters, BBC and ITV interviewers, came to meet him, so what had been planned as a small homely village effort turned into a unique and nationwide exhibition.

During the months after the exhibition he and Michael discussed the possibility of his painting the Last Judgement to be commissioned by the church and hung in the church. This was a subject he had longed to paint for many years and of which he already had many drawings, which he showed us. An important feature of the painting was the thrones on which the Apostles were to sit judging the twelve tribes. These were a variety of chairs, including a commonplace windsor chair, and others. He continued to make reference to this painting up to the time of his last illness. His mind always teemed with work he wished to complete.

The following Christmas he was taken ill and admitted to the Canadian War Memorial Hospital near Cliveden. Cancer was diagnosed and he underwent a colostomy operation. He was confident that he would fully recover and continually talked about the urgency of getting on with his work. When he came out of hospital he came to the vicarage, where we looked after him for two months. He wanted to start work immediately, so the great unfinished *Christ Preaching at the Cookham Regatta* canvas, measuring 21ft long, was rolled up and taken down from the wall in his bedroom at Cliveden View and tacked to the wall of his bedroom at the vicarage. Because of its height, a stool was placed on top of a trestle table on which he sat to paint, perched like a bird. Our children John and Jane loved to watch him painting the coloured lanterns in the punts. On

Michael's birthday he came down to breakfast and announced with his impetuous generosity that his present would be a portrait of Rachel, which he commenced later that day. When tucked up in bed each evening Rachel used to take him a hot drink and would find him absorbed in some part of the Bible, which he expounded to her at length, sometimes having to persuade her to curl up at the end of the bed under the eiderdown, 'as I have not finished telling you about this yet.'

Playing the piano in the drawing room (generally a piece by Bach) gave him much pleasure, and being part of a family again gave him peace and a sense of 'belonging' after his lonely years at Cliveden View.

He accepted the inconvenience of the colostomy with typical fortitude and by April was well enough to move to Fernlea, which had been bought for him. We were much involved with the move and entrusted with helping him sort many writings, drawings and paintings with special instructions about the boxes under the bed.

That summer was a happy one although he was often in pain and far from well. He had many meals in The Torquil, the little café next to Fernlea, run by an Australian couple, the Barratts. When Mrs Barratt complained about the grease in the kitchen he painted her a small picture of two roses as a 'grease remover'. The café was renamed 'The Two Roses' and the picture hung in a place of honour.

In June when he was to be knighted Rachel bought him a new waistcoat to go with his one tidy suit and sent him off to the Palace with Shirin and Unity.

By November he was seriously ill again and re-admitted to the hospital. Nothing could be done except to relieve the pain. Rachel visited him each day and during that time read him *The Wind in the Willows*, which he loved. Michael came each evening and he loved him to read to him from the psalms and give him a blessing before leaving for the night. Aaron's blessing from the *Book of Numbers* (Chapter 6 verses 24–26) which Michael used always brought him great comfort.

'Preserved by its beauty it is indestructable', he used to say. He loved seeing visitors and many came. As the days went by he grew weaker. On December 14th Rachel visited him in the morning and read him the last chapter of *The Wind in the Willows*. Shirin and Unity were with him in the afternoon. Knowing he did not like to be left alone Rachel returned in the evening and noticed a great change in him. She had taken him a small book of reproductions, as he often liked to look at 'pictures' instead of trying to talk or write messages. He spurned it saying, 'plenty of time to look at these, sit where I can look at you'. His gaze was similar in intensity to when he had painted her but interspersed with beaming smiles. She helped him try to eat his supper which he found difficult and seemed at times to be far away. The Sister came in to say 'Good night', and he said to her 'Your cloak is a beautiful colour'. Rachel thought it unlikely that he would be conscious when she next came to see him, so she kissed him goodbye, saying she would send Michael to sit with him and give him a blessing. Michael came soon afterwards, prepared to sit with him until he fell asleep. They had snatches of conversation, but seeing how exhausted he was Michael said, 'You are tired; shall I leave you?' Stanley took up his pad and pencil and wrote, 'I most certainly am not. I am never weary, never bored. Why should you think I am? Sadness and sorrow is not me.' So Michael stayed on and soon the nurse came to give him his injection for the night. 'Beautifully done', he said. They were his last words, as soon afterwards he turned his head away to the right and stretched out his left arm. It was a moment or two before Michael realised that he had gone, so quietly. Before calling the nurse, Michael knelt by him and commended his soul to God.

Chronology

1891	Stanley Spencer born 30 June at Fernlea (now Fernley) in Cookham-on-Thames, Berkshire, seventh son of William, organist and piano teacher. Only schooling at morning classes run by his sister Annie.
1907	At Maidenhead Technical Institute.
1908–12	Student at Slade School (under Tonks), travelling daily from Cookham.
1912–15	Painted at home some of his best religious work, e.g. *Zacharias and Elizabeth*, *Joachim among the Shepherds*.
1915–18	Joined Royal Army Medical Corps. Posted to Beaufort War Hospital, Bristol, July 1915. August 1916 sent to Macedonia. August 1917 volunteered for infantry and served with Royal Berkshires till end of war. Returned home December 1918.
1919	Painting in Cookham. Finished *Swan Upping*, begun before military service.
1920–2	Lived at Bourne End (near Cookham) with Slessers for about a year. Summer 1921 accepted invitation to stay with Muirhead Bones near Petersfield, later taking lodgings over a teashop, where painted four pictures to form predella for *The Betrayal*.
1922	Visited Jugoslavia with Carlines during summer. December moved to Hampstead.
1922–3	Stayed for a year with Henry Lamb at Poole, Dorset, where made detailed drawings for *Resurrection, Cookham* and worked out designs for mural decorations that were later embodied in the Memorial Chapel, Burghclere, Berkshire. Returned to Hampstead October 1923 and started painting *Resurrection*, using Lamb's studio in Vale of Health.
1925	Married Hilda Carline at Wangford, near Southwold, Suffolk. Two daughters, Shirin and Unity born, 1925 and 1930.
1926–7	Completed *Resurrection*, acquired for Tate Gallery from his first one-man exhibition 1927. Moved to Burghclere, where he lived, at Chapel View, from May 1927 until early 1932.
1932	Returned to Cookham, living at Lindworth and finishing his last Burghclere panels there. In October Dudley Tooth became his sole dealer. Remained painting at Cookham – many landscapes – till 1938.
1933	Visited Switzerland, at invitation of Edward Beddington-Behrens, with Patricia Preece. (Went again with Beddington-Behrens in 1936.)
1937-8	Married Patricia Preece 29 May 1937, living alone at Lindworth and then in lodgings.

1938	Left Cookham in October, staying with John and Elizabeth Rothenstein 'in Fellows Road, Hampstead, and then with Malcolm Mc Donald till December, when he lodged in Constance Oliver's house in Adelaide Road, where painted first four of series *Christ in the Wilderness*.
1939	Moved, 30 July, to White Hart Inn, Leonard Stanley, Gloucestershire, with George and Daphne Charlton.
1940	Commissioned to paint shipyard pictures by War Artists' Advisory Committee. Made several visits to Port Glasgow, and continued them till end of war, putting up at Glencairn boarding house.
1941	Moved to Epsom, staying with Mrs Harter (Sydney Carline's mother-in-law), who looked after his daughters.
1942	Returned to Cookham, 7 January, as tenant of cousin, Bernard Smithers, at Quinneys, the house attached to Lindworth, where he stayed till May 1944.
1943–4	Seeing a Port Glasgow cemetery sent him 'back to the bottle' – drawings for a new *Resurrection* series, whose first two panels were painted in Port Glasgow 1945, the rest occupying him at Cookham till 1950.
1945	Returned to Cookham, to Cliveden View. Frequent visitor of Carlines and of Hilda in hospital.
1950	C.B.E. Hilda died November.
1952–3	Made series of some sixty drawings for *Christ preaching at Cookham Regatta*; began work on the paintings 1953.
1955	Retrospective exhibition at Tate Gallery.
1958	Knighted. Exhibition at Cookham Church and vicarage.
1959	Died aged 68, 14 December, at Canadian War Memorial Hospital, Cliveden.

Appendix

At last I can say my say about my pictures.

Before the 1914 war I had to be very convinced about a picture before I drew it or painted it. The drawing or painting of the thing was the experiencing of heaven: it would have been unthinkable that I should or might find hitches or snags. The ability I might need in carrying out the work was dependent on there being no such possibility. This state of sureness continues to about 1922-3, when I did the *Betrayal*. At this time I did the series of drawings for the Burghclere Memorial and also the drawing for the 1927 *Resurrection*. So that all the painting I was to do from 1922 to 1932 was settled in nearly every detail: ten years of solid bliss was ahead of me. But I knew in 1922-3 that I was changing or losing grip or something.

I was, I feared, forsaking the vision and I was filled with consternation. All the ability I had was dependent on that vision. I knew of this in 1922-3 but I felt and hoped that having been able to do the *Resurrection* drawing and the Burghclere drawings that while carrying out this work I might recover my vision. I hoped so especially as I wanted when I had finished the Burghclere work to do not a chapel to do with war but to do with the more vital meaning of peace.

This change in my work only becomes more glaringly apparent in 1932-3 because up to this time I was only carrying out what had been done in 1922-3.

I recovered partially from this loss and in 1933 the next 'chapel' (built also in the air as was first the Burghclere Chapel, that is to say not commissioned) was to be planned somewhat thus: the Village Street of Cookham was to be the nave and the river which runs behind the street was a side aisle. The *Promenade of Women* and the *Sarah Tubb and the Heavenly Visitors* and the *St Francis and the Birds* and *Villagers and Saints* are fragments of the street scenes and the more recent *Listening from Punts* Regatta scene is a river aisle fragment. The whole work was far too big for me to undertake unless I could devote the whole of my time to it and this I was far from being able to do. This not being able to see the *whole* of my way had the same effect on the way I painted as occurred if and when I painted in a state of doubt. I knew if I could spare the time I could do it. But I was doing a lot of landscapes and portraits and this took almost all my time.

I could never have borne to have to start a painting where the success was entirely dependent and reliant solely on the degree of ability I managed to achieve: where the chance of success was such as one could only hope for in a war: entering something fraught with untold difficulties. I am no fighter. In the village there is a plate on a house near some hotels which says 'all fighting to be over by 10 o'clock' and with me all fighting and all associated with it has to be over by the time I begin to draw a picture or paint it and the kind of heaven I enter when I do begin to paint I find not at all insipid.

The spectator – ever on the scout for complaisance on the part of the artist – is never happy unless he feels assured I have had a hell of a time and am evidently utterly wretched in doing some painting. In fact I once or twice rightly deduced when I was hating a thing I was doing, that that would mean that I would sell it. Failure for me has its bright side.

The result of having my work held up by doing so much landscape has caused my other work to accumulate. In the days before the 1914 war nothing had accumulated. As I finished one painting I had no drawing or sketch or notion as to what would be the next painting. I only felt confident there would be something. I woo'd the empty air in front of me. Each succeeding painting seems to celebrate and illustrate the joy that followed the joy which the former painting illustrated. And so they seem to belong to each other and to adhere in some way not through any conscious attempt to make them do so but just that at some time when I was feeling this joy they kicked their way through my mind and made their appearance as paintings of that joy.

The paintings I do now are 'selected' from hundreds of drawings which I have had by me for many years. And if you consider the works I have done say since 1950 you will see that while in the pre-1914 collection there is something auspicious like succession of children in a family in their unrelated sequence, in that of 1950 to the present day there is something almost haphazard in the succession as they appear.

My work falls into various periods in which I appear to be developing some theme or some particularised outlook and then abruptly it stops without point or purpose. I get so far with some series of paintings and hope to get round and complete it but the central theme which gives sense to the rest never turns up.

Today I was shown the list of works that were included in this exhibition and I found my interest waning as I came chronologically into the 1930s and I never recovered the interest or confidence that I had felt about the works earlier than 1932.

All the figure pictures done after 1932 were a part of some scheme, the whole of which scheme when completed would have given the part the meaning I know it had. Having completed a memorial chapel in which I seek to express the joys of peace in spite of being in the midst of war, I then hoped to express the same peace in its more positive state in times of peace.

I was making big demands on life at the time and had to paint far more than I would have wished. This has always been a bad thing with me. From 1933 the landscape work began and left me with snatches of time and much depleted energy for these schemes I hoped to realise and carry out. So completely was I swamped with doing the landscapes that I saw that unless I painted a few 'excerpts' from one or other of these figure picture schemes nothing at all of these schemes would ever be done.

But as and when I painted them, I never felt the joy I would have experienced doing this work had I known that I could complete the scheme. The work suffered. They have not the conviction that comes with that joy. As I have done them the knowledge that the final meaning may never be clear has had a crushing effect.

To try and give an idea as to what I mean. How could I rejoice in painting the people listening in the punts (as it is necessary to do if I am to do what I want) when what is being listened to, namely, Christ preaching, is not in this picture? There are nineteen paintings in the Burghclere memorial and among the eight smaller ones there is one of a man scrubbing the floor and a man carrying groceries stepping over him. This is a 3ft + 6ft painting. Had I not known and been completely assured that this painting was to form part of a scheme in which there would be a final painting of a resurrection in which Christ would be receiving the resurrected soldiers I would not have been able to compose that picture of the man scrubbing the floor. If this listening from punts and the others of this series of pictures were seen together with the big picture of Christ preaching from a barge (which is drawn on the canvas at present) their meaning would be clearer. If I know that a certain result will arise from a certain experience I value the experience and I feel quite sure long before I have seen the result. For instance I believe in my associations and always have done. I believe in them as having the power of realising the meaning I seek because they are guided by another and deeper belief, namely that only goodness and love and Christian and other benign beliefs are capable of creative works.

17 August 1955

Index